British Television Policy: A Reader

British Television Policy: A Reader provides a forum for the significant policy debates which have informed and shaped television broadcasting since the Peacock Committee Report on the financing of the BBC was published in 1986. The Reader presents key documents and critically analyses their impact on the organisation, financial resources, programme content, editorial philosophy and the regulatory environment of television broadcasting.

Recognising that policy making is not wholly a prerogative of government, *British Television Policy* provides readers with access to a wide range of statutory and non-governmental documents that have affected British broadcasting legislation. The Reader brings together materials from a range of sources: Acts of Parliament; Private Members' Bills; White Papers, such as *A New Future for Communications*; Select Committee Reports; official statements by Ministers; parliamentary inquiries, such as the Davies Report; policy documents prepared by interest groups, such as the Campaign for Quality Television and the Voice of the Listener and Viewer; policy announcements from the ITC; statements from the BBC and ITV; public lectures by media owners and executives, such as Rupert Murdoch and Richard Eyre; commentaries from media academics and media analysts.

Beginning with a comprehensive editorial introduction which details television policy since 1945, the Reader is arranged in thematic sections which explore the purposes of television broadcasting, television financing, broadcasting policy and programming, regulation and the relationship of broadcasting and politics. Each section is accompanied by an editor's introduction and commentary, and the Reader is supported by a glossary and a guide to further reading.

Bob Franklin is Professor of Media Communications in the Department of Sociological Studies at the University of Sheffield. His publications include *Making the Local News*, *Social Policy, the Media and Misrepresentation*, *Hard Pressed: Newspaper Reporting of Social Work* and *Newszak and News Media*.

British Television Policy: A Reader

Edited by Bob Franklin

London and New York

First published 2001
by Routledge
11 New Fetter Lane, London EC4P 4EE

Simultaneously published in the USA and Canada
by Routledge
29 West 35th Street, New York, NY 10001

Routledge is an imprint of the Taylor & Francis Group

Typeset in Perpetua and Bell Gothic by RefineCatch Limited, Bungay, Suffolk
Printed and bound in Great Britain by
TJ International Ltd, Padstow, Cornwall

British Library Cataloguing in Publication Data
A catalogue record for this book is available from the British Library

Library of Congress Cataloging in Publication Data
British television policy: a reader/edited by Bob Franklin.
p. cm.
Includes bibliographical references and index.
ISBN 0–415–19871–2 (alk. paper) — ISBN 0–415–19872–0 (pbk.: alk. paper)
1. Television broadcasting — Great Britain. 2. Television broadcasting policy — Great Britain. I. Franklin, Bob, 1949– II. Title.
PN1992.3.G7 B76 2001
384.55′0941—dc21
2001019503

ISBN 0–415–19871–2 (hbk)
ISBN 0–415–19872–0 (pbk)

To Jay Blumler

With thanks

This book is dedicated to my good friend and ex-colleague Jay Blumler who, almost single-handedly, pushed open the door to political communication scholarship in Britain during the greater part of the three decades spanning the 1960s to the 1990s. Many of us owe him an enormous intellectual debt for so kindly leaving the door ajar.

CONTENTS

CRITICAL VOICES

FINANCING THE BBC

PART FOUR
Television Broadcasting Policy: Regulation 129

PROGRAMME CONTENT

MEDIA OWNERSHIP

CONVERGENCE IN THE DIGITAL AGE

GLOSSARY

ABC	An American network station (see also NBC and CBS).
Anglia Television	A Channel 3 licence holder.
Annan Committee	A committee of inquiry into broadcasting. It was chaired by Lord Annan, reported in 1977 and recommended a new television channel should be launched: Channel 4 came on air in 1982 (see Appendix B).
BBC	Since 1927 the British Broadcasting Corporation. Between 1922 and 1927 the BBC was the British Broadcasting Company.
BCC	Broadcasting Complaints Commission. Established in 1981 to hear complaints from individuals concerning invasion of privacy and unfair treatment in programming. Following the Broadcasting Act 1996, the BCC was merged with the Broadcasting Standards Council in 1997 to form the Broadcasting Standards Commission.
BBC Resources	One of six directorates of the BBC announced in a policy statement by John Birt in June 1996: BBC Resources provides broadcasting resources for all BBC programmes. The Davies Review Panel recommended selling this Directorate.
BBC Worldwide	A directorate of the BBC responsible for the marketing, sales and distribution of BBC products. The Davies Review Panel recommended that a substantial share of this directorate should be sold.
BECTU	Broadcasting, Entertainment, Cinematograph and Theatre Union.
Beveridge Committee	A committee of inquiry into the financial and organisational structures of the BBC television services. The Committee's report (1949) included a significant minority report by Selwyn Lloyd which recommended the development of an independent broadcasting sector (see Appendix B).
Biggam, Sir Robin	Chairman of the ITC.
Birt, Sir John	Director General of the BBC between 1991 and April 2000.
Board of Governors	The regulatory authority of the BBC which is appointed by the government and entrusted to defend the independence of the BBC. The Board also serves to protect the public interest, to ensure that the BBC's programme services maintain standards of excellence and reflect the programming requirements of the audience. The Board oversees the BBC managers who are responsible for the day-to-day making of programmes.
Border Television	A Channel 3 licence holder.
BRU	The Broadcasting Research Unit. Established in 1980, the BRU

	initiated independent research into broadcasting policy until it closed in the early 1990s.
BSB	British Satellite Broadcasting. The second satellite station to be launched in the UK in April 1990. After a costly battle to establish a market lead above its rival Sky Television, the company merged with Sky in November 1990 to form BSkyB.
BSC	Broadcasting Standards Council established in May 1988, given statutory recognition by the Broadcasting Act 1990 and merged with the BCC to form the Broadcasting Standards Commission in April 1997.
BSComm	Broadcasting Standards Commission (see BSC and BCC above). A regulatory body merging the functions of the BCC and BSC.
BSkyB	The new satellite broadcasting company which emerged from the November 1990 merger of the two rivals Sky television and BSB (see BSB above).
CBS	An American network station (see also ABC and NBC).
CEEFAX	The BBC's Teletext Service (see Teletext). A system of information retrieval, usually presented in the form of sequentially numbered pages, which can be superimposed over television images.
CNN	Cable News Network (Critics' nickname is Chicken Noodle News). A twenty-four-hour news service owned by US media magnate Ted Turner and based in Atlanta, USA.
CPBF	Campaign for Press and Broadcasting Freedom. A media-based interest group advocating regulation of media ownership to ensure diversity and range in programming which the Campaign argues is crucial to the operation of democratic political systems.
CQT	Campaign for Quality Television. Established in 1988 by a number of senior programme makers in both the public and private sectors of broadcasting following the publication of the White Paper *Broadcasting in the '90s*.
Cable Authority	The Cable Authority was established by the Cable and Broadcasting Act 1984 with a loose regulatory responsibility for the Cable TV industry. After the Broadcasting Act 1990, the functions of the Authority were transferred to the Independent Television Commission (see ITC).
Central Television	A Channel 3 licence holder.
Channel 3	The commercially funded, regionally based, television network previously known as the ITV network before the Broadcasting Act 1990. It includes the fourteen regional companies such as Carlton Television, Central Television and Granada as well as the Breakfast contractor GMTV.
Channel 4	Created by the Broadcasting Act 1982, Channel 4 was given a brief to broadcast radical and innovatory programming which appealed to minority audiences not provided for by the then ITV network.
Channel 5	A new commercial terrestrial channel launched on 30 March 1997 with a programme philosophy described by its Chief Executive as 'modern mainstream'.
Channel Television	A Channel 3 licence holder.
Community Radio	A fourth tier of radio alongside national, regional and local radio

either in the form of a low power transmitter broadcasting to the immediate neighbourhood, with a close involvement of the community, or a station broadcasting across a wider area to a 'community of interest' such as an ethnic minority community.

Convergence — The prospect offered by the development of digital technology to amalgamate the functions of televisions and computers.

CPS — Centre for Policy Studies. An independent but right-of-centre think-tank. It publishes reports on a wide range of subjects including broadcasting.

Crawford Committee — The second committee of inquiry into the subject of broadcasting. It was chaired by Earl Crawford and reported in 1926 (see Appendix B).

Davies Review — In October 1998, the Secretary of State for Culture, Media and Sport established the Davies Independent Review to conduct a review of the licence fee and the future funding of the BBC. Chaired by Gavin Davies, the committee reported in July 1999 and recommended retention of the licence fee and the establishment of a digital licence supplement to help fund the launch of the BBC's digital television services.

DBS — Direct Broadcasting by Satellite. Television signals are transmitted from a broadcasting station to a satellite (uplink) which, in turn transmits the signals (downlink) to small 'dishes' (aerials) for reception as pictures on a television set. This allows broadcasters the opportunity to reach much greater audiences since a fixed station in a single country can transmit via satellite to audiences in a number of different countries.

DCMS — The Department of Culture, Media and Sport which is responsible for most aspects of broadcasting policy. The DCMS replaced the Department of National Heritage in 1997 following the election of the Labour Party to government. One strand in the argument for the change was that the name 'National Heritage' was too backward-looking and placed insufficient emphasis on the dynamism inherent in the media industries.

Demos — An independent think-tank launched by Geoff Mulgan, its first director. Demos publishes reports on a wide range of issues including broadcasting policy.

Digital technology — A newly developed technology which can be used for creating and delivering television images with considerably improved sound and picture quality. It offers the possibility of interactive television in which viewers can influence programme contents by, for example, calling up instant replays of a goal in a football match from any one of eight camera angles, or by choosing from a range of possible endings to a particular film or play.

DTI — The Department of Trade and Industry which exercises some regulatory functions over the broadcasting industry.

Dumbing down — A phrase which has come to imply that the nature of television programmes has changed to meet the circumstances of multi-channel competition. The suggestion is that broadcasters have 'gone downmarket' or 'dumbed down' in order to 'chase ratings'

	and win audiences in the increasingly competitive market for media audiences both in private and public sectors of broadcasting.
Dyke, Greg	Director General of the BBC since April 2000. A leading figure in Channel 5 Broadcasting, the company which won the franchise auction for the new Channel 5. He was previously at LWT and, until recently, was perhaps most well known for his rescue strategy of the ailing breakfast broadcaster TV-AM whose programme fortunes were revived by the introduction of the puppet character Roland Rat.
Footprint	The area in which the signal of a particular television service can be received.
Franchise auction	The method for allocating Channel 3 and Channel 5 broadcasting licences. Companies must convince the ITC that their programming intentions meet clearly specified requirements, but then bid in a 'blind' auction for the franchise. The highest bidder is awarded the licence in other than 'exceptional circumstances'.
Free to air	A phrase used to describe a television service funded *solely* by advertising: in truth, it describes channels such as Channels 3, 4 and 5 which are funded *largely* by advertising but also broadcast sponsored programmes, although these form a modest part of each channel's core funding. Since there is no payment demanded from viewers in the form of licence fee, or subscription charges since all the station's costs are met by advertising revenues, the channel offers programmes which are free to air.
GMTV	Holder of the Channel 3 franchise for the breakfast television service.
Grampian Television	A Channel 3 licence holder.
Granada Television	A Channel 3 licence holder.
Hankey Committee	A committee of inquiry into re-establishing television broadcasting after the Second World War: the committee reported in 1945 (see Appendix B).
HTV	A Channel 3 licence holder.
Hunt Committee	A committee of Inquiry examining the development of cable television services and broadcasting policy; the committee reported in 1982 (see Appendix B).
IBA	The Independent Broadcasting Authority: the predecessor to the ITC established by the Broadcasting Act 1990. The IBA was responsible for the regulation of commercial television (the ITV network and Channel 4).
ILR	Independent Local Radio.
INR	Independent National Radio.
IPPR	The Institute of Public Policy Research: an independent but left-leaning policy think-tank which publishes reports on a wide range of subjects including broadcasting.
ITC	The Independent Television Commission. The ITC regulates all commercially funded television services: terrestrial, satellite and cable. It allocates the licences to broadcast in the Channel 3 regions including breakfast television, monitors their compliance with

	their franchise programme commitments and publishes an annual review of programme standards. It drafts and polices programming codes, advertising codes and codes concerning the technical requirements of service delivery.
ITN	Independent Television News was established in the early days of commercial television to provide national and international news to the various regional television companies which comprised the ITV network. The ITV companies jointly funded and owned ITN until the Broadcasting Act 1990 changed these rules of ownership and required the ITV companies to 'hold less than 50 per cent shares' in the company.
ITV Network Centre	The ITV Network Centre is the administrative and organisational centre of the ITV network. It has significant functions concerning the scheduling of programmes on the network. It was the Centre, for example, which took the decision in 1999 to move *News At Ten* from its traditional position in order to 'free up' the schedules and allow the Centre to schedule programmes – uninterrupted by news – which might attract larger audiences and advertising revenues.
LWT	London Weekend Television, a Channel 3 licence holder broadcasting in the London region at weekends only. Carlton Television is the weekday contractor.
Meridian Television	A Channel 3 licence holder, successor to Television South (TVS) following the 1991 franchise round.
Modern Mainstream	The description of the programming philosophy for Channel 5. In its bid to the ITC for the Channel 5 licence, Channel 5 Broadcasting declared that it would offer 'a user friendly schedule of programmes for everyone'.
NBC	An American network station (see also ABC and CBS).
OFT	The Office of Fair Trading. An organisation with regulatory responsibilities for financial and competitive aspects of media.
OFCOM	The new regulatory body proposed by the White Paper *A New Future For Communications*. The body is to incorporate the Broadcasting Standards Commission, The Independent Television Commission, Oftel, the Radio Authority and the Radiocommunications agency. OFCOM's major regulatory brief is to protect consumers' interests and sustain programme quality. OFCOM has regulatory powers based on competition act principles and can levy financial penalties.
OFTEL	The Office of Telecommunications.
ORACLE	The ITV Teletext Service (see TELETEXT).
Off-air	A term used to distinguish broadcasts by transmitters (tower on a hill top TV) from other delivery systems such as cable or satellite.
Pay-per-view	A system of funding programming which involves paying to view particular programmes or channels. In the UK this is usually associated with large sporting events such as boxing title fights, etc.
PBS	Public Broadcasting Service in the USA.
Peacock Committee	The committee on financing the BBC, it was established by the Conservative government in 1985 under the chairmanship of

	Professor Alan Peacock; it reported in 1986. The committee's brief was to explore possible funding mechanisms for the BBC, including advertising revenues. The committee decided against advertising in favour of retaining the licence fee in the short term, but moving to subscription funding of services in the longer term when technology allowed the establishment of a free broadcasting market.
Pilkington Committee	A committee of inquiry into broadcasting, chaired by Sir Harry Pilkington. The committee, which reported in 1962, offered a critical review of the new commercial services introduced in 1955 and suggested a new television channel for the BBC (see Appendix B).
Producer choice	The name given to John Birt's policy initiative for funding programme production at the BBC. Somewhat akin to an internal market, producer choice allowed producers of television programmes to choose production services from outside the BBC if these proved more cost-effective than 'in house' production services.
Public interest broadcasting	A phrase coined by Richard Eyre, then head of the ITV Network Centre, to describe the broadcasting philosophy which he believed should replace public service broadcasting. Eyre believes that viewers' choices must be at the heart of any sustainable broadcasting system.
Public service broadcasting	An approach to broadcasting which has informed both BBC and independent television broadcasting in the UK. The philosophy is captured in John Reith's maxim that broadcasting should seek to 'inform, educate and entertain'.
RTS	The Royal Television Society is an industry forum which organises conferences and public meetings via its seventeen regional centres. It publishes the journal *Television*.
Quality threshold	When bidding for a Channel 3 licence, television companies must convince the regulatory authority, the ITC, that their plans for programmes meet certain requirements which are specified in law (The Broadcasting Act 1990). This set of requirements is known as the quality threshold.
S4C	The Welsh Fourth Channel.
Scottish Television	A Channel 3 licence holder.
Selsdon Committee	A committee of inquiry into the early development of television which was concerned with adjudicating between alternative technical systems for producing televisual images. The committee reported in 1935 (see Appendix B).
Sky Television	The first satellite television station to broadcast in the UK. It was launched on 5 February 1989, owned by Rupert Murdoch and transmitted via the Astra satellite. Sky offered four channels (Sky News, Sky Sport, Sky Movies and Sky1): its arrival in the UK doubled the number of television channels available.
Subscription	A mechanism for funding television services. It was much favoured by the Peacock Committee because it represented a mechanism for consumers (viewers) to express their programming preferences directly in a broadcasting market.

Sykes Committee	A committee of inquiry into broadcasting. It was chaired by Frederick Sykes and reported in 1923 (see Appendix B).
TV-AM	The holder of the Breakfast contract, which lost to rival GMTV in the franchise auction for the Channel 3 breakfast licence in the 1991 round of bidding.
Teletext	A system of transmitting information as text (see CEEFAX).
Terrestrial	A delivery system for television images which uses land-based transmitters rather than satellites or cable.
Thames Television	A leading independent production company. Before 1991, the company held the contract to provide weekday television services in greater London: its bid in the 1991 franchise auction was unsuccessful and Carlton television replaced Thames as the licenced contractor.
Tyne Tees	A Channel 3 licence holder.
Ullswater Committee	A committee of inquiry into highly significant issues of the finance and organisational structures of the developing television broadcasting industry. The committee reported in 1936 (see Appendix B).
UVT	Ulster Television, a Channel 3 licence holder.
UNM	United News and Media, a conglomerate with wide-ranging media interests formed by the merger of Lord Hollick's MAI group and Lord Stevens's United Newspaper group.
VLV	Voice of the Listener and Viewer, a consumers' organisation which articulates the views of listeners and viewers on all matters concerning programming and policy in television and radio broadcasting, the VLV is especially concerned with issues of programme quality and range. The VLV organises conferences and public meetings and commissions research studies on broadcasting topics.
Westcountry Television	A Channel 3 licence holder and successor to South West Television (TSW) following the 1991 franchise round.
Windlesham/Rampton Report	An inquiry into the conduct of broadcasters at Thames Television and the making of the programme *Death on the Rock*. The report concluded that the programme was a journalistically fair account of the shooting of three members of the IRA by British soldiers at Gibraltar.
Yorkshire Television	A Channel 3 licence holder.

ACKNOWLEDGEMENTS

The following is a list of permissions to reproduce material within this Reader, for which the editor and publishers are grateful.

The BBC for material from John Birt, *The BBC: Past and Present*, 1993 (2.10); News Release, *BBC Response to Licence Panel Fee Report*, 1999 (2.13); *Extending Choice: The BBC's Role in the New Broadcasting Age*, 1992 (3.5); *People and Programmes*, 1995 (3.6); *Governing Today's BBC: Broadcasting, the Public Interest and Accountability*, 1997 (4.1); *Regulating Communications: Approaching Convergence in the Information age* (4.15); John Birt, Lecture, 1999 (4.17); Stephen Coleman, *Electronic Media, Parliament and the People*, 1999 (5.9); The Broadcasters' Consortium, *Consultation Paper on the Reform of Party Political Broadcasting*, 1998 (5.10, 5.11, 5.12).

The British Film Institute for material from Geoff Mulgan (ed.), *The Question of Quality*, 1990 (3.2).

The Broadcasting Standards Commission for material from Jay G. Blumler and Daniel Biltereyst, *The Integrity and Erosion of Public Television for Children: A Pan-European Survey*, 1998 (3.14).

The Campaign for Press and Broadcasting Freedom for material from *21st Century Media: Shaping the Democratic Vision*, 1996 (4.9).

The Campaign for Quality Television (45 Loftus Road, London W12 7EH) for material from *The Purposes of Broadcasting*, 1998 (1.10); *Serious Documentaries on ITV*, 1998 (3.11); Steve Barnett and Emily Seymour, *Changing Trends in British Television: A Case Study of Drama and Current Affairs*, 1999 (3.12); *The Purposes of Broadcasting*, 1998 (4.4, 4.10, 4.13).

© Crown copyright. Reproduced with the permission of the Controller of Her Majesty's Stationery Office: *Report of the Committee on Financing the BBC*, 1986 (1.3, 2.2, 2.7); *The Future of the BBC: A Consultation Document*, Cm 2098, 1992 (1.4, 2.8, 3.4); *The Future Funding of the BBC*, 1999 (1.6, 2.11); *A New Future for Communications*, 2000 (1.7, 4.6, 4.11, 4.18); *Broadcasting in the '90s: Competition, Choice and Quality*, Cm 517, 1988 (2.3); Broadcasting Act 1990 (2.4, 4.3); Broadcasting Act 1996 (4.5); *Funding the BBC* (2.14); *Media Ownership: The Government's Proposals*, Cm 2872, 1995 (4.8); *Regulating Communications: Approaching Convergence in the Digital Age*, Cm 4022, 1998 (4.12). © Department of Culture, Media and Sports. Crown copyright is reproduced with the permission of the Controller of Her Majesty's Stationery Office: Chris Smith, Lecture to the Royal Television Society, 1999 (4.16); *The Big Switch? Digital Future – Turn-On or Turn-Off? (1.5).*

Demos Publishers (Elizabeth House, 39 York Road, London SE1 7NQ) for material from Ian Hargreaves, *Sharper Visions: The BBC and the Communications Revolution, 1993.*

Greg Dyke for material from MacTaggart Memorial Lectures, 1994 (5.4) and 2000 (3.8).

The Edinburgh Film and Television Festival for material from Rupert Murdoch, MacTaggart Memorial Lecture, 1989 (1.8); Dennis Potter, MacTaggart Memorial Lecture, 1993 (1.9); MacTaggart Memorial Lectures, 1994 (5.4) and 2000 (3.8); Richard Tyre, MacTaggart Memorial Lecture, 1999 (1.11); Michael Grade, Speech delivered at the Edinburgh Festival, 1996 (2.6).

Richard Eyre for material from a public lecture, 1999 (3.13).

Faber and Faber for material from *The Windlesham/Rampton Report on Death on the Rock*, 1989 (5.2). © 1988 Thames Television Limited, A Pearson Television Company.

The *Guardian* Newspaper for extract from 'A Tax Too Far', 16 August 1999 (2.12); 'World in Action Meets Yoof TV . . .', 18 January 1999 (3.9); John Pilger, 'A Code for Charlatans', 8 October 1990 (5.5).

HarperCollins for material from Margaret Thatcher, *The Downing Street Years*, 1993.

The Independent Television Commission for material from *ITC Sets Out Terms For Renewal of Channel 3 Licences*, News Release, 109/98, 25 November 1998 (2.5); *Annual Reports and Accounts*, 1998 (3.10); The ITC Programme Code (4.2); Sir Robin Biggam, 'The Future of Regulation', Speech, 1999 (4.14).

Simon Jenkins for material from 'In Defence of Quality', *Listener* lecture, 6 July 1989 (3.1).

Oxford University Press for material reprinted from *Parliamentary Affairs*, 1986.

© Parliamentary copyright. Reproduced with the permission of the Controller of Her Majesty's Stationery Office on behalf of parliament: Chris Smith, Statement on BBC Funding, *Hansard*, 21 February 2000 (2.15); Lord Hussey's contribution to the debate on Public Service Broadcasting, *Parliamentary Debates*, 2 March 1999 (3.7); Chris Mullin in *Hansard*, 11 January 1995 (4.7); 'Broadcasting and Terrorism', *Parliamentary Debates*, 9 October 1988; The Broadcasting Act 1990 (5.4); Michael Foot, 'Televising the House', *Parliamentary Debates*, 20 November 1985 (5.7).

Routledge for material from Roger Gale, 'Sceptic's Judgement of Televising the Commons', in Bob Franklin, *Televising Democracies*, 1992 (5.8).

The Times Newspapers Limited for material from 'Whither The BBC?', 14 January 1985 (1.2).

The Voice of the Listener and Viewer for material from BRU, *The Public Service idea in British Broadcasting: Main Principles*, 1985 (1.1); BRU, *Quality in Television: Programmes, Programme-makers, Systems*, 1989 (3.3).

Particular thanks are owed to Jay Blumler for the many stimulating discussions about this project, to Chris Cudmore at Routledge for his helpful editorial insights and to Anthony Smith for writing the book *British Broadcasting* which inspired the current volume.

While the publishers and editor have made every effort to contact authors and copyright holders of works reprinted in *British Television Policy: A Reader*, they would welcome correspondence from individuals or companies they have been unable to trace so as to rectify any omissions in future editions.

TELEVISION POLICY POST-PEACOCK

An Introduction

WHEN BRITISH TELEVISION BROADCASTING was renewed in June 1946 following the Second World War, audiences were modest. The BBC enjoyed a broadcasting monopoly. The Corporation's programmes, which were transmitted using 'tower on a hilltop' technology, were watched by the 14,560 holders of the new combined sound and vision licences. In 1946, programmes were broadcast for an average of twenty-eight hours each week (Seymour Ure, 1991: 186). By the end of 1947 a mere 34,000 television sets had been installed in 0.2 per cent of households (Briggs, 1979: 242). Audience reach was limited further by the relatively primitive broadcasting technology which could not extend the signal beyond a forty-mile radius of the Alexander Palace transmitter. Expenditure on television programming was equally modest. In 1948, for example, the BBC spent around £6.5 million on radio while expenditure on television services was only £716,666 (Briggs, 1979: 8). In these early days, television was seen as little more than a natural extension of sound broadcasting, and consequently both politicians and broadcasters believed that the principles of public service broadcasting should regulate television finance, organisation and programming priorities (Hood, 1983: 60).

Fifty years on, the picture of broadcasting looks radically different. Television sets are in place in 96 per cent of households: 58 per cent of homes have two or more televisions, 83 per cent have a video recorder (VCR), 27 per cent have two or more VCRs and UK households possess a total of 22,300,000 television sets (European Audiovisual Observatory, 1999: 37). The BBC competes with commercial broadcasters for viewers' attention and more than half of the BBC's income now derives from the Corporation's commercial activities (BBC, 1999). Five terrestrial channels and more than 250 digital channels provide round-the-clock programming, which is available via terrestrial, satellite and cable delivery systems. At the turn of the millennium, viewers can choose from more than 40,000 hours of programming in any single week (DTI and DCMS, 2000: para 1.1.2). Technological developments in multi-media enable growing numbers of people to watch television programmes on their personal computers, or to send e-mails via their television sets, and pose signficant questions about regulation in an age of 'media convergence'. Television, moreover, has become a highly significant industry which makes a substantial economic contribution to

Britain's GDP. The manufacture and sales of television receivers, video recorders, DVDs and recorders, combined with the making and selling of television programmes, constitute a multi-million pound industry which competes in an expansive market with a global reach.

A succession of government broadcasting policies has helped to shape and direct this expansion in the provision of television programmes, hardware and services. Policy disputes have been commonplace both within and between different governing parties. In turn, government policy has been influenced by technological developments which have posed new policy 'problems' requiring distinctive solutions. In addition, in democratic political systems, governments are obliged to take account of the competing policy ambitions of particular and interested groups. In the case of broadcasting policy, this includes broadcasters (both public and private sector), media owners, broadcasting organisations, trade unions and broadcasting-related pressure groups like the Voice of the Listener and Viewer or the Campaign for Press and Broadcasting Freedom (CPBF). This book attempts to detail the various twists and turns of these policy debates since 1986 when the report of the Peacock Committee on financing the BBC established itself as a significant landmark on the broadcasting policy landscape.

This brief introduction is in three parts. The first examines the conclusions and recommendations of the Peacock Committee which succeeded in establishing a policy agenda for British broadcasting across the subsequent fifteen years. The second contextualises the Peacock Committee's report by setting its concerns against the broader backcloth of developments in British television broadcasting since the Second World War. The third sets out the broad ambitions of the book and addresses some of the difficulties which inevitably arise when selecting particular documents, from a considerably larger candidate group, in order to try to provide a balanced and well-rounded account of policy debates and developments.

'Ideological dementia'? The Peacock Committee

To suggest that the publication of the Peacock Committee on financing the BBC was not well received invites challenge for understatement. Labour's Shadow Home Secretary, Gerald Kaufman, denounced the report's conclusions as 'ideological dementia' which 'should be put in the waste paper basket' (Elstein, 1999, lecture 5: 16). The Committee's brief was guaranteed to incite controversy. Peacock was invited to 'assess the effects of the introduction of advertising or sponsorship on the BBC's Home Services, either as an alternative or a supplement to the income now received through the licence fee' (Peacock, 1986: 1). Many broadcasters, television regulators, broadcasting trade unions, academics and MPs, especially those in the then opposition Labour Party, were uncharacteristically united in their opposition to a report which they alleged represented a government-orchestrated attack on the BBC (Negrine, 1998: 4). Successive Conservative governments under Margaret Thatcher's leadership had certainly displayed a growing frustration with the BBC. The Corporation was part of an entrenched broadcasting oligopoly resilient to the broad thrust of Thatcherite economic policy that wished to privilege market forces as the organisational principle informing broadcasting policy above the provision of television on a public service basis (Franklin, 1997: 170–174). Politically too, there were tensions. In the early 1980s there had been some very public and well-documented spats between the government and the BBC, exemplified by the BBC's reporting of the Falklands' War which prompted allegations of 'treason' by some Conservative backbenchers: the *Panorama* programme devoted to IRA activities in Carrickmore and the BBC's *Real Lives* programmes triggered Thatcher's celebrated remark about the need to deny terrorists the 'oxygen of publicity' (Bolton, 1990: 52, 127).

Peacock: composition, critics and conclusions

Established in this context of a nadir in the relationship between government and broadcasters, no other inquiry into broadcasting has proved so contentious; hyperbole abounded in many responses to Peacock. A Conservative Minister, for example, dismissed the report as 'a dead duck' while the Independent Broadcasting Authority (IBA) claimed Peacock's proposal that Channel 4 should sell its own advertising would 'wreck' the fledgling broadcaster. The ITV companies joined the growing chorus of invective and somewhat bemused disbelief triggered by some of the proposals. Christopher Bland, then Head of London Weekend Television (LWT), argued that Peacock's idea of auctioning regional television franchises to the highest bidder was a 'pretty loopy procedure . . . a Friday afternoon suggestion' (Elstein, 1999, lecture 5: 16). A special issue of the trade paper *Broadcast* described the auction as 'a shark's charter' and noted that 'seldom has a government set up a committee with clearer instructions on precisely what it was expected to report . . . seldom has a committee so disappointed and defied its political masters' (*Broadcast*, 1986).

However, while many observers remained sceptical about the Committee's conclusions, few doubted that Peacock had expended great energy and considerable industry to achieve this near universal opprobrium. Established on 27 March 1985, the Committee commissioned a total of twenty research studies exploring various aspects of British television including: the public's attitude to the funding of the BBC (BMRB); the impact of advertising on the range and quality of BBC programming (West Yorkshire Media in Politics Group, 1986); and the effects of introducing advertising on BBC television services on the ITV and other media (National Economic Research Associates (NERA)) (Peacock, 1986: 177). Public interest in the issue of funding the BBC was considerable. Peacock received written submissions of evidence from organisations which ranged alphabetically from the Adam Smith Institute and the General Synod of the Church of England, via the Independent Television Companies Association (ITCA), the Local Radio Association and the National Union of Journalists, to the Writers Guild of Great Britain, Yorkshire Television plc and eleven anonymous writers: an impressive total of 843 submissions from interested parties and individual observers (Peacock, 1986: 158–164). In addition, Committee members made ten visits to governments and television broadcasting organisations in America, Japan and a number of European countries (Peacock, 1986: 165).

This extensive crop of research studies, combined with the great number of expert and public views canvassed by the report, as well as Peacock's undoubted academic skills, should have produced an authoritative policy document. But from the outset, the integrity of the report was challenged by politicians and broadcasters who were sceptical about the independence of the Peacock Committee as well as the government's motives in establishing the Committee. The appointment of Peacock to chair the Committee – a distinguished economist well known for his advocacy of liberal, free-market economics – seemed portentous. The widely held view was that the government would proceed to 'stack' the Committee with members ideologically disposed to favour an outcome congenial to its policy ambitions for broadcasting; 'the outcome of its inquiries was assumed to be a formality' (Barnett and Curry, 1994: 33). The announcement of the other members of the Committee did little to allay these concerns and suspicions. Members included Lord Quinton, the right-of-centre philosopher and President of Trinity College Oxford, conservative industrialist Sir Peter Reynolds CBE and – to many observers' surprise given the politically sensitive character of the inquiry – Samuel Brittan, the economic correspondent of the *Financial Times*, but also brother of Home Secretary Leon Brittan who had established the Committee. Some measure of balance seemed to be provided by the inclusion of Alastair Hetherington, the distinguished ex-editor of the *Guardian*, but many journalists continued to believe that 'the cast list of Professor Peacock's committee . . . has done little to dampen doubts that herself intended it to provide the rationale for bringing in the ads' (O'Malley, 1992: 94).

But those who anticipated that the findings of the Peacock inquiry would be resonant with government policy intentions were surprised in at least four respects by the Committee's eventual recommendations. First, Peacock extended the Committee's original remit to consider and make recommendations concerning the financing of the BBC, to embrace a considerably broader range of issues within both the public and commercial sectors of the broadcasting industry. Peacock argued that consideration of the financing of television required discussion of a logically and chronologically prior question: namely, what are the purposes of broadcasting? 'It would have been tempting' claimed Peacock

> to confine ourselves to a limited examination of the case for and against the introduction of advertising on the BBC . . . But . . . our terms of reference also require us to examine the financial and other consequences of any changes for a wide range of broadcasting and other media, and in particular their 'range and quality'. We therefore agree with those witnesses who have maintained that before we can devise guidelines for the finance of broadcasting, we have to specify its purposes.
>
> (Peacock, 1986: 125, para 546; Blumler and Nossiter, 1991: 5)

Second, Peacock concluded that there was much to praise in the existing broadcasting arrangements. 'The BBC and the regulated ITV system' he argued,

> have done far better in mimicking the effects of a true consumer market, than any purely *laissez faire* system, financed by advertising could have done under conditions of spectrum shortage . . . We would go further . . .

> they have provided packages of programmes to audiences at remarkably low cost . . . The intertwining of information, education and entertainment has broadened the horizons of great numbers of viewers . . . The notion of cross-fertilisation of programmes is inherent in BBC practice – and in ITV practice too – and of great value . . . All that is in accord with the Reithian tradition: deriving from Reith's own dictum in 1924 that you have to mix a little education with a lot of entertainment to carry people with you.
>
> (Peacock, 1986: 131, paras 581–582)

Third, the Committee 'disappointed the Prime Minister' by not delivering the policy agenda for change at the BBC which so many observers believed was a foregone conclusion given the committee's composition, its ideological predispositions and the government's policy ambitions (Barnett and Curry, 1994: 60). Indeed many of the government's most cherished policy aspirations (see 2.1) were explicitly rejected by Peacock. The Committee, for example, rejected advertising as a source of funding for the BBC, preferring to argue for retaining the licence fee which it recommended should be index-linked to the rate of inflation and continue to provide the BBC's major revenue stream, at least in the medium term (Peacock, 1986: 137, paras 615 and 620). Thatcher's 'disappointment' reflected the forceful political opposition she confronted from senior Cabinet colleagues, such as William Whitelaw, to any suggestion that the funding base of the BBC should be altered by advertising: she had hoped that Peacock might prove a political ally (O'Malley, 1992: 115).

Finally, although Peacock was established to consider the funding of BBC television services, few of the Committee's substantive recommendations involved the BBC. By contrast, many of its key proposals were to prove highly influential in reshaping the financial and organisational structures, as well as the regulatory regime, of the commercial sector of broadcasting. It was the Peacock Committee, for example, which proposed a blind franchise auction with licences to broadcast being awarded to the highest bidder and with franchise periods extended to ten years. Peacock also suggested that both the BBC and ITV should be required to increase to a minimum of 40 per cent the proportion of programmes supplied by independent producers, that the financial basis of Channel 4 should be radically changed by giving the channel the option of selling its own advertising and that all restrictions on pay-per-view should be removed for terrestrial as well as cable and satellite services (Peacock, 1986: 142–146). It is perhaps not surprising that Alastair Hetherington described the government's 1988 White Paper *Broadcasting in the '90s: Competition, Choice and Quality*, which contained each of these policy recommendations, as the 'progeny of Peacock' (Hetherington, 1989).

Peacock's legacy

Notwithstanding these unanticipated outcomes, the Peacock report established a policy agenda for broadcasting for the subsequent decades and marked a decisive watershed or 'landmark' in British broadcasting policy (Blumler and Nossiter, 1991: 3; O'Malley, 1992: 88). David Elstein, Chief Executive of Channel 5, claimed the 'sheer power of Peacock's arguments' made it 'easily the most brilliant of the five such inquiries since the war . . . at its best, the intensity of his logic and the clarity of his vision dwarf his failings. The reverberations of his report' have been 'felt for a decade or more' (Elstein, 1999, lecture 5: 17).

Peacock argued against specific policy proposals, such as the replacement of the licence fee by advertising, but offered a forceful advocacy of more general policy principles closely congruent with government thinking. The Committee argued for the supremacy of market forces and asserted the need for consumer sovereignty in shaping broadcasting services; the Committee was also highly critical of many aspects of existing broadcasting practice. Peacock concluded,

> British broadcasting should move to a sophisticated market based on consumer sovereignty. That is a system which recognises that viewers and listeners are the best ultimate judge of their own interests which they can best satisfy if they have the option of purchasing what they require from as many alternative sources of supply as possible . . . Our consumer sovereignty model is, of course, an ideal, a standard and a goal; not a fully specified mechanism to be pulled from the shelf tomorrow by a trigger-happy central planner. A satisfactory broadcasting market requires full freedom of entry for programme makers, a transmission system capable of carrying an indefinitely large number of programmes, facilities for pay-per-view or pay-per-channel and differentiated charges for units of time . . . The difficulty of course, is how to move from the present regulated system now under stress to the full broadcasting market.
>
> (Peacock, 1986: 133–134, paras 592–598)

Peacock offered a transition strategy. Broadcasting should move in three stages towards the 'full market system'. In the first stage, the BBC should continue to be funded by an inflation-linked licence fee rather than by advertising. In stage two, the licence fee would increasingly be supplanted by subscription. The third stage marks the transition to the 'functioning broadcasting market' characterised by multiple channels, delivery systems and a diversity of charging and payment systems. The transition to a market system based on consumer sovereignty would have obvious implications for public service broadcasting which, up to that point, constituted the foundation stone of British broadcasting. Public service broadcasting may now be judged unnecessary and inappropriate because of technological developments (there is no longer spectrum scarcity nor any need for public control); because it is undesirable (public service is based on paternalism); because it is anachronistic (competition and convergence signal that broadcasting policy should reflect industry requirements not the aspirations of a cultural elite); or because it is simply no longer a sustainable ambition (in the context of multi-channel television services, consumers will be unwilling to finance public service broadcasting via a licence fee) (Graham and Davies, 1997: 8; Graham, 2000).

The fifteen years since the publication of the Peacock report have witnessed a flurry of policy activity. The 1988 White Paper *Broadcasting in the '90s: Competi-*

tion, Choice and Quality, the Broadcasting Acts of 1990 and 1996, the White Papers *Media Ownership; the Government's Proposals* (1995) and *Regulating Communications: Approaching Convergence in the Digital Age* (1998), have transformed many aspects of the financial, organisational and regulatory landscape of television broadcasting. The results for the commercial sector of broadcasting have been considerable. The period since Peacock has witnessed the emergence of a more competitive commercial sector reflecting a revamped Channel 3, new funding arrangements for Channel 4, the launch of Channel 5 in 1997, the expansion of cable and satellite services and the explosion of digital television services since 1998.

Policy change has been equally evident in the public sector of broadcasting. The National Heritage report *The Future of the BBC* proposed retention of the licence fee (Cmnd 2098, 1992: 31), while the White Paper *The Future of the BBC: Serving the Nation Competing World Wide* (1994) encouraged the BBC to expand its commercial services at home and abroad. In 1999 the Davies report on the future Funding of the BBC recommended a digital licence fee supplement to assist the BBC to develop digital television; it also proposed the sale of the BBC Resources directorate as well as the sale of a 49 per cent share of BBC Worldwide. In February 2000 Chris Smith, the Secretary of State for Culture, Media and Sport, rejected the proposed sales of directorates and the digital supplement. He offered the BBC a £3 increase in licence fee, encouraged the BBC to make savings of £1 billion and argued the case for subjecting the BBC accounts to audit by the National Audit Office (see 2.15).

For their part, broadcasters have contributed with apparent enthusiasm to this proliferation of policy. At the BBC, *Extending Choice: The BBC's Role in the New Broadcasting Age* (1992), *Responding to the Green Paper* (1993), *People and Programmes: Continuity and Change in BBC Programming* (1995) and John Birt's influential speech 'The BBC; Past and Present' (1993) committed the BBC to a number of policy initiatives intended to reduce costs and improve efficiency – including 'producer choice' – while sustaining the range and quality of programming characteristic of a public service broadcaster in a multi-channel setting. In the commercial sector, Richard Eyre, then chief executive of the ITV Network Centre, argued for the replacement of *public service* broadcasting with *public interest* broadcasting, speaking against centralised regulation by the Independent Television Commission (ITC) and reasserting the role of audiences in shaping programme contents (1999). In summary, the period since the Peacock Committee report has been a period of substantial policy making and implementation resulting in considerable changes in the British broadcasting system, but these developments need to be contextualised in the broader setting of television policy in the post-war period.

Peacock and post-war television policy

Jay Blumler identifies five distinctive, but overlapping, phases in the development of British television broadcasting since 1946 (Blumler, 1996): this classification of broadcasting history and the associated developments in television policy shares many affinities with Smith's earlier periodisation of broadcasting (Smith, 1974: 16–17).

The first period may be termed 'monopoly'. It began with the onset of the BBC's early television broadcasts in 1936 (television broadcasting was suspended during the war and reintroduced in 1946) and concluded with the Television Act 1954 and the launching of ITV in 1955. For the greater part of this period, television was judged to be little more than an adjunct to radio: television was 'radio with pictures'. Sir William Haley, the first post-war Director General, believed that television 'was the natural extension of sound' and consequently the new medium was, from the outset, steeped in the traditions of public service broadcasting associated with Reith (Briggs, 1979: 4). The financial and organisational principles and structures which Sykes and Crawford had established for radio were grafted unquestioningly on to television (Franklin, 1997: 160). Television, like radio, was organised as a public service monopoly, which was funded by licence fee, regulated by the Board of Governors and broadcast to the whole nation a wide range of programmes intended to 'educate, inform and entertain'. In this latter respect, however, it differed from radio, being judged less serious and too frivolous because of the undue emphasis which the new medium placed on entertainment. But these perceptions of television shifted markedly following the broadcasting of the Coronation in 1952 which revealed the potential of television to provide serious commentary on significant national events while simultaneously capturing the spectacle of the occasion in a fashion which radio was unable to match. The age of monopoly ended when the Conservative Party's victory in the 1951 general election ushered in the new 'Independent' television services in 1955, despite Beveridge's support for retaining the BBC's monopoly (see Selwyn Lloyd's minority report to Beveridge in Appendix B).

The second period, which might be dubbed 'creative competition', extends from 1955 to 1962. At this time, policy debates became preoccupied with the impact of the new commercial television services on programme standards – which were allegedly being debased on ITV – while at the BBC one beneficial consequence of the arrival of commercial broadcasting seemed to be that the BBC was becoming less remote and more sensitive to audiences. The period ends with the publication of the Pilkington report, the rejection of programme populism and the establishment of BBC 2. But Blumler identifies 'creative competition' as a time of some considerable blossoming for television services in the UK which 'advanced the medium's programming powers and viewers' all round enjoyment' (Blumler, 1996). ITV programming targeted neglected 'mass tastes', especially for entertainment, provided regional programmes which undermined the metropolitan flavour of much BBC output and delivered programmes (especially news) in a more informal style: the net effect was to trigger a plummeting of BBC audience figures. For the first time, but certainly not the last, there was considerable pressure on the BBC to justify its claim for licence fee funding based on its audience share. The BBC responded with an invigorated programming schedule which included enhanced provision of sports and children's programmes, the development of television drama and situation comedy alongside what were to become legendary news and current affairs programmes such as *Tonight* and *Panorama*. These programming innovations seem to offer retrospective endorsement of Selwyn Lloyd's view expressed in a minority report to Beveridge that 'independent competition will be healthy for broadcasting' (Beveridge, Cmnd 8116, Minority Report, para

20). Not everyone was convinced of the desirability of competition however. In 1962, Pilkington rewarded the BBC for the quality and diverse range of its programming with a new channel: BBC 2. But Pilkington was highly critical of ITV for the alleged triviality of much of its programming, its too frequent portrayals of violence, combined with the narrow range of programmes broadcast, especially at peak points in the schedule. Pilkington was also critical of the Independent Television Authority (ITA) which it claimed was an ineffective regulator that needed to place a tighter control on programming output and advertising (Pilkington, Cmnd 1753, para 572).

A third period, 'stable competition', extended across 1963 to 1970 and witnessed broadcasting in confident (perhaps over-confident) mood, partly reflected in the broadcasting of an entirely new range of programmes. This new mood of confidence, questioning and modernism at the BBC was captured by the widely quoted suggestion that Hugh Greene, the new Director-General, had 'dressed Auntie in a mini skirt'. The new programmes (both factual and fictional) exemplified broadcasters' more critical posture towards society. Reith's dictum that programmes should educate, inform and entertain was supplemented by the additional requirement to question and challenge, especially the most powerful figures in society. The satirical programme *That Was The Week That Was* exemplified these trends and moods. Blumler also lists social dramas such as *Cathy Come Home*, unprecedentedly realistic police dramas such as *Z Cars*, socially conscious comedy *'Til Death Us Do Part* and sitcoms set in northern towns such as the *Likely Lads*, and argues that each illustrated this new confident mood among broadcasters which seemed increasingly to require them to make programmes characterised by social realism and social criticism (Blumler, 1996).

The fourth period, 'broadcasting under cultural attack', which lasted from 1970 to 1983, reflected a public backlash to the previous period of broadcasting confidence: there were loudly articulated public demands for mechanisms to make broadcasters more accountable. In Smith's words, there was 'a growing belief that television had grown over-dominant, that it was beginning to "trivialise" politics and to be careless of its effects on public morals, on the level of violence and on respect for authority' (Smith, 1974: 17). Blumler cites particular examples of programmes and oppositional groups to 'flesh out' Smith's more schematic point: the broad ideological range of television's critics seemed considerable. Politicians across all parties, for example, objected to the 'flippant' tone of *Yesterday's Men*, a programme about the Labour Party and its leader Harold Wilson. Mary Whitehouse's Viewers and Listeners Association grew in numbers and strength of opposition to what they argued were too frequent and explicit portrayals of violence and sexual behaviour in programmes, while studies by media academics, especially the Glasgow Media group, proved corrosive of television news' treasured claims to impartiality and objectivity in news coverage of industrial disputes. The policy preoccupations which dominated this period were consequently the need for additional forms of regulatory control of programme contents and public accountability. In addition, from both 'left and right there were demands to break the broadcasters' editorial stronghold, and substitute forms of free public access to the camera and the microphone' (Smith, 1974: 17). At the same time, a different critique emerged from within broadcasting itself. There was a growing unhappiness with the broadcasting duopoly of the BBC and ITV which was increasingly seen as conservative with a small 'c', obsessed with preserving and protecting its own interests, with a consequent stultifying effect on creative and artistic work.

The BBC responded by creating a Community Programming Unit to facilitate community-based groups' access to programme making. Annan's response was an enthusiastic advocacy of an Open Broadcasting Authority. But Blumler argues that the most important policy outcome of this period was the establishment of Channel 4 in 1982 with its special remit to seek out minority audiences and make innovative programmes (Blumler, 1996). Commercially funded via a complex arrangement whereby advertisements for the new channel were sold by the ITV companies, Channel 4 retained an independence from advertisers' pressures to seek out large audiences, but was guaranteed sufficient funding to commission quality programming. Channel 4 was given a public service mission which was to be funded by a private sector mechanism: a wonderfully British squaring of the circle between quality and market forces.

The fifth period of 'deregulation and markets' from 1984 to the present is characterised by the emergence of the market as the organisational principle for broadcasting and the enthronement of the consumer as the sovereign guarantor of popular (rather than quality) programming. The policy preoccupations have been with finance, public service and (de)regulation. The 'curtain raiser' for the unleashing of this 'tide of radically revisionist commercialism' was the Peacock Committee on financing the BBC (Blumler, 1996). During this current policy period, television has been subject to extraordinary changes in its financial, organisational and regulatory aspects both in the commercial and public sectors of the industry. Technological developments such as the emergence of cable, satellite and digital delivery systems have heightened the pace and intensity of policy change. During the late 1990s, for example, the development of digital services, the burgeoning of new television channels and the prospect of media convergence has prompted a reappraisal of structures for regulation including the suggestion that media convergence might signal regulation convergence with a single regulatory body to supplant the existing bodies with their overlapping regulatory briefs. The publication of the White Paper *A New Future For Communications* on 12 December 2000 transformed this 'suggestion' into a concrete proposal.

Another notable tendency during this period has been the continuing trend towards the concentration of media ownership invested in large conglomerates, with interests in a wide range of media, prompting an inevitable growth in cross-media ownership. This process was exemplified in July 2000 when Granada bought Meridian, Anglia and HTV from Lord Hollick's United News and Media for £1.75 billion. The purchase made Granada the dominant broadcaster within Channel 3. The addition of these new licences to Granada's existing holdings in Tyne Tees and Yorkshire Television gave the company a 12.8 per cent market share, broadcasting to fifteen million homes and anticipating advertising sales of £1 billion. Prior to publication of *A New Future For Communications*, many of the larger broadcasters and newspaper groups were lobbying to secure a relaxation of existing ownership rules, suggesting that the process of concentration of ownership was a necessary prerequisite for competing effectively in a global market (see, for example, the submissions of News International, Trinity Mirror and the ITC to the consultation process at www.culture.gov.uk/

creative/dti-dcms_comms-reform_white_paper.html). The White Paper's recommendation that the 15 per cent limit on share of television audience should be removed, along with the prohibition on ownership of the two London ITV licences, undoubtedly paves the way for a merger between Granada and Carlton and the creation of a single ITV company.

Finally, a continuing and prominent policy issue in this most recent period has been the perennial question of the adequacy of the licence fee as a funding mechanism for the BBC. In late 1999, the Davies report suggested a digital licence supplement, an option rejected by the Select Committee on Culture, Media and Sport in December 1999 and by the Minister in an announcement in Parliament on 21 February 2000. The reports of the Davies Committee, the Select Committee and the Minister's statement address questions concerning the legitimacy of the licence fee, the level of the fee, related issues regarding the character of public service broadcasting and the implications of funding for the quality of television programming which could have been, and were, raised by previous inquiries into television broadcasting. The policy concerns of the current period signal a continuity rather than any break with the policy preoccupations of previous periods. The policy documents collected here provide in great detail the narrative of these policy developments and broadcasting changes since the publication of the Peacock report.

Television policy documents: structure and problems

The idea for this collection of broadcasting policy documents reflects little more than a self-conscious attempt to replicate and develop an earlier book which is currently out of print and substantially out of date. Anthony Smith's *British Broadcasting* (1974) provided the model for what is offered here. As a researcher, I have used Smith's book extensively and know that other media scholars have also found it useful. For students, it is simply a delight, a near comprehensive account of developments in radio and television broadcasting accompanied by authoritative commentary. *British Television Policy: A Reader* updates Smith's analysis and hopes to provide a similarly useful 'reference' or 'source' text for students and others with interests in media policy. The ambition is to provide a forum for the significant policy debates that have informed and shaped television broadcasting since the publication of the Peacock Committee report. The book selects, presents and analyses key policy documents and critically appraises their impact on the organisation, financial resources, programme content, editorial philosophy and regulatory environment of television broadcasting.

British Television Policy has a number of broad objectives. First, it seeks to provide readers with access to a wide range of statutory and non-governmental policy documents relating to television broadcasting, which are organised thematically. Second, it aims to present a range of critical assessments by academics, broadcasters and policy makers of these recent developments in television policy. Third, it offers authoritative commentary on television policy developments. Fourth, it attempts to signal and explore the diversity and range of beliefs and theoretical stances, as well as the plurality of policy ambitions, which are evident in the policy process. Fifth, it identifies and discusses a number of historically overlapping stages in the development of television policy making and implementation, while arguing for an essential continuity of policy concerns. Sixth, it provides an assessment of the impact of media policy on the organisational structures, financial arrangements, programme content and regulatory environment of television broadcasting and, finally, it attempts to contextualise recent television policy within successive governments' broader policy ambitions.

The selection of documents

The ambition to produce a reader of policy documents which catalogues the various twists and turns of television policy in recent years confronts an immediate and obvious question: Which documents should be included? Other questions follow promptly. What constitutes a 'key' policy document? How are these policy documents to be identified? Ultimately the process of selection requires consideration of even broader questions about the policy process itself. It involves, for example, an acknowledgement that policy making is not wholly or simply a prerogative of government. Governments enact legislation under the critical eye of Parliament and, in that process, legislation may be amended in substantive ways. But, in democratic polities, the policy activities of governments are subject to scrutiny by a much wider policy community constituted of a number of groups with their own policy ambitions that they seek to incorporate into the policy mix. These groups share differing degrees of ideological and policy proximity to the government of the day, and consequently their potential and effectiveness in shaping policy outcomes varies considerably. As governments are removed and replaced during the electoral cycle, moreover, new policy agendas are established, creating variable possibilities for policy influence for these members of the policy community across time.

In the context of television policy, this policy community embraces: the various political parties; Members of Parliament; interest groups such as the Voice of the Listener and Viewer (VLV), the Campaign for Press and Broadcasting Freedom (CPBF) and the Campaign for Quality Television (CQT); broadcasting regulators (the BBC and ITC); the broadcasting organisations: terrestrial (the BBC and Channels 3, 4 and 5), satellite (Sky Channel) and cable (Fantasy TV, the Parliament Channel and the Black Music Channel); individual media owners, broadcasters, academics and politicians. Each of these members of the policy community contributes to the broad policy debate by generating policy statements and is thereby a player in the process of policy formulation. Consequently, the documents collected here include:

- Acts of Parliament (*The Broadcasting Act 1996*);
- White papers (*A New Future For Communications*, 2000, *Media Ownership: The Government's View* 1995);
- Private Members Bills (Chris Mullin MP, A Bill To Regulate for Media Diversity, 1995);
- Select Committee reports (The report of the Select Committee on Culture, Media and Sport, *Funding the BBC*, 20 December 1999);

- Official statements by ministers (Chris Smith's formal rejection of the licence fee supplement in *Hansard*, 21 February 2000);
- Inquiries into various aspects of television broadcasting (the Davies Independent Review of the future funding of the BBC);
- Policy statements by think-tanks (*Privatising the BBC*, demos);
- Policy documents prepared by interest groups (the Campaign for Quality Television's *The Purposes of Broadcasting*, 1998);
- Policy statements by regulatory bodies (*The Future of Regulation*, Sir Robin Biggam, 1999, ITC);
- Policy statements by broadcasting organisations (the BBC's *People and Programmes*, 1995);
- Public lectures by media owners, distinguished broadcasters and media executives (The MacTaggart Lectures by Rupert Murdoch, 1989, Dennis Potter, 1993 and Richard Eyre, 1999);
- Commentaries by academics (Stephen Coleman's study of the declining television coverage of Parliament, 1999);
- Newspaper articles and leaders (*The Times*, 'Whither the BBC?', 1985);
- And finally, extracts from the memoirs of significant policy actors (*Margaret Thatcher: The Downing Street Years*, 1993).

Two points emerge from even the most cursory glance at this fairly lengthy list of sources: accordingly, two 'health warnings' must be posted at the outset. First, the different policy documents listed here are not equal in terms of their policy significance measured either by their capacity to command wide-ranging support, consensus and respect, nor by the actual impact they make on the institutions and processes of television broadcasting; in this latter sense, legislation is evidently the most significant of policy statements. Second, the process of selection involves substantial opportunity costs. Given limited word space, every selection has been made at the expense of another document that necessarily has been excluded. Consequently, the selection of documents inevitably steers the reader towards the consideration of some aspects of policy at the expense of ignoring others. Further opportunity costs are incurred in the selection of a short extract from what is often a very lengthy document, with all the attendant risks of offering readers a partial and subjective account of what constitutes the significant policy kernel within any particular document. Given these potential problems, it is essential to establish and make clear the criteria of selection, which have informed decisions concerning the inclusion of some documents in this collection and which explain the discarding of others. Six criteria emerged as significant. Documents were selected because of (1) their consequences and significant impacts on broadcasting; (2) the authority and primacy of the document (legislation has been prioritised above newspaper articles); (3) the significance of a particular policy document's contribution to a policy debate; (4) the need to achieve a comprehensive discussion of policy issues; (5) the desire to produce a well-rounded and even-handed account of the range of viewpoints on broadcasting issues, and (6) the need to include the widest possible range of relevant and pertinent contributions to policy discussions embracing legislation, policy statements emanating from broadcasting organisations as well as policy reviews by academic observers and broadcasters.

The historical or thematic grouping of documents?

A second major concern in structuring a collection of television policy documents is whether to organise the various documents 'historically' or 'thematically'. Anthony Smith's *British Broadcasting* treats its subject matter historically, beginning with extracts from the Sykes Committee (1923) and concluding with Sir Hugh Greene's Guildhall lecture detailing a general plan of reform for television (1972). This approach enjoys the evident merit of allowing the complex development of argument and debate about television policy across fifty years to unravel in a step-by-step fashion for readers. But the current *Reader* focuses on a period of fifteen years' intense policy activity which is arguably too brief to be the subject of any historical sweep or review.

The preferred approach, which is adopted here, involves identifying the key questions that have informed recent television broadcasting policy. These central questions have been:

1. What is the purpose of television broadcasting? What is its mission? Should television still seek to educate, inform and entertain? Has the balance between these elements in broadcasting's fundamental purpose shifted? Is television still to be informed by public service principles?
2. How is broadcasting to be financed – and by whom? Does advertising, subscription, pay-per-view, a direct tax on viewers or the licence fee provide the most satisfactory mechanism for funding broadcasting?
3. What are the likely implications of different patterns and forms of broadcasting finance for the range and quality of television programming? Is the increasingly competitive character of the commercial sector of broadcasting compatible with the provision of quality programming? What has been the policy response and programming strategy of the BBC when confronting a multi-channel environment for television programmes and services?
4. How is broadcasting to be regulated? How can broadcasters be held accountable to ensure their programmes comply with popular standards of 'taste and decency'? Should television programme content be subject to a different style of regulation (perhaps regulated with a 'lighter touch') in the context of a more competitive market environment? What form should economic regulation assume in order to prevent monopoly concentrations of ownership which might, in turn, diminish the range and quality of programming? How might regulatory regimes need to be reconfigured in the light of developing broadcasting technologies such as cable, satellite and digital?
5. How is broadcasting related to the wider political system? What is the nature of politicians' relationships with television broadcasting? Is the relationship adversarial or collusive? Does the ability of government to legislate for change in broadcasting (including the censorship of broadcasters) make them the

dominant partner, or are governments and politicians subject to the constraints imposed by vigilant broadcasters who function as a fourth estate?

These central problems and dilemmas, which television policy has tried to resolve since the mid-1980s, provide the various section headings under which the wide-ranging policy documents will be grouped: (1) Public service broadcasting; (2) Broadcasting finance; (3) Programmes; (4) Regulation, and (5) Broadcasting and political communications.

Perhaps more significantly, these five inquiries seem to represent what might be termed 'perennial questions' which have been at the centre of policy concerns since the very beginnings of broadcasting; radio before television! (see Appendix B). However, while the questions have been perennial, the considerably changed social, economic, political and cultural context of broadcasting in which they have been posed, in tandem with striking developments in broadcasting technology, has often generated distinctive and novel solutions on different historical occasions.

The persistency of these perennial concerns is evident across the various inquiries into broadcasting during the twentieth century. The Sykes Committee (1923), for example, considered questions of finance such as whether advertising and sponsorship might provide suitable revenue sources for the BBC. The committee concluded that advertising would 'lower' the 'high standard of broadcast programmes' but offered 'no objection' to sponsorship (Sykes, Cmd 1951, 1923: 19). Crawford explored the organisational and funding structures of broadcasting and recommended that broadcasting should remain a monopoly, financed by licence fees on receivers and administered by an independent public corporation (Crawford, 1926, Cmd 2599: 14–15). Selsdon (1935) addressed issues arising from early developments in television technology but also argued against 'letting private enterprise nurture the infant service' preferring, on the ground of 'public Interest' that responsibility for developing television services should 'be laid on the British Broadcasting Corporation' (Selsdon, 1935, Cmd 4793: paras 39–40). The Ullswater Committee confirmed the policy mood against advertising and sponsorship and in favour of the licence fee, but suggested that the government had 'a right directly to control broadcasting during a national emergency' (Ullswater, 1936, Cmd 5091: para 57). Beveridge argued that political broadcasting should be increased and, with the exception of a minority report by Selwyn Lloyd, that the BBC should remain a monopoly; it also suggested that any retreat from the BBC's monopoly would lead to the trivialising of programmes (Beveridge, 1949, Cmd 8116: paras 326–335). After Beveridge, Pilkington looked at competition between broadcasters following the introduction of independent commercial television services and its effects on programme quality. The committee concluded, 'there was . . . a preoccupation in many programmes with the superficial' and 'the cheaply sensational', with many programmes being 'vapid and puerile, their content often derivative, repetitious and lacking in real substance' (Pilkington, 1962, Cmnd 1752: paras 97–100). Indeed the sense of *déjà vu* can be overwhelming when the debates about the impact of competition for advertising revenues on programmes quality, which appeared at the time of the Peacock report, are compared with Richard Hoggart's discussion of similar concerns during the Pilkington Committee (ibid.). The Annan Committee, as well as illustrating how changing political circumstances can influence policy outcomes (the day after Annan was announced, Harold Wilson dissolved Parliament and, following the election of a Conservative government, Annan's appointment was rescinded), argued in support of public service broadcasting, made recommendations to guarantee the editorial independence of broadcasters from political pressure and proposed a new structure for broadcasting to ensure diversity outside the 'straitjacket of the existing duopoly of the BBC and the IBA' (Annan, 1977, Cmnd 6753: para 30.1).

This posing of perennial questions has been noted previously. Asa Briggs in his *History of Broadcasting in the United Kingdom* (vol. 1), for example, reproduced what he described as a 'fascinating document' retrieved from the Sykes Committee hearings which explored possible organisational, financial and regulatory arrangements for the emerging broadcasting industry. It is difficult to demur from Briggs' judgement that the tantalising document explores 'all the right questions without giving any of the answers' (Briggs, 1995: 8–9). But the thoughtful if precocious document, by posing perennial questions, anticipates many of the key concerns which continue to inform debates about broadcasting policy. Entitled 'Questions Concerning Scheme That Would Be Recommended if Government Had Free Hand With No Commitments', it asks 'Should broadcasting be entrusted to one organisation only, or to more than one?' If to more than one, 'should the service at each centre be thrown open to tender?' Again, if broadcasting is entrusted to a single organisation, 'should it be to a government department or to a company working under a government licence?' 'If the latter, should the company's operations be controlled – or advised on – by a committee representing various "interests"? If so . . . should it exercise any financial supervision?' And finally, 'about what annual revenue would the company require to give satisfactory service?' (Briggs, 1995: 8–9).

This posing of perennial questions has, on occasion, evoked 'perennial answers'. Peacock's suggestion that licences to broadcast should be allocated to the highest bidder, for example, has a considerable pedigree which can certainly be traced back to the 1950s: the extract from the Sykes hearings quoted above suggests that the idea of bidding for broadcasting licences may even have its origins in the 1920s. Fifty years on in the 1970s, Labour Cabinet Minister Harold Lever suggested that ITV franchises should be treated in much the same way as the newly discovered North Sea oilfields, as scarce, publicly owned assets whose revenues should be maximised when allocating licences to drill. Subsequently an appendix in the Annan report on 'The Profits of Advertising Financed Television' suggested that companies which wished a licence to broadcast should 'bid a price . . . in competition with other potential users' (Annan, 1977, Cmnd 6753, Appendix). In rejecting the idea, Annan quoted with approval Pilkington's assertion that there was 'no natural connection between the best all round qualification to provide a public service and the amount of money an applicant might offer or think it prudent to offer' (Elstein, 1999, lecture 6: 3).

Consequently, a thematic approach to television policy which considers these perennial questions (and sometimes perennial answers) captures the essence of policy preoccupations since the beginnings of television broadcasting. It also illustrates what Smith describes as the 'certain unity' and 'stability of debate' in the 'whole discussion of broadcasting in Britain' which is evident when 'reading through all the material thrown up by successive Acts of Parliament and periodic investigations into broadcasting' (Smith, 1974: 15). That certain unity identified by Smith almost thirty years ago is no less evident in current discussions of television policy.

References

Barnett, S. and Curry, A. (1994) *Battle for the BBC*, London: Aurum Books.

BBC (1999) *Annual Report and Accounts*, London: BBC Publications.

Blumler, J.G. (1996) 'British Television', in H. Newcomb (ed.) *The Encyclopaedia of Television*, New York: Frank Dearborn.

Blumler, J.G. and Nossiter, T. (1991) *The Financing of Television: A Handbook*, Oxford: Oxford University Press.

Bolton, R. (1990) *Death on the Rock and Other Stories*, London: W.H. Allen/Optomen Books.

Briggs, A. (1979) *A History of Broadcasting in the United Kingdom*, vol. 4 *Sound and Vision*, Oxford: Oxford University Press.

Briggs, A. (1995) *A History of Broadcasting in the United Kingdom:* vol. 1 *Competition 1955–1974*, Oxford: Oxford University Press.

DTI and DCMS (2000) *A New Future For Communications*, London: Stationery Office.

Elstein, D. (1999) *The Political Structure of UK Broadcasting, 1949–1999*, unpublished lectures delivered at Oxford University, Hilary term.

European Audiovisual Observatory (1999) *Statistical Yearbook: Film, Television, Video and New Media in Europe*, Strasbourg: Council of Europe.

Franklin, B. (1997) *Newszak and News Media*, London: Arnold

Graham, A. (2000) 'Public Policy Issues for UK Broadcasting', in *e-britannia*, Luton: University of Luton Press, pp. 93–108

Graham, A. and Davies, G. (1997) *Broadcasting, Society and Policy in the Multimedia Age*, Luton: John Libbey Media.

Hetherington, A. (1989) 'The White Paper: Thatcher, Peacock and Who Remembers Reith?', unpublished paper presented to the Conference on the Future of Broadcasting, York, 24–25 February.

Hood, S. (1983) *On Television*, London: Pluto.

Negrine, R. (1998) *Television and the Press Since 1945*, Manchester: Manchester University Press.

O'Malley, T. (1992) *Closedown*, London: Pluto Press.

Peacock, A. (1986) *Report of the Committee on Financing The BBC* (Chair Professor Alan Peacock), London: HMSO, Cmnd 9824, July.

Seymour Ure, C. (1991) *The British Press and Broadcasting Since 1945*, Oxford: Blackwell.

Smith, A. (1974) *British Broadcasting*, Newton Abbot: David and Charles.

West Yorkshire Media in Politics Group (1986) *Financing the BBC: A Research Report*, London: HMSO.

PART ONE

Television Broadcasting Policy: Public Service Broadcasting

JOHN REITH the first Director-General of the BBC, was convinced that broadcasting should constitute a public service rather than being organised according to free-market principles, with funding derived from advertising or sponsorship and with the profit motive impelling programming decisions. 'I wonder if many have paused to consider' he mused, 'the incalculable harm which might have been done had different principles guided the conduct of the service in the early days' (Reith, 1925: 31). His commitment to public service broadcasting was captured in the phrase – quoted so frequently that it risks becoming a cliché – that broadcasting should seek to 'inform, educate and entertain'. Within this Reithian trilogy, the concern to 'inform' suggested the need for a comprehensive news service, international news, current affairs programming and documentaries. The emphasis on the need to 'educate' argued for the provision of quality schools' programming but, more significantly, a broader mission to 'improve' the audience. In Reith's words, 'our responsibility is to carry into the greatest possible number of homes everything that is best in every department of human knowledge, endeavour and achievement' (Reith, 1924: 34). With hindsight, this commitment to 'educate' has been interpreted critically, with some observers suggesting that 'for 50 years British television has operated on the assumption that the people could not be trusted to watch what they wanted to watch . . . it had to be controlled by like-minded people who knew what was good for us' (see 1.8). Reith himself was conscious of contemporary allegations of paternalism which he dismissed too frequently in language suggestive of arrogance. 'It is occasionally indicated to us' he claimed, 'that we are apparently setting out to give the public what we think they need – and not what they want, but few know what they want, and very few what they need. There is often no difference . . . in any case it is better to over estimate the mentality of the public, than to underestimate it' (ibid.).

Reith believed that public service broadcasting was founded on four principles. First, broadcasting should be protected from commercial pressures and the profit motive. Second, broadcasting should provide radio and television services to the whole community; broadcasting's reach should be national. Third, broadcasting must be characterised by 'unified control', by which Reith meant the 'brute force of monopoly', rather than any regional or sectional interest. Finally, broadcasting must be closely regulated to establish high standards and ensure that broadcast programmes were of high quality.

Since Reith was appointed, the philosophy of public service broadcasting was not simply an abstract set of principles on which to base a broadcasting system, but an account of the particular organisational form which broadcasting assumed in both the public and private sectors of British broadcasting. The reports of the various committees of inquiry into broadcasting published over the past seventy-five years – from Sykes to Hunt (see Appendix B) – have built on Reith's initial conception and further shaped the resilient but changing character of public service broadcasting.

The arrival of a commercial television service (ITV) in 1954 posed a particular challenge to the public service tradition. The new network's popular programmes attracted considerable audiences and prompted a review of programmes at the BBC. But the Pilkington Committee's (see Appendix B) highly critical appraisal of ITV programmes resulted in the 1963 Television Act obliging the commercial sector to reconsider and buttress its public service commitments.

During the early 1980s, developments in broadcasting technology prompted the emergence of cable and satellite television delivery systems. These developments, combined with the newly elected Conservative government's commitment to deregulate broadcasting – as part of a broader agenda to subject all aspects of the public sector to the rigour of market forces – created an expectation of a new inquiry into broadcasting: a series of editorials published in *The Times* during January 1985 articulated the growing public expectation (1.2). In 1985 the Peacock Committee was established to examine the funding of the BBC. It was widely anticipated that the Committee's report would recommend the replacement of the licence fee with advertising revenues. However, contra contemporary predictions, the Committee's eventual suggestion was in favour of retaining the licence fee but moving in stages to a 'full broadcasting market' in which the BBC would be funded by subscription. In the short run the pubic service tradition was secure. But Peacock's emphasis on market mechanisms, on a competitive broadcasting system to be driven by consumer choice and funded by subscription – with the inevitable fragmentation of the audience – signalled that in the longer term, public service broadcasting would become a residue or mere adjunct of commercial broadcasting with modest and truncated ambitions, consigned to making programmes which a market-based broadcasting system would have little incentive to produce; i.e. programmes which viewers are willing to support in their capacity 'as taxpayers . . . but not directly as consumers' (Peacock, 1986, para 580. See 1.3). The Davies Review Panel looking at the funding of the BBC offered a similar formulation to Peacock's view of public service when its report argued that 'beyond simply using the catch-phrase that public service broadcasting must "inform, educate and entertain", we must add "inform, educate and entertain in a way which the private sector left unregulated would not do"' (Davies, 1999: 136. See 1.6). The White Paper *A New Future For Communications* (December 2000) restated the significance of public service broadcasting in the digital age but argued for a different system of regulation to deliver it (1.7). This growing emphasis on market forces in broadcasting, and the considerable challenge it has posed to the principles informing the public service tradition since the early 1980s, prompted communications scholar Jay Blumler to describe such principles as 'vulnerable values' (Blumler, 1992). A decade later, the situation seemed more dramatic; the hyperbole was certainly greater. Using the James MacTaggart lecture as his platform, Richard Eyre announced the imminent demise of public service broadcasting. 'It's a gonner' he claimed, because 'free school milk doesn't work when the kids go and buy Coca-Cola because it's available, they prefer it and they can afford it. So public service broadcasting will soon be dead . . . public interest broadcasting not public service will be the salvation of the BBC' (see 1.11).

This chapter examines various and developing understandings of public service broadcasting. The selected extracts are gathered under two headings; within each the ordering is chronological to allow the various strands of the argument and debate to unfold. Extracts in the first group present the changing definitions of public service broadcasting over the past fifteen years. The second collection of extracts presents the views of recent critics of public service broadcasting. These include critics who believe that the market offers a superior organisational mechanism for broadcasting (Murdoch, 1.8 and Eyre, 1.11), as well as others who regret what they consider to be the inappropriate 'intrusion' of market forces into broadcasting and criticise the public service tradition on precisely that ground (Potter, 1.9 and the Campaign for Quality Television, 1.10).

References

Blumler, J. (1992) *Television and The Public Interest: Vulnerable Values in West European Broadcasting*, London: Sage and the Broadcasting Standards Council.

Reith, J. (1924) *Broadcast Over Britain* London: Hodder and Stoughton.

Reith, J. (1925) *Personality and Career*, London: George Newnes.

CHANGING UNDERSTANDINGS AND PERCEPTIONS

1.1 The Broadcasting Research Unit and Public Service Broadcasting

In 1985, when the Peacock Committee was commissioned to examine the funding of the BBC, the Broadcasting Research Unit (BRU) – an organisation concerned to research issues of broadcasting policy, chaired by academic Richard Hoggart who had been a member of the Pilkington inquiry into broadcasting (see Appendix B) – conducted an opinion survey of broadcasters working both in the commercial and public sectors of television, in an effort to establish a definition of public service broadcasting which might assist Peacock in its investigations; the key elements in the BRU definition are included in Peacock's final report (para 33).

[T]he purposes served by the main provisions of public service broadcasting in Britain go far beyond the policing of a shortage, serve far more important democratic aims and that, though the structure we have is not perfect, nor perfectly operated, in general it has served us extremely well; that the continuance of its aims cannot be ensured simply by the operation of market mechanisms; and that, no matter how many outlets for delivery systems the new technologies offer, the essential elements of pubic service broadcasting should be retained. They are a unique device serving our highest interests and are by now an integral part of the social fabric. if they are lost we shall be diminished as a nation.

Main principles

1. Universality: Geographic – broadcast programmes should be available to the whole population.
2. Universality of appeal: – broadcast programmes should cater for all interests and tastes.

3 Minorities, especially disadvantaged minorities, should receive particular provision.
4 Broadcasters should recognise their special relationship to the sense of national identity and community.
5 Broadcasting should be distanced from all vested interests, and in particular from those of the government of the day.
6 Universality of payment: – one main instrument of broadcasting should be directly funded by the corpus of users.
7 Broadcasting should be structured so as to encourage competition in good programming rather than competition for numbers.
8 The public guidelines for broadcasting should be designed to liberate rather than restrict the programme makers.

The Broadcasting Research Unit (1985) *The Public Service Idea in British Broadcasting: Main Principles*, Luton: John Libbey, pp.25–32.

1.2 *The Times* Critique of Public Service Broadcasting

In January 1985, Rupert Murdoch's *The Times* published a series of editorials criticising the BBC and arguing that the arrival of commercial television, the launch of a second BBC channel, the development of BBC local radio and breakfast television, the opportunities for time-shifting offered by VCRs and a changed political climate in which the regressive licence fee requires some justification, had each eroded the BBC's claims to public service broadcasting and required public investigation and discussion. *The Times* urged the 'government to consider quickly the establishment of a new broadcasting commission . . . to begin the process of redefining public service broadcasting' (16 January). In the final analysis, the editorial argued, the BBC's case for public service broadcasting 'is reduced to the simple unproven assertion that without it programme quality will fall' (15 January).

Whither the BBC?

Tomorrow the Labour MP, Mr Joe Ashton, launches a Bill calling for the BBC to take advertising. Last month, on the very day that the BBC began its campaign for a 41% increase in its licence fee, the Prime Minister let it be known that she too favoured BBC advertising. The BBC is today accused, with varying degrees of fairness, of inefficiency, unaccountability, self-aggrandisement, feather bedding its employees – everything from impoliteness to John Selwyn Gummer to failing to make *Jewel In The Crown*.

Are the critics justified? In their main principles: yes. The Cabinet is to make a decision on the size and duration of the next licence fee in the next few weeks. In the present climate that can only be an interim announcement. The debate must – and will – go much further. The BBC should not survive this Parliament at its present size, in its present form and with its present terms of reference intact.

To justify the changes it is necessary to look much more deeply at the nature of the BBC than has been done hitherto. With the Annan Committee's Report still not 10 years old, tired BBC executives may feel that they have been examined to death. They have not. Since the very foundation of the BBC there has been a paradox at its heart. Radio and television are considered to have a role as a public servant. Their service – while not an essential one to be funded from tax like the police or the army – is nonetheless a public good, at least in part. But because that part contains its political reporting and analysis, politicians have always been shy of defining to the public what that public service broadcasting should be.

For more than 60 years the licence fee has provided an acceptable screen behind which the question could be fudged. The BBC has been allowed to evolve its own concept of public service broadcasting. The essence of this is the idea of a seamless robe, that there is no point in a daily broadcasting diet at which entertainment ends and the public service begins. Not everyone in the BBC believes this convenient diktat for the same reasons. To the true disciples of Lord Reith, the meat and the pudding are both necessary parts of the same well-balanced meal; it is as much a component of the public good that the quiz show be a suitable family treat as that the news programmes keep the electorate properly informed of world events. To the more cynical broadcasters, the role of the quiz shows is to bring in the size of audience necessary to justify a licence fee which comes from everyone who owns a television set regardless of whether he/she watches BBC or not.

The system still has its defenders – and not just in the BBC. The licence system has reached the status of an acceptable institution in its own right. And the duopoly in which the BBC alone takes the licence fees and the independent companies alone broadcast advertising might have continued for ever were it not for a number of pressures that now look set to burst it apart.

First, since the arrival of independent television, the BBC has found it harder to win the audience necessary to justify to itself its licence fee monopoly. As was pointed out in a study for the Annan Committee in 1977, professionalism is the prized epithet of praise for the modern BBC man. The realists quickly triumphed over Lord Reith's true believers in public service. The BBC's seamless robe has long looked remarkably similar to that of its commercial competitors.

Secondly the BBC expanded *pari passu* to meet the general expansion in broadcasting. The seamless robe has stretched to take in local radio, a new television channel and breakfast television. Costs rose sharply and are still rising sharply. For the BBC, unlike its competitors, every extra hour of broadcast presents no revenue, only extra bills. In the future looms the enormous cost of technical enhancement from satellites in space and cables beneath the city streets.

Thirdly, those same technical advances – plus others in the fields of home computers and videos – are extending consumer choice, making it still harder for the BBC to achieve its chosen level of domination in the market.

Fourthly, the political climate has changed. Today a duopoly has to be justified. So does a poll tax such as the BBC licence fee, particularly one that is fast rising and looks set on present policies to rise still faster. The fact that 70% of the BBC's licence fee increase is allegedly required to meet its own special 29% rate of 'broadcasting inflation' makes the present Government especially and rightly suspicious. Moreover the spiralling of the licence fee has accentuated its essentially 'regressive nature'. The family with the single parent and the single television set pays the same as the opera-loving tycoon with a television in every room; and the tycoon's favourite television Shakespeare is subsidised by the very quiz shows that so successfully keep the children quiet.

As a result of these pressures, various questions should now be asked – and answered – by politicians and broadcasters. We hope to identify them in this and two further leading articles. What is public service broadcasting? Is the existing BBC concept of PSB the only one? Are not some aspects of PSB more important than others? If a licence fee is thought acceptable in principle but too large in practice, cannot a reasonable public contribution to broadcasting be concentrated on those areas most central to public service?

The Times (1985) 'Whither the BBC?' 14 January, p.9. See also *The Times*, 15 January, p.13, and 16 January, p.15.

1.3 Peacock and Public Service Broadcasting

The establishment of the Peacock Committee generated substantial controversy. Many observers believed it would recommend the abolition of the licence fee and its replacement with advertising revenues as the major source of funding for the BBC; the corrosion of the tradition of public service broadcasting was, allegedly, inevitable. Peacock's view of public service broadcasting turned out to be considerably more complex than anticipated. The Committee concluded that, in conditions of spectrum scarcity, public service broadcasting had provided viewers with a wide range of cost-effective and high-quality programmes more successfully than might have been achieved by an advertising-financed system. Defining public service television as 'any major modification of purely commercial provision resulting from public policy', Peacock concluded that in circumstances of the 'full broadcasting market' which the Committee envisaged and endorsed, the role of public service broadcasting would be to deliver programmes which viewers 'are willing to support in their capacity of taxpayers and voters but not directly as consumers'.

578. We had some difficulty in obtaining an operational definition from broadcasters of public service broadcasting. But . . . its meaning is reasonably clear from its usage. Most broadcasters have insisted on: –

(i) The duty to 'inform, entertain and educate', a duty which is reaffirmed in the introductory section of the BBC Charter
(ii) The principle of geographic universality. In other words there is a commitment to ensure that television and radio services reach as high a proportion of the population as possible.

579. In the early stage of our Inquiry stress was laid by BBC representatives on the incompatibility of advertising on the BBC with public service principles. Any such move would, it was argued, drive both the BBC and ITV much further into a battle for ratings. Later more stress was laid on the argument that public service covered the BBC's light entertainment as well as other programmes and that the Corporation must not be drawn into a so-called 'Arts Council Ghetto'.

580. The best operational definition of public service is simply any major modification of purely commercial provision resulting from public policy. Defined in this way the scope of public service will vary with the state of broadcasting. If a full broadcasting market is eventually achieved, in which viewers and listeners can express preferences directly, the main role of public service could turn out to be the collective provision . . . of programmes which viewers and listeners are willing to support in their capacity as taxpayers and voters, but not directly as consumers . . .

563. The Committee has its own views on the types of programmes suitable for public patronage and which form a large part of its concept of Public Service Broadcasting . . . Four key words we would suggest here are knowledge, culture, criticism and experiment. To be more specific:

(i) There should be news, current affairs, documentaries, programmes about science, nature and other parts of the world, as well as avowedly educational programmes, all of which require active and not passive attention and which may also contribute to active citizenship.
(ii) There should be high quality programmes on the Arts (music, drama, literature, etc.) covering not only performance but also presentation of and comment on the process of artistic creation.
(iii) There should be critical and controversial programmes covering everything from the appraisal of commercial products to politics ideology, philosophy and religion.

564. The case for public support of programmes of this type can be accepted by those who believe that viewers and listeners are in the last analysis the best judges of their own interests because:

(i) Some people may come to enjoy what they do not do already as a result of new opportunities being presented.
(ii) Some people will accept guidance or stimulus from others on matters where they perceive that their knowledge or taste is limited.
(iii) Many people would like high quality material to be available even though they would not willingly watch or listen to it themselves in large enough numbers for it to be paid for directly.

565. Public patronage of broadcasting can go further. There may be a case for experimenting with types of entertainment or popular programmes of a different standard to the ones which viewers and listeners would have demanded unprompted. The only *a priori* stipulations are that state support should be direct and visible and not achieved by cross-subsidisation or 'leaning' on programme makers, and that such patronage should account for a modest amount of total broadcasting.

566. We have stated that the case for trying to enlarge the range of choice facing the public beyond what would otherwise be viable . . . If one believes that people should be allowed to make their own decisions, and they appear content with a diet of manufactured junk food, then we can support all kinds of activities designed to enlarge their tastes and inform them of the merits of other foods, But if after all these efforts they still make for junk food, that is their privilege in a free society.

581. But in the highly imperfect broadcasting market we have known and which continues to exist, the role of public service is much wider. So long as the number of television channels is severely limited by spectrum shortage and there is no direct payment by viewers and listeners, an unregulated advertising-financed broadcasting system, so far from satisfying consumer demand, can actually distort it. In particular it provides an inadequate supply of medium appeal and 'minority programmes', which most people want to see or hear some of the time. In these circumstances – quite apart from their role in stimulating a taste for demanding programmes – the public service institutions have been necessary to provide the viewer and listener with what he or she wants as a consumer. The BBC and the regulated ITV system have done far better in mimicking the effects of a true consumer market than any purely *laissez-faire* system, financed by advertising could have done under conditions of spectrum scarcity . . .

582. We would go further. The broadcasting authorities have not only mimicked the market; they have provided packages of programmes to audiences at remarkably low costs (measured by the licence fee and by the implicit cost to the consumer of ITV advertisements and judged by the standards of other forms of leisure and entertainment and by international standards). We can also pay tribute to the way in which the packaging of programmes has satisfied and developed audience tastes. The intertwining of information, education and entertainment has broadened the horizons of great numbers of viewers and listeners. The notion of cross-fertilisation of programme categories is inherent in BBC practice – and in ITV practice too – and of great value. Thus we have 'Yes Minister', a programme series conceived as entertainment but, some of us think, providing effective education in the ways of British government. Comparable examples can be found in 'Crimewatch', 'Tomorrow's World', 'Mastermind', 'The World About Us' and a host of other programmes . . . All that is in accord with the Reithian tradition; deriving from Reith's own dictum in 1924 that you have to mix a little education with a lot of entertainment to carry people with you . . . It must be admitted that, today, entertainment values at times appear to have taken over in some news and current affairs programmes, with the inevitable consequences of triviality and dilution of information. Broadly speaking, though, the concept of providing indirect education and information through some entertainment programmes still prevails.

583. The practice of providing a mixed diet at low cost is one that we wish to see continued. It is, in our view, compatible with the recommendations that follow for future financing of the BBC through subscription. It is indeed important that in moving towards the changes of the mid-1990s . . . that we do not prematurely dismantle or destroy the 'packaged' terrestrial broadcasting services that give good value today.

584. There are also weaknesses in the public service system. Despite the investment of both the BBC and ITV sectors in sophisticated market research, there is an absence of true consumer sovereignty and of market signals, which only direct payment by viewers and listeners could establish. Because of its dependence on public finance and regulation, the system is vulnerable to political pressure and vulnerable to trade union and other special interest groups. The BBC's administrative structure seems to generate more than the usual amount of tension associated with large corporations organised on hierarchical lines. The unpopularity whether deserved or not, of the financial mechanism associated with the BBC and the near impossibility of the IBA to be seen to be discharging fairly its award of franchises are other problems likely to grow rather than diminish in time.

585. A further problem of the public service institutions is its endemic weakness in the control of cost or pursuit of efficiency in the sense of value for money. No amount of scrutiny by accountants or consultants can be a substitute for the direct pressure of a competitive market. Indeed the inflation of costs in broadcasting probably has its origins on the ITV side. Inevitably, the profits theoretically obtainable from a monopoly franchise in a large and prosperous region are shared between the programme contractors and the unions, with the taxpayer – the real freeholder of the franchised public asset – coming a poor third through the levy.

586. Thus tributes to the success of publicly regulated broadcasting cannot absolve policy makers from permitting and encouraging technological developments which may eventually make a fully developed consumer market possible. The past effects of packaging and channelling in developing viewers' and listeners' tastes do not justify a paternalistic attitude which could prevent them from making less constrained choices in the future. In many walks of life it is possible to accept that earlier constraints and restrictions may have had beneficial side effects, while insisting that consumers should be regarded as the best judges of their own welfare in formulating future policy.

Report of the Committee on Financing the BBC (1986) (Chair Alan Peacock), London: HMSO, Cmnd 9824, July.

1.4 The Future of the BBC and Public Service Broadcasting

In the White Paper *The Future of the BBC*, the government wished to invite opinions and promote discussion about the future of public service broadcasting (in the commercial as well as public sector of broadcasting) in the context of rapid and considerable changes in broadcasting, triggered by developments in communications technology which were resolving problems of spectrum scarcity, providing new delivery systems (cable and satellite) for television services and prompting – in tandem with government broadcasting policy – a burgeoning of television channels.

3.6 The original justification for public service broadcasting – that a small number of services should be used for the benefit of the public as a whole – no longer exists. More services and greater choice have been made possible by developments in technology . . .

3.11 If public service broadcasting is to continue in the 21st Century in the United Kingdom, what will be its objectives and how will it differ from other forms of broadcasting? Some public service broadcasting objectives may be shared, to some extent, by other broadcasters. However, there may be a number of objectives which, taken together, are uniquely suitable for a public service broadcasting organisation which, like the BBC, is operating throughout the world.

3.12 Setting objectives for public service broadcasting in new and rapidly changing circumstances calls for careful consideration, rather than slogans or nostalgia. The government would welcome views on whether the future objectives of public service broadcasting should embrace:

Focus on the audience. Public service broadcasting should be provided for the benefit of viewers and listeners. The audiences should take priority over other possible interests, the broadcasters, advertisers, shareholders or political parties.

Quality. The Government aims to promote quality in all public services. Quality in broadcasting is difficult to define and can be achieved in different ways and in all kinds of programmes, in light entertainment or sports coverage, as well as news, documentaries and drama.

Diversity and choice. A wide range of programmes can be achieved on one service or through a multiplicity of services. In the past, public service broadcasting has included all types of programmes, entertainment, information and education, and programmes which appeal to large audiences and those for minority audiences. Public service broadcasters have introduced experiments in programming. They have broadened the horizons of many viewers and listeners and encouraged new interests. With more entertainment services available to audiences, public service broadcasters could be required to concentrate on programmes which inform and educate, including news and current affairs, and to cut back the proportion of entertainment programmes. However, reducing entertainment and popular programmes would conflict with an objective of accessibility.

Accessibility. There are two forms of accessibility: geographical coverage of services and broadcasting programmes which many people find enjoyable and interesting. Public service broadcasters have planned both to reach people throughout the country and to broadcast programmes which appeal to people with a wide range of tastes and interests, of different ages and backgrounds and living in all parts of the country. This contrasts with services which cannot be received throughout the country or which are available only to those who pay more for them; both limit the opportunities for people to explore a diverse range of programmes.

Editorial independence. It has been an essential feature of public service broadcasting in this country that decisions about programmes have been taken by broadcasters or broadcasting authorities, not by the Government or other interest groups. Editorial independence enables broadcasters to resist pressures from those who wish to manipulate audiences for their own purposes, but it carries the risk that broadcasters may become self-indulgent and unresponsive to public criticism.

Efficiency and value for money. All public services, whether or not they are financed from public funds, should be efficient and give value for money in the services they provide.

Accountability. Public service broadcasters should be held to account for what they do. They should be clear about their objectives, the services they are expected to provide and the standards they are expected to meet. If services are paid for from public funds, there should be ways of ensuring public money is used effectively and is not.

National identity. Public service broadcasters have taken the view that they should reflect the national interests and cultural traditions of their audiences. They can create a sense of community. They can ensure that national occasions can be seen and heard by the majority of the population. They can promote better understanding of current events in the United Kingdom, in Europe and throughout the world, and greater participation in the processes of Parliamentary democracy through news and current affairs programmes. They can celebrate and enhance the national heritage and encourage people to enjoy it.

The Department of National Heritage (1992) *The Future of the BBC*, Cm 2098, London: HMSO.

1.5 No Change?

Public service broadcasting in the digital age

In his speech to the Royal Television Society on 14 October 1998, the Secretary of State for Culture, Media and Sport set down his understanding of public service broadcasting in the digital age. The terrestrial channels will have a central role in the digital era while the BBC should maintain its role as a 'high quality, comprehensive public service producer-broadcaster'. The understanding of public service broadcasting presented here is more comprehensive, suggesting 'an approach to broadcasting' rather than merely a 'safety net providing only those kinds of programming which are not of interest to the purely commercial broadcaster'.

The public service channels: the BBC and channels 3, 4 and 5 will continue to have a central role. The viewing figures demonstrate that these services are important to the overwhelming majority of our viewers. Even in cable and satellite homes they account for almost two-thirds of television viewing. The viewing of certain popular shows and events continues to be a collective experience – I've heard it described aptly as part of the cement that binds our society together . . . I know the situation is not static and the share of the terrestrial broadcasters has diminished, but it does not seem to me to be changing at a rate which suggests a fundamental change in viewers' habits or their expectations. People still look to the terrestrial channels for a variety of quality programmes which speak to their day to day concerns, which keep them informed and entertained, which offer everything from the undemanding sheer entertainment of popular soaps and gameshows to challenging innovative drama and documentary. I see this as a basic entitlement for all our citizens. It leaves plenty of scope for purely commercial services in the multi-channel environment, and they have an important role. They will add to the richness and variety of what is on offer. And I do not delude myself that quality programmes are only to be found on public service channels.

But public service broadcasting is not a niche. It is not a safety net providing only those kinds of programming which are not of interest to the purely commercial broadcaster. Rather it is an approach to broadcasting which has as its driving force the need to serve the community, rather than the purely economic considerations which motivate non-public service broadcasters. I do not deny that they serve their audience too. But the public service broadcasters inform, educate, and challenge it in a way that few purely commercial enterprises are free to do.

If I may . . . I would like briefly to set out my vision for the BBC. Put simply, it is for a BBC strongly committed to maintaining its traditional ethos, principles and purpose in the digital era. And it is for a BBC that is capable of adapting, surviving and prospering in the fragmented modern market.

There are five key principles:

- the BBC should act as a benchmark for quality, driving up standards across the board;
- it should provide something for everybody, making the good popular and the popular good;
- it should inform, educate and entertain, expanding people's horizons with new and innovative programming;
- it should operate efficiently and effectively and provide value for money for licence fee payers;
- it should stimulate, support and reflect the diversity of cultural activity in the United Kingdom, acting as a voice for the nation.

The BBC has a central role in articulating and delivering these objectives. It must, for instance, maintain and enhance its primary role as a high quality, comprehensive public service producer-broadcaster, delivering distinctive and creative programmes to the public. The BBC must also continue to nurture and support talent not only in the audio visual field, but throughout the creative industries. These industries are a central concern of my Department and, accordingly, the BBC plays a central role in our aspirations.

BBC viewers and listeners expect and will continue to want programmes they can trust to be beholden to no one, and to expand their horizons rather than to cater for tastes they already knew they had, and formulas they have already solved. If the BBC is to thrive, it needs not simply, or even primarily, to retain its existing strong audience share. Audience share is likely to fall as the years go by. What it needs most to retain public confidence is to continue to be true to its distinctive public service ethos and programming range. That way, it will continue to sustain near universal reach and its near universal public respect.

Secretary of State for Culture, Media and Sport (1998) 'The Big Switch? Digital Future – Turn-On or Turn-Off?', Speech to the Royal Television Society Autumn Symposium, 14 October.

1.6 Davies and Public Service Broadcasting

Like its predecessor the Peacock Committee, the Davies review panel believed it could not discuss the financial requirements of the BBC without first establishing the ambitions, purposes and scope of BBC broadcasting. This promptly led the panel to a discussion of the 'conundrum' of public service broadcasting. Like an elephant, public service broadcasting is hard to define but 'we know it when we see it'. The panel believed that three broad principles informed common understandings of public service broadcasting. Public service broadcasting in the British setting requires a mixed broadcasting ecology which combines 'creative and market pressures to achieve the public good'.

Many people who gave evidence to the panel said – quite logically – that we could not decide how much extra money the BBC might need without first attempting to define what the BBC should do. They added almost as a throwaway, that this would mean establishing a new definition of the role of public service broadcasting.

We have not managed anything so ambitious in the six months we have had at our disposal. When we each tried to define public service broadcasting, some very familiar words started to appear – information, education, extension of horizons, impartiality, independence, universal access, inclusivity, service of minorities, lack of commercial motivation, etc, etc. We decided that we might not be able to offer a tight new definition of public service broadcasting, but we nevertheless each felt we knew it when we saw it.

And not only did we all share some basic conceptions of what it meant, but we believed that these would be common to many people, probably the majority, in our society. Here are some broad principles:

> The first is that, while the BBC is a public sector broadcaster, this does not mean that everything it does is public service broadcasting. Still less does it mean that the output of other broadcasters falls outside the definition of pubic service. To support the continued existence of the BBC as the recipient of a universal compulsory charge, we need to believe both that a large share of the Corporation's output falls into the public service category and also that by no means all of the private sector's output does so.
>
> The second principle is that some form of market failure must lie at the heart of any concept of public service broadcasting. Beyond simply using the catch-phrase that public service broadcasting must 'inform, educate and entertain', we must add 'inform, educate and entertain in a way which the private sector left unregulated, would not do'. Otherwise, why not leave matters entirely to the private sector?
>
> The third principle is that, in order to believe in a full scale BBC, we need to accept that a combination of the private sector's profit motive plus regulation, is insufficient to repair the market failure and deliver what we want. After all, the existence of public service broadcasting on ITV, and the success of Channel Four, shows that a fair ration of public service output can be generate from the private sector. In order to argue in favour of maintaining an expensive organisation dedicated to public service television, we need to be satisfied that regulation of the private sector is not, of its own, enough.

The panel unanimously believed that the adoption of these three principles today would make out a strong case for a comprehensive broadcaster like the BBC in the UK market. The present outcome in the broadcasting market seems broadly satisfactory. We were cautioned several times by our witnesses against claiming that the UK has the best television in the world, but we would claim it has the best television *for a British audience* in the world. This may not be saying much. But since the alternative might be to import even more American television, designed for American tastes, it is probably an argument in favour of the present structure. The panel would go further and say that in the present state of technology, it would be a very risky act to try to do without a full-scale BBC, since it has proven itself able to condition the whole marketplace (the broadcasting 'ecology') for the better (pp.9–10).

Some organisations believe that public service broadcasting has had its day and that the public will be well served by the growing number and diversity of television and radio channels. Others, including the government, have argued that there will continue to be an important role for public service however defined.

Again there are different views about how large that role should be. Some believe that public service broadcasting should concentrate on the types of programme which would not be provided by commercial broadcasters. Others believe that public service broadcasting consists of more than the provision of particular programmes, mainly for minority audiences. They regard public service broadcasting as an approach, which influences the choice of programme subjects, and how programmes are made and scheduled, as well as the scope of the services. Others again believe that public service broadcasters should compete in providing every form of broadcasting.

For there is a basic conundrum that puzzles everyone who looks at this subject objectively. The natural definition of public service broadcasting is that it is broadcasting which, for one reason or another is desirable, but which the market will not provide or will provide in insufficient quantity. It is impossible to argue for a public service broadcaster unless market failure can be shown. There are reasons for believing that the basic causes of market failure will persist in the digital age. Indeed some of them may become more rather than less important. The best means of funding such broadcasting yet devised is a licence fee. However, broadcasting which the market will not provide may (almost by definition) be broadcasting that is not very popular. At least it will not necessarily be the kind of 'lowest common denominator' which can command the largest audiences. And people naturally resist the proposition that they should pay for programmes that they do not wish to watch. Hence we have a debate which veers dangerously between the purist view of public service broadcasting, the so-called 'Himalayas' view, which has it just producing programmes at the top end of the market, and the impure view which interprets 'public service' as potentially embracing any broadcasting, however populist, which a public broadcaster chooses to put on air.

We have not resolved the conundrum, perhaps because it is unresolvable. We do believe that public service broadcasting, however defined, can play an important role in the competitive and complex broadcasting environment of the multi-channel, digital future. There is good reason to suppose that the market, left to itself, will not provide the broadcasting which our society wishes to foster.

Public service broadcasting exists to serve the community by providing distinctive programmes which inform, educate and entertain. It can help to ensure that the benefits of the information age are available to all at a reasonable cost and that viewers and listeners have access to quality services which cater for a wide range of interests. In all these respects, it can correct the tendency of the market to pull too far in the opposite direction.

There is a continuing need to support the public policy aims of quality, diversity, choice and accessibility. Pluralism is not guaranteed in the multi-channel age, where the economics point towards a fragmentation of audience and concentration of ownership. Public service broadcasting can act as a counterweight to private concentration of ownership and, provided that public service broadcasters are broadcasting distinctive schedules, this will exert pressure on commercial competitors to do the same. Many of our witnesses drew attention to what they described as the 'ecology' of broadcasting where a variety of institutions and funding mechanisms provide a mixed economy which is neither pure Reithian public broadcasting not pure market, but which in a rough and ready kind of way, reconciles conflicting objective (pp.136–137).

What our society should be looking for is a public service broadcasting model, which combines creative and market pressures to achieve the public good. And this requires a balance between giving public support to programmes which the market simply would not provide while sustaining programmes with a wider appeal in a way that seeks to maintain overall standards of broadcasting quality. It is not 'either-or'. It requires a sustainable and defensible mix, just as it always has.

In striking this balance, the BBC's performance should not just be judged by ratings. It should also be linked to whether it offers something of real value to audiences not guaranteed elsewhere. Too often, the BBC in effect behaves as if public service broadcasting is everything the BBC chooses to put out. We welcome the BBC's remarkable success in more or less preserving the market share of BBC One and BBC Two in the face of increasing competition. But we worry that this has to some extent been achieved by 'dumbing down' in a way that has upset that balance (pp.136–139).

The Future Funding of the BBC (1999) Report of the Independent Review Panel, Chaired by Gavyn Davies, Department of Culture, Media and Sport, 28 July, 210pp.

1.7 The End of Public Service Broadcasting?

In the early days of television broadcasting, spectrum scarcity limited the number of television channels and hence viewer choice. Public service broadcasting, with its commitment to public ownership, diversity and quality in programming and broadcasters' independence and impartiality, provided one necessary solution to these shortcomings. But when public service television includes the commercially funded Channels 3, 4 and 5, when 250 'purely commercial' channels are available in UK homes and when the Internet makes radio and television programmes available from around the world, is the idea of public service broadcasting at the end of its useful life? *A New Future For Communications* argues that public service broadcasting will continue to play a 'key role' in the digital future although the way public service broadcasting is regulated will need to change.

5.2.5 Some argue that the end of spectrum scarcity means the end of public service broadcasting. Without scarcity, there will be many competing providers and a vibrant market. We do not have public service magazines – why should we have public service television, radio or Internet services?

5.2.6 This White Paper rejects that argument. It argues that public service broadcasting will continue to have a key role to play in the digital future, potentially an even more important role than it has now . . . However, the way in which that public service role is regulated and delivered by the broadcasters will have to change, to reflect the new market conditions in which they operate.

5.3.1 The Government believes that we will continue to rely on public service broadcasting for one clear reason – it works.

5.3.2 We welcome the growth of new channels and the much greater competition and choice it brings. Whole areas of broadcasting have been transformed, for the better, by the multi-channel revolution – in particular films, sport and news. Satellite and cable television shook up an industry that had sometimes tended towards complacency and a lack of competition. New industries and companies have grown, thanks to pay television, and the UK has managed to secure a healthy share of these markets.

5.3.3 Nevertheless, public service broadcasting remains the best way we have yet found of creating a wide range of UK-made, original programmes of the kind people want. The public service broadcasters still command 61.6% of the total audience in multichannel homes and 70% in peak time. They continue to produce original and high quality programmes, and to be bold and popular.

5.3.4 That success is not an accident. It is founded on the economic, democratic and cultural characteristics of our broadcasting.

5.3.5 The economics of broadcasting are complex and unique . . . radio and television markets have natural tendencies to concentrations of market power. The end of spectrum scarcity does not mean therefore that broadcasting will automatically become a perfectly functioning market.

5.3.7 Television and radio are what economists call 'public goods'. Once a programme has been made, it is virtually free to make the next copy. By making access free at the point of use, we increase the audience without increasing costs. So the public interest is maximised by having everyone pay a relatively small amount, through advertising, or the licence fee, rather than charging a subscription which would restrict access.

5.3.8 In summary, we believe now that mixed schedule networks, free at the point of use, funded through advertising or a licence fee, continue to be the best way of funding the production of mass audience, high quality, varied, UK-originated programmes. That could change as the market evolves; but it would be a foolhardy move to frame our policy for a potential, contentious future, rather than on the current, successful reality.

5.3.9 The democratic importance of public service broadcasting is as great as the economic justification. First, public service broadcasting ensures that the interests of all viewers are taken into account . . .

5.3.10 Second, public service broadcasting is a counter-balance to fears about concentration of ownership and the absence of diversity of views. It means news and current affairs are available in peak time, as part of mixed schedules, where citizens are most likely to see them. It guarantees the availability of full and balanced information about the world at local, regional and global levels.

5.3.11 Finally, there are strong cultural justifications for public service broadcasting. The value of information, education and entertainment is not limited to how much we are prepared to pay for them. Whether arts or sciences, fiction or documentaries, entertainment or news, the subjects of television and radio are central to how we live our lives and how we understand each other. They allow our community to talk to itself.

5.3.12 Public service broadcasting is there to make sure those wider cultural goals are achieved . . . The public service broadcasters have provided a guarantee and benchmark of quality for the rest of the market, halting any slide towards lowest common denominator content. That mixed ecology of broadcasting is worth fostering, indeed is essential for the digital world.

DTI and DCMS (2000) *A New Future For Communications* London: Stationery Office, Cm 5010, Sections 5.2.5–5.3.12.

CRITICAL VOICES

1.8 Freedom in Broadcasting versus the Public Service Tradition

Murdoch criticises public service broadcasting, denouncing it as an ideology deployed by 'propagandists' to protect the interests of a narrow broadcasting elite, but with debilitating consequences for British broadcasting; most significantly, public service broadcasting militates against viewer choice. This ideology misrepresents an economically inefficient, paternalistic and unaccountable broadcasting system, as the only organisational structure capable of delivering quality programmes and encouraging creative risk taking in programme making. Murdoch argues that the market-led American television system generates much greater quality and diversity of programming.

For 50 years British television has operated on the assumption that the people could not be trusted to watch what they wanted to watch, so that it had to be controlled by like-minded people who knew what was good for us. As one of those guardians, my distinguished friend Sir Denis Foreman, explained a few years ago, even so-called commercial television in Britain 'is only an alternative method of financing public broadcasting, and that method itself has depended on the creation of tightly held monopolies for the sale of advertising and programme production'. So even though the lure of filthy lucre was to become part of the British television system with the advent of ITV from the mid-1950s, it was done by subordinating commerce to so-called public service . . .

I start from a very simple principle: in every area of economic activity in which competition is available, it is much to be preferred to monopoly. The reasons are set forth in every elementary economics text book, but the argument is best proved by experience rather than theory.

Competition lets consumers decide what they want to buy: monopoly or duopoly forces them to take whatever the seller puts on offer. Competition forces suppliers to innovate products, lest they lose business to rivals offering better; monopoly permits a seller to force outdated goods onto captive customers. Competition keeps prices low and quality high; monopoly does the opposite. Why should television be exempt from these laws of supply and demand?

The consensus among established broadcasters, however, is that a properly free and competitive television system will mean the end of 'quality' television and that multi-channel choice equals multi-channel drivel – wall-to-wall Dallas is the sneering phrase most commonly trotted out to sum up this argument. Put aside the fact that the BBC is happy to run Dallas at prime time (and to repeat it as well); put side to the simple economic truth that if 15 channels were to run it wall-to-wall, 14 of them would quickly go bust. I want instead to concentrate on the assumption that is behind the establishment broadcasters' case: that only public service television can produce quality television.

There are real problems of definition and taste here. For a start I have never heard a convincing definition of what public service television really is . . . My own view is that anybody who . . . provides a service which the public wants at a price it can afford is providing a public service. So if in the years ahead we can make a success of Sky Television, that will be as much a public service as ITV . . . But quality is in the eye of the beholder, or in the current debate in Britain, the propagandist.

Much of what is claimed to be quality television here is no more than the parading of the prejudices and interests of the like-minded people who currently control British television. It may well be that at its very best, British television does produce what most viewers would regard as some of the world's best television. Examples have been given to prove the case, though the fact that the same examples are trotted out all the time, and they are all getting a bit long in the tooth, suggests to me that the case is weaker than generally believed.

Moreover, the price viewers have had to pay for these peaks in quality has been pretty high. The troughs of British television, such as much of the variety, situation comedies, sporting coverage, and other popular fare, are not particularly special by international standards . . . This public-service TV system has had, in my view, debilitating effects on British society, by producing a TV output which is so often obsessed with class, dominated by anti-commercial attitudes and with a tendency to hark back to the past . . .

People often say to me, however, that the current British system encourages creative risk taking, and that a market-led system would not fund all manner of excellent programming currently on show. 'Without public-service television, there would be no Dennis Potter plays on television' was how the argument was put at a recent seminar organised by the Broadcasting Standards Council . . . My argument, however, is not that television can be left entirely to the market . . . What I am arguing for is a move from the current system of public broadcasting, in which market considerations are marginal, to a market system in which public broadcasting would be part of the market mix but in no way dominate the output the way it does at present. I suspect that the market is able to provide much more variety, and risk taking, than many of you realise . . .

This brings me to my next point. Contrary to conventional wisdom in this country, there is much to admire about American television . . . because America provides the best example of a market-led television system and because it has been so disgracefully misrepresented by propagandists in this country . . . I watch television regularly on both sides of the Atlantic; when there were only four channels on this side, I was regularly frustrated by the lack of choice; and given the quality of much of the prime-time programming it was always difficult to believe that I was tuning in to a cultural citadel which had to be preserved at all costs.

At News International, we stand for choice. I say this aware of the fact that some of our critics accuse us of stifling choice in the media because we are supposed to own so much of it . . . in television; our role is that of a monopoly destroyer, not a monopolist. At present, we have less than 1% of the TV audience. Our critics cannot make up their minds if Sky Television is a threat to the existing broadcasters or destined to be seen by fewer people than have seen the Loch Ness monster.

The truth is that, even by the time Sky is in several million British homes it has no prospect of dominating the medium. For just as Wapping so lowered the cost of newspaper production as to enable *The Independent* and others to enter, so Sky has paved the way for non-Sky channels . . . in Britain cross-ownership of media is a force for diversity. Were it not for the strength of our newspaper group, we surely could not have afforded to have doubled the number of television channels available in Britain . . . We could not have created Sky News, which has become a third force in British television news alongside the BBC and ITN.

Public-service broadcasters in this country have paid a price for their state-sponsored privileges. That price has been their freedom. British broadcasters depend on government for protection: when you depend on government for protection, there will come a time when that government, no matter its political complexion, will exact a price. The pressure can be overt or, more likely, covert. The result is the same either way: less than independent, neutered journalism. I cannot imagine a British Watergate, or a British Irangate, being pursued by the BBC or ITV with the vigour that the US networks did. British broadcasters are now constantly subject to inhibiting criticism and reporting restrictions . . . if, like the BBC, you're dependent on the government to set the licence fee, you think twice before offending powerful politicians . . .

Across the world there is a realisation that only market economies can deliver both political freedom and economic well-being, whether they be free market economies of the right or social market economics of the left. The freeing of broadcasting in this country is very much part of this democratic revolution and an essential step forward into the Information Age with its golden promise.

It means freeing television from the lie of spectrum scarcity; freeing it from the dominance of one narrow set of cultural values; freeing it for entry by any private or public enterprise which thinks it has something people might like to watch; freeing it to cater to mass and minority audiences; freeing it from the bureaucrats of television and placing It in the hands of those who should control it – the people.

Rupert Murdoch (1989) 'Freedom in Broadcasting', MacTaggart Memorial Lecture, Edinburgh International Film Festival, 25 August.

1.9 Defending Public Service Broadcasting from 'Occupying Powers'

In his 1993 MacTaggart Lecture entitled 'Occupying Powers', playwright Dennis Potter offered an articulate, eloquent and very personal defence of public service broadcasting which he believed was under severe attack from market forces and the growing trends towards cross-media ownership, the interventions of politicians and, most significantly, a director-general and board of governors which had lost its sense of mission and which was stifling creativity with bureaucracy. Potter offers a number of policy prescriptions to escape this malaise: with tongue planted firmly in cheek, he concludes by announcing his candidacy for the post of director general.

Our television has been ripped apart and falteringly reassembled by politicians who believe that value is a monetary term only, and that a cost-accountant is thereby the most suitable adjudicator of what we can and cannot see on our screens. And these accountants or their near-clones are employed by new kinds of media owners who try to gobble up everything in their path. We must protect ourselves and our democracy, first by properly exercising the cross-ownership provisions currently in place, and then by erecting further checks and balances against dangerous concentrations of the media power which plays such a large part in our lives. No individual, group or company should be allowed to own more than one daily, one evening and one weekly newspaper. No newspaper should be allowed to own a television station, and vice versa. A simple act of public hygiene, tempering abuse, widening choice, and maybe even returning broadcasting to its makers.

The political pressures from market-obsessed radicals, and the huckster atmosphere that follows, have by degrees, and in confused self-defence, drawn the BBC so heavily into the dogma-coated discourses of so-called 'market efficiency' that in the end it might lose clear sight of why it, the BBC, is there in the first place. I fear the time is near when we must save not the BBC from itself but public service broadcasting from the BBC . . .

Thirty years ago, under the personal pressures of whatever guilt, whatever shame and whatever remaining shard of idealism, I found or I made up what I may unwisely have termed a sense of vocation. I have it still. It was born, of course, from the already aborted dream of a common culture which has long since been zapped into glistening fragments by those who are now the real, if not always recognised, occupying powers of our culture. Look in the pink pages and see their mesh of connections. Open the *Sun* and measure their aspirations. Put Rupert Murdoch on public trial and televise every single second of it. Show us who is abusing us, and why. Ask your public library – if there is one left – to file the television franchise applications on the shelf hitherto kept for Fantasy, Astrology and Crime bracket Bizarre bracket.

I was exceptionally fortunate to begin my career in television at a time when the BBC was so infuriatingly confident about what public service broadcasting meant that the question itself was not even on what would now be called the agenda. The then ITV companies shared much more of this ethos than they were then willing to acknowledge. Our profession was then mostly filled with men and women who mostly cared about the programmes rather than the dividend. And the venomous hostilities of the small minority who are the political right – before its ideological transformation into the type of venal, wet-mouthed radicalism which can even assert without a hint of shame that 'there is no such thing as society' – before those who had yet launched their poisoned arrows. Clunk! they go. Clunk! Clunk! And, lo and behold, we have in the fullness of such darkness sent unto us a Director-General who bares his chest to receive these arrows, a St Sebastian eager for their punishing stings.

The world has turned upside-down. The BBC is under governors who seem incapable of performing the public trust invested in them, under a Chairman who seems to believe he is heading a private fiefdom, and under a Chief Executive who must somehow or other have swallowed whole and unsalted the kind of humbug-punctuated pre-privatization manual which is being forced on British Rail or British Coal. But I do not want to end on a malediction . . . I first saw television when I was in my late teens. It made my heart pound. Here was a medium of great power, of potentially wondrous delights, that could slice through all the tedious hierarchies of the printed word and help to emancipate us from many of the stifling tyrannies of class and status and gutter-press ignorance. We are privileged if we can work in this, the most entrancing of all the many palaces of varieties. Switch on, tune in and *grow*.

I hope it is clear by now that I happen to care very much about the medium that has both allowed and shaped the bulk of my life's work, and even my life's meaning. However, I do have the odd hour or two in each day in which to pretend to be a St George rather than a St Sebastian. I therefore hereby formally apply in front of witnesses of substance, here at the Edinburgh International Television Festival, for the post of Chairman of the Governors of the British Broadcasting Corporation. (pp.53–56)

Dennis Potter (1993) 'Occupying Powers', MacTaggart Memorial Lecture, Edinburgh Film Festival, reprinted in Dennis Potter (1994) *Seeing The Blossom*, London and Boston, MA: Faber and Faber, pp.33–56.

1.10 The Campaign for Quality Television and Public Service Broadcasting

In its 1998 pamphlet *The Purposes Of Broadcasting*, the Campaign for Quality Television argued that the BBC's extensive commercial broadcasting activities were undermining its public service commitments. A separate company should be established to oversee the commercial sector of the BBC, leaving the governors to regulate the public service sector of the BBC.

5 The BBC and its public service commitment

We have already expressed our view that the BBC has become distracted by its commercial activities, an involvement resulting from a realistic concern about its income in the absence of firm political undertakings about future funding through the licence fee, but also, damagingly, of its wish to demonstrate its zeal for the market philosophy of the previous government. As a result, the commercial tail has been wagging the dog. The development of the substantial commercial activities now carried on by BBC Worldwide, a wholly owned subsidiary of the Corporation, may have widened the BBC's room for financial manoeuvre, but has led to a sacrifice of the BBC's independence to an extent perhaps inadequately realised. We therefore suggest that the commercial exploitation of the BBC 'brand' should be conducted by an independent body under a strict licensing agreement. Since the 1990 Broadcasting Act, the BBC's commercial operations have been regulated by the Independent Television Commission and the new body should be overseen by the new content regulator. In summary, our proposal is:

- The role of the Governors, under the terms of the Charter and Licence, should focus solely upon the Corporation's public service responsibilities.
- The BBC should license a separate company to market its programmes and run its commercial channels. The commercial product should he linked to the value of the BBC 'brand', but distinguished from it by the choice of name, as has already been done in the case of the 'Beeb' services. The terms of the licence would provide for a proper financial return to the BBC and thus a fair return to the licence payer who provided the original funding.
- The independence of the Board of Governors should be preserved and the Board should have a free hand in its direct dealings with the Government over the level of the receiving-licence fee or issues arising from individual programmes.
- We believe that the performance and accountability of the BBC should be continuously scrutinised and, if, after a period of five years, there remain grounds for dissatisfaction, an appropriate form of external regulation should be instituted (pp.19–20).

Campaign for Quality Television (1998) *The Purposes of Broadcasting*, London: CQT, 26pp.

1.11 Public *Interest* Broadcasting

In his 1999 MacTaggart Memorial Lecture, Richard Eyre announced the imminent demise of public service broadcasting because of: its reliance on regulators (in an age when regulation imposes inequities in the broadcasting market); its reliance on an active broadcaster and passive viewers (in an age when 'free school milk doesn't work' because 'the kids go and buy Coca-Cola'); its lack of any precise definition. Public service broadcasting must give way to public interest broadcasting which will be the salvation of the BBC.

It is a great privilege and a fearsome responsibility to be giving the final James MacTaggart Memorial Lecture of the millennium. The more so since my subject is the future of public service broadcasting and the lecture is named for a man whose life's work was devoted to crafting some of the best examples of public service broadcasting we have seen . . .

I'm billed as posing the question: Is there a post-Reithian model of public service broadcasting that can thrive in the communicopia of the future? I hope I can make a contribution to what will be a continuing discussion of this. But I also want to use this unique opportunity to talk about our responsibilities as the people who shape British television in a future in which I believe it will not be realistic for the state and its trustees to determine what we do.

Here is my answer to the question: Public service broadcasting will soon be dead. It will soon be dead because it relies on an active broadcaster and a passive viewer. Once upon a time, viewers (and listeners) could be reasonably expected to eat what they were given, because we, the broadcasters knew it was good for them. As a model it's been the defining structure of the last 75 years but as we reach the millennium and the final MacTaggart of the decade, it's a gonner. It's a gonner because given the choice at the end of a tiring day viewers don't always choose what's good for them. Many will always pass on the wholesome, healthy and carefully crafted in favour of the easily digestible, pre-packaged, and the undemanding. They devour the entertainment, play with the information and leave the education on the side of their plates thank you very much.

Public service broadcasting will soon be dead because it relies on regulators who will, in time, no longer be able to do a comprehensive job, because the vast number of sources of broadcast information will be impossible to monitor. And because it will be unfair to apply constraints to some and not all market participants. Public service broadcasting will soon be dead for lack of definition – or at least a definition that will endure for the next 75 years. The ITC haven't got it taped. As one learned member said to me, 'we keep trying to get our heads around it, but we don't get very far.' The unsustainable in pursuit of the undefinable.

In the next 50 minutes I'd like to tackle an agenda with three items: public service broadcasting, the role of television in our culture, and our role in television.

In the first 40 years of the BBC, the animus is one of improvement . . . Aim above their heads so they have to grow a bit. So giving them what we think is good for them, the driving force of the first phase of British broadcasting, has had it as a rationale for television content. Broadcasting is clearly different on a scale that Reith would not have envisaged.

This means the market has control, doesn't it? Free school milk doesn't work when the kids go and buy Coca-Cola because it's available and they prefer it and they can afford it. So public service broadcasting will soon be dead. What will replace it? Have we reached that point when we're obliged to let the market decide? And does that mean it's all over for quality television?

Well, no. Because it is not true to say that broadcasters can thrive without reference to the public interest. Not into a lowest common denominator free for all but into a notion of broadcasting that is sustainable without minute by minute content regulation.

Because, though we are right now blessed with plenty of regulators to help us get it right, their job in the next five to 10 years will become impossible. Effective regulation needs teeth and an ultimate sanction. If content regulation is no longer realistic, does this mean an end to quality television? Because no one went broke underestimating the taste of the public, are we inevitably in for free licence in broadcasting? Lowest common denominator broadcasting? Well, yes it does. To an extent we've already got it.

It's a fact of life that future broadcasters will push the boundaries of taste and decency and some people will be very uncomfortable. Will ITV go that route? Absolutely not. ITV must be a public interest broadcaster if it is to continue to draw large audiences. So must the BBC, S4C and Channel 4. And Channel 5.

Public interest broadcasting doesn't need a regulator to sustain it. Public interest broadcasting, not public service, will be the salvation of the BBC, because it will force the corporation to engage with viewers and listeners more wholeheartedly. The BBC must be held to deliver the things that the commercial sector cannot. The BBC must engage in the full breadth of viewers' interests, even those which are not most sought out by commercial broadcasters. Above all, the licence fee needs consensus. My worry is the slipping away of public consensus. You may have read in the papers that this lecture was to be a wild swing at the corporation. No. I think it is a superb creation. But I worry because I believe our culture would be desperately impoverished without a vibrant BBC confidently wearing its mantle of benchmark broadcaster. So what about ITV? ITV is designated a public service broadcaster. But if it is to continue to thrive in the new market competition, ITV cannot be regulated with reference to the BBC while forging its way against legions of other channels that are not similarly bound.

Meanwhile the advertising community wants, not more viewers of any old sort, but more lighter viewers of television. The market common sense is that our most unique selling proposition to advertisers is the sheer scale of ITV's audiences. How then does that market imperative to preserve high reach affect ITV? Quality and diversity of output. The highest levels of domestic production. News, drama, sport, current affairs, comedy, documentary, arts, entertainment, children's programmes, movies, a selection of the best acquired programmes, regional services, deals with the very biggest talent names.

Commercial common sense will sustain an ITV that is unequivocally in the public interest. Because public interest broadcasting is the economic mainstay of mass television. The interrelationship of a BBC pursuing weekly reach and the ITV that I have described sustains them both. In this model, the BBC is the benchmark. If it stops being a benchmark and tries to become just another of the players it will destabilise that interrelationship that works so strongly in the public interest because a BBC and an ITV slugging it out for share points will produce programme decisions that will devalue the deal for the public. And at that point there will be no argument to prevent the Incorporated Society of British Advertisers from winning their relentless case – driven by American companies – that the BBC should carry ads.

So the evolution of the system then needs careful husbandry, but I'd say that even after the death of public service broadcasting I'm optimistic about the potential shape of broadcasting in the UK. I do though believe that much of the debate about the future has been inadequate. In particular the debate about the future shape, scope and cost of the BBC hasn't really happened. Shouldn't the public be involved – or do we think they wouldn't understand?

The death of public service broadcasting isn't going to leave us as bereft as we thought. And a changed and reduced role for the regulator in the future won't necessarily mean wholesale change in the standards, but there are aspects which concern me. Television is without peer as the most influential advertising medium in the world. What about the editorial? The editorial is of course more influential than the ads.

One of our principal problems is that, because we've always been very heavily regulated, the public has been conditioned to believe we won't behave responsibly without it. We've never been fully put to the test, but we're about to be. I believe that together we now have a job to do on the reputation of television. My experience of television is that we are not cynical. The way I see it is that those of us who are in broadcasting are all responsible for the direction of our craft. If one shines, the gleam reflects off all of us; if one sinks, in some way it drags us all down.

In the long run, regulation as a sort of conscience by rulebook won't exist. What will replace it? You and me . . . and the viewers. Doesn't sound like a very big finish, does it? But there is no other grand design. If we pass on the responsibility because we somehow feel that there's a corporate or an industry agenda that is bigger than us, then not only broadcasting, but our society will be impoverished. But if together we pick up that responsibility because we recognise the incredible power of the medium to work in the public interest and because we acknowledge that we hold the reins to the potential of television to enthral and enlighten, but also to influence and inspire, then we too can have a share in greatness.

Richard Eyre (1999) 'Public Interest Broadcasting', MacTaggart Memorial Lecture, Edinburgh International Film Festival, 27 August.

PART TWO

Television Broadcasting Policy: Finance

MARGARET THATCHER believed that television broadcasting should become part of her radical agenda for change in Britain. She was convinced that many of the ills which appeared to plague broadcasting might be cured by a healthy dose of the same free-market medicine she had prescribed so liberally to other sectors of British industry. Television, at least in its BBC variant, was paternalistic, funded by a licence fee (which she had once inadvertently described as a 'poll tax') and was unresponsive and unaccountable to the programming choices of viewers. More generally, broadcasting was judged to be economically inefficient because of its duopoly structure and the restrictive practices that she believed characterised so many spheres of its operation. Her favoured policy was to abolish the licence fee and privatise Channel 4, but she was frustrated by opposition from broadcasters and political opponents: not least her formidable Cabinet allies William Whitelaw and Douglas Hurd (2.1). The Peacock Committee on financing the BBC was established in 1985 to consider whether advertising revenues might replace the licence fee as the key funding mechanism. Thatcher believed that the introduction of advertising would provide for greater competition within broadcasting, choice for viewers and efficient use of resources by broadcasters. But funding via advertising seemed to offer additional benefits: it might undermine the BBC's apparent indifference to public criticism, break the monopoly of the ITV companies and lower the costs of advertising.

These policy ambitions foundered on the rock of Peacock's suggestion that funding the BBC by advertising would compromise the quality of BBC programming and undermine the financial basis of the ITV companies. But Peacock's general conclusion that it was necessary to move in stages towards a 'functioning broadcasting market' in which consumer programme choices would be sovereign, proved much more congenial to the Thatcherite project and became highly influential in debates concerning broadcasting finance policy across the next fifteen years (2.2). The subsequent policy agenda for broadcasting has been dominated by concerns to deregulate broadcasting, subject it to the disciplines of the market, and to establish consumers' preferences as central in shaping the structures of television broadcasting.

Peacock was established to consider the funding of the BBC, but many of the committee's proposals for broadcasting finance, which found a prominent place in the government's subsequent White Paper *Broadcasting in the '90s*, focused on the commercial sector of broadcasting. The White Paper embraced Thatcher and Peacock's commitment to a 'more open and competitive broadcasting market' which placed 'the viewer at the centre of broadcasting' (2.3). A key policy proposal of the White Paper, included in the Broadcasting Act 1990, was the suggestion that licences to broadcast in the different regions of Channel 3 should be allocated by inviting companies to tender blind bids in a competitive auction, with licences going to the highest bidder (2.4). Critics of the auction protocol argued that it prompted overbidding and failed to include a reserve price mechanism, which meant some franchises were secured for low bids and achieved little in terms of enhancing competitiveness among broadcasters: in 1991 three licences were awarded without a competitive bid. But the prospect of further deregulation of broadcasting and the possible privatisation of Channel 4 remained a persistent theme throughout the 1990s. When the Broadcasting Act 1996, for example, revised the financial relations between Channel 4 and Channel 3 by abolishing what became known as the 'safety net levy', Channel 4's revenues increased by £90 million per annum and fuelled speculation that the then Conservative government might try to privatise the company. Chief Executive Michael Grade offered a spirited rebuttal of such a policy (2.6). The White Paper *A New Future For Communications* (December 2000) finally stemmed such speculations. The auction procedure to allocate the licence for Channel 5 revived familiar criticisms to observers of the 1991 auction for Channel 3 licences. On air in 1997, the new channel incurred considerable set-up costs because of technical difficulties, had limited audience reach with consequent loss of advertising revenues but, as a 'free to air' channel, enjoys cost advantages over subscription rivals.

Questions about the financing of the BBC, combined with growing concerns about the legitimacy of the licence fee as a funding mechanism in circumstances of declining audience share in a multi-channel environment, have dominated policy concerns in the public sector. Peacock proposed retention of the licence fee but its gradual replacement by subscription in a phased move to a more efficient broadcasting market (2.7). The Department of National Heritage's White Paper *The Future of the BBC* seemed to support the licence fee only in the absence of any better funding option (2.8). Other policy suggestions have ranged from: a proposal to abolish the licence fee as an indefensible, regressive tax which is costly to collect (Boulton, 1991); to an argument to retain the licence fee but distribute it by a newly created Public Service Broadcasting Authority intended to fund all public service broadcasting and not only the BBC (Green, 1991); to the suggestion that the BBC might be fully privatised (2.9). The BBC has responded to these financial proposals with policies such as producer choice which attempts to create an internal market for production resources within the BBC and make cost-efficiency savings (2.10), and by requests for an increase in licence fee to fund new services (Birt, 1996).

More recently, technological changes such as the development of digital television have placed the issue of the financing of the BBC in sharper focus. The need to develop new digital services, to compete in a burgeoning multi-channel television market, has created renewed demands from the BBC for greater financial resources. In 1998 the Davies Independent Review was established to explore the possible funding options for the BBC, including the question of the licence fee. Davies reported in July 1999, arguing for a digital licence supplement to be paid, as an interim measure, by viewers with digital television sets (2.11). Commercial television companies promptly rejected this policy option, suggesting that it would delay the roll-out of the new digital services (2.12) while the BBC complained that it would provide insufficient revenue to adequately resource the Corporation's plans for new services (2.13). The Select Committee on Culture, Media and Sport argued forcibly against the supplement, signalling a highly critical attitude to some of the new BBC television services and suggesting that an independent assessment of the BBC's financial requirements was required (2.14). On 21 February 2000, the Secretary of State for Culture, Media and Sport announced his decision not to move ahead with a digital licence fee supplement. The BBC, he argued, must finance new services from cost efficiencies supplemented by inflation-linked rises in the licence fee. The Corporation must also develop new regulatory mechanisms to guarantee transparency in its financial operations (2.15).

Part two examines these developing themes in television finance policy across the period since 1986. The extracts are structured into three groups. The first explores the broad policy agenda established by Thatcher and the Peacock Committee, the second examines policy in the commercial sector of television, and the final group details financial policy developments at the BBC. In each group extracts are presented in approximately chronological order to enable the unravelling argument to follow the order of the policy debate.

References

Birt, J. (1996) *A Glorious Future: Quality Broadcasting in the Digital Age*, Edinburgh: James MacTaggart Memorial Lecture, Edinburgh Film and Television Festival.

Boulton, D. (1991) *The Third Age of Broadcasting*, London: Institute for Public Policy Research (IPPR).

Green, D. (1991) *A Better BBC: Public Service Broadcasting in the '90s*, London: Centre for Policy Studies (CPS).

THATCHER AND PEACOCK SET AN AGENDA

2.1 Television Broadcasting Policy

Margaret Thatcher's Analysis and Policy Prescriptions

Margaret Thatcher's memoirs articulate the problems which she believed plagued television broadcasting (especially at the BBC): programming was paternalistic, funded by the licence fee, failed to reflect public demand and was too often at odds with public standards of taste and decency. Broadcasting, moreover, was economically inefficient because of its duopoly structure and restrictive practices. Thatcher suggested that television broadcasting, like any other industry, would benefit from being subject to the discipline of the market. She also believed that the deregulation of broadcasting required the abolition of the licence fee and the privatising of Channel 4. While this extract from her memoirs makes clear that there was opposition – not least from within her Cabinet – to some of these policy proposals, it is equally certain that her analysis and perception of the problems confronting broadcasting helped to shape the broad policy agenda for a decade beginning in the mid-1980s.

Broadcasting was one of a number of areas – the professions such as teaching, medicine and the law were others – in which special pleading by powerful interest groups was disguised as high-minded commitment to some greater good. So anyone who queried, as I did, whether a licence fee – with non-payment subject to criminal sanctions – was the best way to pay for the BBC, was likely to be pilloried as at best philistine and at worst undermining its 'constitutional independence'. Criticism of the broadcasters' decisions to show material which outraged the sense of public decency or played into the hands of terrorists and criminals was always likely to be met with accusations of censorship. Attempts to break the powerful duopoly which the BBC and ITV had achieved – which encouraged restrictive practices, increased costs and kept out talent –

were decried as threatening the 'quality of broadcasting'. Some of Britain's television and radio was of very high quality indeed, particularly drama and news. Internationally it was in a class of its own. But the idea that a small clique of broadcasting professionals always knew what was best and that they should be more or less immune from criticism or competition was not one I could accept. Unfortunately, in the Home Office the broadcasters often found a ready advocate. The irony that a Reithian rhetoric should be used to defend a moral neutrality between terrorism and the forces of law and order, as well as programmes that seemed to many to be scurrilous and offensive, was quite lost.

The notion of 'public service broadcasting' was the kernel of what the broadcasting oligopolists claimed to be defending. Unfortunately when subject to closer inspection that kernel began rapidly to disintegrate. 'Public service broadcasting' was extremely, difficult to define. One, clement was supposed to be that viewers or listeners in all parts of the country, who paid the same licence fee should be able to receive all public service channels – what was described as the concept of 'universality'. More, important, though, was the idea that there should be a proper balance of information, education and entertainment offered through a wide range of high quality programmes. More recently, the public service obligation had been extended to cover particular 'minority' programmes. The BBC and the IBA – which regulated the independent television companies – mainly gave effect to this public service obligation by their influence over scheduling. So much for the somewhat nebulous and increasingly outdated theory. The practice was very different. BBC1 and ITV ran programmes that were increasingly indistinguishable from commercial programming in market systems – soap operas, sport, game shows and made-for-TV films. To use Benthamite language, the public broadcasters were claiming the rights of poetry, but providing us with pushpin. Good fun perhaps. But did our civilisation really depend on it?

Furthermore the duopoly was being undermined by technological developments. Scarcity of available spectrum had previously determined that only a very few channels could be broadcast. But this was changing. It seemed likely that ever higher-frequency parts of the spectrum would be able to be brought into use. Cable television and direct broadcasting by satellite (DBS) also looked likely to transform the possibilities. There was more opportunity for payment – per channel or per programme – by subscription. An entire new world was opening up.

I believed we should take advantage of these technical possibilities to give viewers a far wider choice. This was already happening in countries as diverse as the United States and Luxembourg. Why not in Britain? But this vastly increased potential demand for programmes should not be met from within the existing duopoly. I wanted to see the widest competition among and opportunities for the independent producers – who were themselves virtually a creation of our earlier decision to set up Channel 4 in 1982. I also believed that it would be possible to combine more choice for viewers and more opportunity for producers with standards – both of production and of taste – that were as high as, if not higher than, those under the existing duopoly. To make assurance doubly sure, however, I wanted to establish independent watchdogs to keep standards high by exposing broadcasters to public criticism, complaint and debate.

The Peacock Committee on Broadcasting, which had been set up by Leon Brittan as Home Secretary in March 1985 and reported the following year, provided a good opportunity to look at all these matters once again. I would have liked to find an alternative to the BBC licence fee. One possibility was advertising: Peacock rejected the idea. Willie Whitelaw too was fiercely opposed to it and indeed threatened to resign from the Government if it were introduced. I felt that index linking the licence fee achieved something of the same purpose – to make the BBC more cost-conscious and business-like. In October 1986 the ministerial committee on broadcasting which I chaired agreed that the BBC licence fee should remain at £58 until April 1988 and then be linked to the RPI until 1991. But I did not drop my long-term reservations about the licence fee as the source of its funding. It was agreed to study whether the licence fee could be replaced by subscription.

At least as important for the future was the need to break the BBC and ITV duopoly over the production of the programmes they showed. My ministerial group agreed that the Government should set a target of 25 per cent of BBC and ITV programmes to be provided by independent producers. But there was a sharp division between those of us like Nigel Lawson and David Young who believed that the BBC and ITV would use every opportunity to resist this and Douglas Hurd and Willie Whitelaw who thought that they could be persuaded without legislation. Douglas was to enter into discussions with the broadcasters and report back. In the end we had to legislate to secure it.

I also insisted, against Home Office resistance, that our 1987 general election manifesto should contain a firm commitment to 'bring forward proposals for stronger and more effective arrangements to reflect [public] concern [about] the display of sex and violence on television'. This produced the Broadcasting Standards Council of which William Rees-Mogg became the very effective chairman and which was put on a statutory basis in the 1989 Broadcasting Act.

After the election there was more time to think about the long-term future of broadcasting. Apart from the opportunities for more channels which technology offered and the continuing discussion about how to achieve the 25 per cent target for independent producers, we needed to consider the future of Channel 4 – which I would have liked to privatise altogether, though Douglas Hurd disagreed – and the still more important matter of how the existing system of allocating ITV franchises should be changed. The Peacock Committee recommended that the system be changed to become more transparent and I strongly agreed with this objective. Under the Peacock proposals, if the IBA decided to award a franchise to a contractor other than the highest bidder it should be required to make a full, public and detailed statement of its reasons. This had the merit of openness and simplicity as well as maximising revenues for the Treasury. But we immediately ran into the morass of arguments about 'quality'.

In September 1987 I held a seminar to which the main figures in broadcasting were invited to discuss the future. There was more agreement than I might have thought possible on the technical opportunities and the need for greater choice and competition. But some of those present took a dim view of our decision to set up a Broadcasting Standards Council and to remove the exemption enjoyed by the broadcasters from the provisions of the Obscene Publications Act. I was entirely unrepentant. I said that they must remember that television was special because it was watched in the family's sitting room. Standards on television had an effect on society as a whole and were therefore a matter of proper public interest for the Government.

We had a number of discussions during 1988 about the contents of the planned White Paper on broadcasting. (It was eventually published in November.) I was pressing for the phasing out of the BBC licence fee altogether to be announced in that document. But Douglas was against this and a powerful lobby on behalf of the BBC built up. In the end I agreed to drop my insistence on it and on the privatisation of Channel 4. But I made more progress in ensuring that Channel 3 should be subject to much less heavy regulation under the new ITC (Independent Television Commission) than under the IBA.

Of course, one could only do so much by changing the framework of the system: as always, it was the people who operated within it who were the key. The appointment of Duke Hussey as Chairman of the BBC in 1986 and later of John Birt as Deputy Director-General represented an improvement in every respect. When I met Duke Hussey and Joel Barnett – his deputy – in September 1988 I told them how much I supported the new approach being taken. But I also did not disguise my anger at the BBC's continuing ambivalence as regards the reporting of terrorism and violence. I said that the BBC had a duty to uphold the great institutions and liberties of the country from which we all benefited.

The broadcasters continued to lobby fiercely against the proposals in the Broadcasting White Paper on the process of auctioning the ITV franchises. My preferred approach was that every applicant would have to pass a 'quality threshold' and then go on to offer a financial bid, with the ITC being obliged to select the highest. Otherwise a gathering of the great and the good could make an essentially arbitrary choice with clear possibilities of favouritism, injustice and propping up the *status quo*. But the Home Office team argued that we had to make concessions – first in June 1989 in response to consultation on the White Paper and then at report stage of the broadcasting bill in the spring of 1990, when they said there would be great parliamentary difficulties otherwise. These unfortunately muddled the transparency which I had hoped to achieve and produced a compromise which turned out to be less than satisfactory when the ITC bestowed the franchises the following year 'in the old-fashioned way'. Still, the new auctioning system – combined with the 25 per cent target for independent producers, the arrival of new satellite channels, and a successful assault on union restrictive practices – went some way towards weakening the monopolistic grip of the broadcasting establishment. They did not break it.

Margaret Thatcher (1993) *Margaret Thatcher: The Downing Street Years*, London: HarperCollins, pp.634–638.

2.2 The Peacock Committee

Terms of Reference and Recommendations for a 'Functioning Broadcasting Market'

The Conservative government established the Peacock Committee in 1985. From the outset, the committee adopted an expansionist view of its terms of reference, suggesting that it was not possible to examine the financing of the BBC without giving some consideration to the wider organisation and regulation of broadcasting. In the committee's words, 'before we can devise guidelines for the financing of broadcasting, we have to specify its purposes' (para 546). In its opening paragraphs the committee mused on its terms of reference. Peacock's broad conclusion was that broadcasting should move in three stages towards 'a sophisticated market system based on consumer sovereignty'. In the first stage, the BBC should continue to be funded by an index-linked licence fee rather than advertising revenues; in stage 2 the licence fee will increasingly be replaced by subscription. The third stage marks the transition to a 'functioning broadcasting market' characterised by multiple channels, delivery systems, and a broad diversity of charging and payment systems. Some sense of the significance of the Peacock report for subsequent broadcasting policy can be gained from the fact that some of its detailed recommendations – for example, the suggestions that franchise contracts for ITV should be put to competitive tender and the idea that Channel 4 should be allowed to sell its own advertising – were included in the 1990 Broadcasting Act.

1. The Home Secretary announced on 27 March 1985 that this Committee was to be established with the following terms of reference:

(i) To assess the effects of the introduction of advertising or sponsorship on the BBC's Home Services, either as an alternative or a supplement to the income now received through the licence fee, including

(a) the financial and other consequences for the BBC, for independent television and independent local radio, for the prospective services of cable, independent national radio and direct broadcasting by satellite, for the press and the advertising industry and for the Exchequer; and

(b) the impact on the range and quality of existing broadcasting services; and

(ii) to consider any proposals to secure income from the consumer other than through the licence fee.

5. It would not have been possible to follow the terms of reference if we had confined ourselves to looking only at the ways in which the BBC might be financed without at the same time considering the whole structure and regulation of broadcasting. Originally the scarcity of airwaves made it necessary for their allocation and use to be policed. But we are now in a period of unusually rapid technological advance in broadcasting . . . The committee has had an eye to the future. To consider the BBC as if it will continue with something like half of the small number of channels available is to fail to grasp the nature of changes which are already taking place and whose intensification seems irresistible.

592. Our own conclusion is that British broadcasting should move towards a sophisticated market based on consumer sovereignty. That is a system which recognises that viewers and listeners are the best ultimate judge of their own interests, which they can best satisfy if they have the option of purchasing the broadcasting services they require

from as many alternative sources of supply as possible. There will always be a need to supplement the direct consumer market by public finance for programmes of a public service kind . . . supported by people in their capacity as citizens and voters but unlikely to be commercially self-supporting in the view of the broadcasting entrepreneurs . . .

598. Our consumer sovereignty model is, of course, an ideal, a standard and a goal; not a fully specified mechanism to be pulled off the shelf tomorrow by a trigger-happy central planner. A satisfactory broadcasting market requires full freedom of entry for programme makers, a transmission system capable of carrying an indefinitely large number of programmes, facilities for pay-per-programme or pay-per-channel and differentiated charges for units of time . . . The difficulty is of course, how to move from the present regulated system now under stress to the full broadcasting market without having to pass in between through a time of troubles which could give us the worst of both worlds and the benefits of neither.

604. It has helped our thinking to envisage three stages.

608. The following table sets out the three stages we envisage. These are presented as a guide rather than a predetermined plan of action.

Table 1 The three stages

Stage	*Likely broadcasting developments*	*Policy regime*
1	Satellite and cable develop, but most viewers and listeners continue to rely on BBC, ITV and independent local radio	Indexation of BBC licence fee
2	Proliferation of broadcasting systems channels and payment methods	Subscription replaces main part of licence fee
3	Indefinite number of channels. Pay-per-programme or pay-per-channel available. Technology reduces cost of multiplicity of outlets and of charging systems	Multiplicity of choice leading to full broadcasting market

A public service provision will continue through all three stages

12.5 Recommendations for stage 1

Preparation for subscription

611. In order to prepare for subscription it is necessary to ensure that television sets are suitably adapted. We therefore set out:

Recommendation 1: All new television sets sold or rented in the UK market should be required from the earliest convenient date . . . to have a peritelevision socket and associated equipment which will interface with a decoder to deal with encrypted signals.

615. *Recommendation 2: BBC television should not be obliged to finance its operations by advertising while the present organisation and regulation of broadcasting remain in being.*

620. *Recommendation 3: The licence fee should be indexed on an annual basis to the general rate of inflation.*

628. *Recommendation 4: To permit the BBC to be the managing agent in the collection of the licence fee, the Post Office should be released from its responsibility as agent to the Home Office for collection and enforcement procedures associate with the licence fee.*

632. *Recommendation 5: On the understanding that the proceeds would be used to reduce the cost of the television licence and not to increase the total sum available for broadcasting, a separate licence fee of not less than £10 should be charged for car radios.*

634. *Recommendation 6: Pensioners drawing supplementary pension in households wholly dependent on a pension should be exempt form the licence fee.*

637. We all agreed:

Recommendation 7: The BBC should have the option to privatise radios 1, 2 and local radio in whole or in part. IBA regulation of radio should be replaced by a looser regime.

In addition, five of us go further:

Recommendation 7a: Radio 1 and radio 2 should be privatised and financed by advertising.

647. *Recommendation 8: The BBC and ITV should be required over a ten year period to increase to not less than 40% the proportion of programmes supplied by independent producers.*

652. *Recommendation 9: The non-occupied night time hours (1.00am to 6.00am) of the BBC and ITV television wavelengths should be sold for broadcasting purposes.*

655. Four of us propose:

Recommendation 10: Franchise contracts for ITV contractors should be put to competitive tender. Should the IBA decide to award a franchise to a contractor other than the one making the highest bid it should be required to make a full, public and detailed statement of its reasons.

657. *Recommendation 11: Franchises should be awarded on a rolling review basis. There would be a formal annual review of the contractor's performance by the Authority.*

658. *Recommendation 12: Consideration should be given to extending the franchise periods, perhaps to ten years.*

659. *Recommendation 13: DBS franchises should be put to competitive tender.*

660. *Recommendation 14: Channel 4 should be given the option of selling its own advertising time and would then no longer be funded by a subscription from ITV companies.*

665. *Recommendation 15: National telecommunications systems (e.g. British Telecom, Mercury and any subsequent entrants) should be permitted to act as common carriers with a view to the provision of a full range of services including delivery of television programmes.*

667. *Recommendation 16: The restriction of cable franchises to EEC-owned operators should be removed.*

668. *Recommendation 17: All restrictions for both Pay-Per-Channel and Pay-Per-Programme as options should be removed not only for cable but also for terrestrial and DBS operations.*

669. *Recommendation 18: As regulation is phased out the normal laws of the land relating to obscenity, defamation, blasphemy sedition and other similar matters should be extended to cover broadcasting media and any present exemptions should be removed.*

12.6 Stages 2 and 3: strategic potential

Stage 2 Subscription

671. The 18 recommendations we have just put forward are for prompt action and are designed to make a major step forward, this decade towards our main objective – of widening consumer choice through the new technologies with a high content of knowledge, culture, criticism, or experiment.

673. In Stage 2, which is likely to begin before the end of the century, we recommend that subscription should replace the licence fee. We regard it as a way in which all public service broadcasting organisations including the BBC, can sell their services directly to the public. We do not see it simply as an alternative way of collecting the licence fee . . . In Stage 2 the BBC and ITV would continue to provide a range of entertainment, information, culture and educational programmes, using their discretion and drawing upon their traditions to allocate expenditure. We envisage that the BBC would look to subscription and ITV to advertising revenue for mainstream income, though there would be no reason why, if they wished to do so, the BBC should not finance some of its operations by advertising or the ITV companies sell some of their programmes by subscription.

674. What then would be the trigger for the changeover to subscription? The answer cannot just be technological. A political decision is required about the minimum proportion of households possessing appropriately adapted television sets before there is a switch to encryption.

Stage 3 Multiplicity of choice

700. The shift of BBC to subscription, the greater role of independents, and the spread of various kinds of satellite and cable will not in themselves create a fully fledged broadcasting market.

701. We hope however, that the time will come for what we have called Stage 3 – i.e. full multiplicity of choice. Its essential characteristics . . . include the following:

(i) Freedom of entry for any programme makers who can recover their costs from the market or otherwise finance their production.
(ii) Viewers to be able to register directly the intensity of their preferences through pay-per-programme or pay-per-channel and not rely entirely on indirect expression through advertising ratings.
(iii) A policy to prevent monopolistic concentration among programme channellers or producers.
(iv) Common carrier obligations upon owners of transmission equipment.

Report of the Committee on Financing the BBC (1986) (Chair Professor Alan Peacock), London: HMSO, Cmnd 9824, July.

FINANCING THE COMMERCIAL SECTOR OF TELEVISION

2.3 Progeny of Peacock

The 1988 White Paper *Broadcasting in the '90s* accepted many of the market-based assumptions which Peacock argued should shape the 'full broadcasting market', as well as a number of specific measures designed to usher in the new regime: proposals which in turn became incorporated into the Broadcasting Act 1990. The deregulatory thrust of the White Paper attempted to 'place the viewer at the centre of broadcasting' by creating a 'more open and competitive broadcasting market', but also proposed a new regulatory body – the Broadcasting Standards Council – intended to 'reinforce standards on taste and decency'; the government suggests that advocacy of both proposals involves 'no contradiction'. The White Paper argued that the BBC should remain ' for the foreseeable future, the cornerstone of British broadcasting' (para 3.2), but also acknowledged that the 'Government looks forward to the eventual replacement of the licence fee' (para 3.10). But the greater part of the White Paper's provisions signalled changes for the commercial, rather than public, sector of broadcasting. Undoubtedly the most significant proposal was the reiteration of Peacock's suggestion that a new regulatory body, the Independent Television Commission (ITC), should allocate Channel 3 franchises via a two-stage auction. In the first stage applicants for licences would be obliged to 'pass a quality threshold' (para 6.17); in the second, applicants would offer financial tenders for the licence' (para 6.17).

1.1 This White Paper sets out the government's proposals for broadcasting in the UK in the 1990s.

1.2 The Government places the viewer and listener at the centre of broadcasting policy. Because of technological, international and other developments, change is inevitable. It is also desirable: only through change will the individual be able to exercise the much wider choice which will soon become possible. The Government's aim is to open the doors so that individuals can choose for themselves from a much wider range of programmes and types of broadcasting. In this field as in others, consumers will rightly insist on safeguards which will protect them and their families from shoddy wares and from exploitation. But the Government believes that with the right enabling framework, a more open and competitive broadcasting market can be attained without detriment to programme standards and quality. Its single biggest advantage will be to give the viewer and listener a greater choice and a greater say. The Government is also clear that there is no contradiction between the desire to increase competition and widen choice and concern that programme standards on good taste and decency should be maintained. Both are essential if the quality of British broadcasting is to be safeguarded and enhanced into the next century.

1.3 Chapters III to XI contain the government's specific proposals. The main ones are these:

- Most viewers will have a major increase in choice with the authorisation of a new *fifth channel*, to be operated as a national channel . . . A *sixth channel* will also be authorised should technical studies show this to be feasible.
- The present ITV system will be replaced by a regionally based *Channel 3* with positive programming obligations but also greater freedom to match its programming to market conditions.
- Provision will be made for at least one body which is effectively equipped to provide high quality *news* programmes on Channel 3.
- Options are canvassed for the future constitution of *Channel 4* on the basis that its distinctive remit is preserved and its advertising is sold separately from that on Channel 3. The *Welsh Fourth Channel Authority* will continue to provide the Fourth Channel in Wales.
- There will be a new flexible regime for the development of multi-channel *local services* through both *cable* and *microwave transmission* (MVDS). This will provide a further major extension of viewer choice.
- The UK's two remaining *Direct Broadcasting by Satellite* (DBS) frequencies will be advertised by the Independent Broadcasting Authority (IBA) early next year. This will provide scope for two further UK DBS channels in addition to the three being provided by British Satellite Broadcasting (BSB).
- Viewers will be able to receive *other satellite services* directly, including those from the proposed medium powered Astra and Eutelsat II satellites. Steps will be taken to ensure that the programme content of all such services is supervised.
- All television services (including those of the British Broadcasting Corporation) will be given freedom to raise finance through *subscription* and *sponsorship* (subject to proper safeguards). All services (except the BBC) will also be free to carry *advertising*.
- A new agency, the *Independent Television Commission* (ITC) will be established in place of the Independent Broadcasting Authority (IBA) and the Cable Authority to licence and supervise all parts of a liberalised commercial television sector. It will operate with a lighter touch than the IBA but will have tough sanctions . . .
- The *BBC* will continue as the cornerstone of British broadcasting. The government looks forward to the eventual replacement of the *licence fee* which will, however, continue for some time to come.

- The *night hours* from one of the BBC channels will be assigned to the ITC. The BBC will be allowed to retain the other set on the basis that it uses it as fully as possible for developing subscription services.
- The part played by *independent producers* in programme making in the UK will continue to grow.
- The Government will proceed with its proposals for the deregulation and expansion of *independent radio*, under the lighter touch regulation of a new *Radio Authority*.
- All UK television and radio services will be subject to *consumer protection* obligations on such matters as taste, decency and balance.
- The *Broadcasting Standards Council* (BSC) established to reinforce standards on taste and decency and the portrayal of sex and violence, will be placed on a statutory footing.
- The exemption of broadcasting form the *obscenity* legislation will be removed.
- There will be a major reform of the transmission arrangements, giving scope for greater private sector involvement.

Broadcasting in the '90s: Competition, Choice and Quality (1988) London: HMSO, Cm 517, November 45pp.

2.4 The Franchise Auction and the Broadcasting Act 1990

The Broadcasting Act (1990) introduced radical changes into the regulation, finance and organisational structures of British broadcasting. The Act: established the Independent Television Commission (ITC) as the new regulatory body with licensing and regulatory responsibilities for all commercial television services (terrestrial, cable and satellite) (Part 1, Chapter 1, Sects 1–2); empowered the ITC to issue a licence for a new Channel 5 (Part 1, Chapter 2, Sects 28–30); required Channel 4 to sell its own advertising but made provision for a 'safety net' levy on Channel 3 companies to fund any revenue deficits (Part 1, Chapter 2, Sects 26–7); and, very significantly, proposed to allocate the licences to broadcast in the various regions of the new Channel 3 by inviting companies to tender blind, competitive bids in a franchise auction (Part 1, Chapter 2, Sects 15–18). The Act bears more than a close resemblance to its predecessor White Paper *Broadcasting in the '90s,* despite the tabling of 440 amendments during the Bill's passage through Parliament. One highly significant amendment articulated the growing concerns of some parliamentarians and broadcasters that the new auction protocols might impact adversely on the range and quality of programming on Channel 3. In February 1990 the Secretary for National Heritage announced that while in most cases licences would be awarded to the highest bidder, 'in exceptional circumstances' a licence could be awarded to a lower bid. The 'primary exceptional circumstance in my judgement' he declared, 'is quality' (*Financial Times*, 5 February 1990). In further response to such concerns, the Act also specified very clear programming requirements – including licence commitments to regional, religious and children's programmes, programmes made by independent producers, and news and current affairs broadcast in peak time (Part 1, Chapter 2, Sect. 16(2)).

In February 1991 the ITC invited bids for the first Channel 3 licences; the 'winners' were announced in November. Critics argued that: the auction had not increased competition since three franchises, including the financially vibrant Central Television, were uncontested and awarded on minimal bids of £2000; the number of applicants was lower than on previous franchise rounds; the auction prompted overbidding by companies eager to retain their licence; the Broadcasting Act left it uncertain whether 'quality of programming' or 'the highest cash bid' was the criterion for success in the auction – in 1991 only five of the sixteen franchises were awarded to the highest bidder. Other critics suggested that the Treasury should have insisted on a 'reserve' price for franchises – a standard auction protocol – and argued that the bidding process required a calculation about financial circumstances across the coming decade which could be little more than informed guesswork.

The auction process for the Channel 5 licence – advertised in May 1995 – attracted criticisms similar to those of the Channel 3 auction round in 1991. The four applicants' bids ranged between £2 million (Rupert Murdoch's New Century) and £36 million (UK TV Developments Limited); the successful bidder was Greg Dyke and Lord Hollick's Channel 5 Broadcasting Limited which tendered the second highest bid of £22 million. There were other problems confronting the new station. The new channel's reach was restricted to 75 per cent of the population – with implications for advertising revenues – and this only after substantial expenditure on retuning VCRs to limit interference from the new channel's signal. The high cost associated with launch advertising, programming costs which were projected to outstrip advertising revenues in the short run combined with increased competition from Channel 4, satellite and cable services, guaranteed that the policy wisdom of launching the new channel in 1997 would be treated with a degree of critical caution by some media analysts and observers.

15. – (1) Where the Commission [ITC] proposes to grant a licence to provide a Channel 3 service they shall publish . . . a notice –

(2) The Commission shall . . . publish with the notice general guidance to applicants . . . which contains examples of the kinds of programmes whose inclusion in the service . . . would be likely to result in a finding by the Commission that the service would comply with the requirements specified in Section 16(2) [this section specifies in considerable detail the programming responsibilities attaching to the licence].

(3) Any application made in pursuance of a notice under this section must be in writing and accompanied by:

(a) the fee specified in the notice . . .
(b) the applicant's proposals for providing a service that would comply with the requirements specified in section 16(2) . . .
(f) the applicant's cash bid in respect of the licence
(g) such information as the Commission might reasonably require as to the applicant's current financial position and his projected financial position during the period for which the licence would be in force; and
(h) such other information as the Commission might reasonably require for the purpose of considering the application . . .

(7) In this Part 'cash bid' in relation to a licence means an offer to pay the Commission a specified amount of money in respect of the first complete calendar year falling within the period for which the licence is in force (being an amount which, as increased by the appropriate percentage, is also to be payable in respect of subsequent years falling wholly or partly within the period).

16. – (1) Where a person has made an application for a Channel 3 licence . . . the Commission shall not consider whether to award him the licence on the basis of his cash bid . . . unless it appears to them:

(a) that his proposed service would comply with the requirements specified below . . .
(b) that he would be able to maintain the service throughout the period for which the licence would be in force . . .

17. – (1) . . . the Commission shall, after considering al the cash bids submitted by the applicants for a Channel 3 licence, award the licence to the applicant who submitted the highest bid.

(2) Where two or more applicants for a particular licence have submitted cash bids specifying an identical amount which is higher than the amount of any other cash bids . . . then the Commission shall invite those applicants to submit further cash bids in respect of that licence . . .

(3) The Commission may disregard the requirement imposed by subsection (1) and award the licence to an applicant who has not submitted the highest bid if it appears to them that there are exceptional circumstances which make it appropriate for them to award the licence to that applicant.

(4) Without prejudice to the generality of subsection (3) the Commission may regard the following circumstances as exceptional circumstances which make it appropriate to award the licence to an applicant who has not submitted the highest bid, namely where it appears to the Commission –

(a) that the quality of the service proposed by such an applicant is exceptionally high; and
(b) that the quality of the proposed service is substantially higher than the quality of the service proposed –
    (i) by the applicant who has submitted the highest bid, or
    (ii) in a case falling within subsection (2), by each of the applicants who have submitted equal highest bids

and where it appears to the Commission, in the context of the licence, that any circumstances are regarded as exceptional circumstances for the purposes of subsection (3), those circumstances may be so regarded by them despite the fact that similar circumstances have been so regarded by them in the context of any other licence or licences.

Broadcasting Act 1990, London: HMSO, 291pp.

2.5 The ITC and the Renewal of Channel 3 Licences

In January 1998, the ITC published guidelines governing the renewal of Channel 3 broadcasting licences; the new rules signalled substantial cuts in the companies' payments to the Treasury. Licences to broadcast in the fifteen regional-based Channel 3 franchises and the GMTV breakfast channel, awarded in 1991, were scheduled to expire in January 2001. But companies – especially those which bid high for their licences in 1991, including GMTV, HTV and Yorkshire Tyne Tees – were allowed to reapply for their licence from June 1998 to try to win some financial relief from their overbidding and, if successful, to begin a new ten-year contract in January 1999. By November 1998, eleven franchise holders had decided to apply early: all but two companies were offered a reduced financial payment to continue their franchise. The overall reduction in payments amounted to approximately £90 million, which almost exactly matched the sum the Channel 3 companies 'lost' as a result of the abolition of the 'safety net' funding of Channel 4 (See 2.7). Companies which decided against accepting the new payment could reapply for their franchise in January 2000.

Sir Robin Biggam, Chairman of the ITC said: 'Our intention when setting financial terms was to ensure these licensees would be able to continue to provide the range and quality of programmes – on a national and regional basis – for which they are justly renowned, whilst providing a fair return to the Exchequer for the right to broadcast to nearly every home in the UK. The terms are derived from a realistic assessment of the value of these licences in an increasingly competitive market. The basis is now much fairer since the majority of the tender payment will be based on a percentage of the advertising revenues earned by the companies. If revenues fall below our expectations, the tender payments will fall accordingly.'

The Broadcasting Act 1990 allows Channel 3 licensees to apply for their 10-year licences to be renewed up to four years before the end of the initial licence term. Eleven Channel 3 licensees expressed an interest on 1 June 1998 to have their licences renewed at the earliest opportunity; i.e. from 1 January 1999. The ITC is required to set tender

Company	*Total tender payments in 1998*	*Total tender payments in 1999*	*Turnover in 1997*	*Advertising revenue*	*Owner*
Anglia	£29.6m	£29m	£140.1m	£124.2m	United News and Media
Border	£0.6m	£0.5m	£15.8m	£12.0m	Border and Cumbria Newspaper Group
Carlton	£81.5m	£72m	£785.7m	–	Carlton Communications
Central	£31.5m	£49m	£391m	£259m	Carlton Communications
GMTV	£50.5m	£20m	£72m	–	Disney, Granada Group, Scottish TV, Carlton Communications, Guardian Media Group
HTV	£25.5m	£9.0m	–	–	United News and Media
Meridien	£64m	£58m	£206m	£191m	United News and Media and Carlton Communications
Tyne Tees and Yorkshire	£70.5m	£46m	£270.8m	£171.1m	Yorkshire Tyne Tees Holdings; main shareholders, LWT, MAI Media Holdings, Allquiet Investments, Granada Group
Ulster	£1m	£2m	£34.5m	£33.2m	Ulster Television
Westcountry	£9.0m	£8.0m	–	–	Carlton Communications

payments to government based on the value of the licence as if it were put out to competitive tender.

ITC Sets Out Terms For Renewal of Channel 3 Licences (1998) ITC News Release, 109/98, 25 November.

2.6 Privatising Channel 4

In June 1996 the Conservative Government announced that it was giving detailed consideration to a plan to privatise Channel 4. The timing was propitious. Channel 4 had recently succeeded in lobbying for the abolition of a 'safety net' levy on Channel 3 companies, which the Broadcasting Act 1990 originally intended as a safeguard for any deficits in Channel 4 revenues following the Act's provision that Channel 4 should sell its own advertising. The continued success of Channel 4 had not only made the levy redundant, but reversed its initial ambitions by requiring Channel 4 to distribute a portion of its excess profits among Channel 3 companies. The abolition of this levy in the Broadcasting Act 1996 meant that Channel 4 had an additional £90 million to allocate to programme making. Channel 4 was also increasingly under attack for having allegedly strayed from its initial remit to seek out minority audiences, preferring instead to schedule ratings-led entertainment programmes such as American imports, sitcoms and repeats. In a speech at the Edinburgh Festival, Michael Grade spoke against privatising Channel 4 on the ground that it would prove corrosive of Channel 4's special remit to broadcast innovative programmes for minority audiences; the market he alleged would prove hostile and ultimately destructive of that remit.

Despite Grade's forceful rejection of the government's ambitions for Channel 4, the intention to privatise remained on the agenda. In May 2000 newspaper speculation that Chancellor Gordon Brown favoured privatising Channel 4 to raise £2 billion for other projects prompted the new Chief Executive Michael Jackson to use the annual Fleming Lecture to the Royal Television Society to state his implacable opposition to such a policy. In an argument reminiscent of Grade's earlier statement, Jackson suggested that Channel 4's investment in costly areas of programming such as news which does not deliver large audiences would not have been possible in the private sector with its requirement to 'maximise revenues from every part of the schedule' (*Guardian*, 11 May 2000, p.8). Once again, the rumours concerning government plans to privatise Channel 4 emerged at a time when the station's financial circumstances were very strong. Within a week Channel 4's annual report revealed a 7 per cent increase in advertising and sponsorship revenues to £600 million, producing profits of £46 million, a rise of £20 million on the previous year. In February 2001, Channel 4 separated its commercial ventures such as FilmFour and the new entertainment channel E4 by establishing a subsidiary, 4 Ventures Ltd, in a move designed to allow the partial selling off of the purely commercial parts of Channel 4. The idea that the core public service television component of Channel 4 might be privatised was finally laid to rest by the publication of the White Paper *A New Future For Communications* in December 2000 (Sect. 5.6.8).

Sorry folks, no jokes this morning; I'm too angry and sad that the privatisation of Channel 4 is even on the political agenda somewhere between the Treasury and Downing Street . . . the debate today . . . must address the following proposition: You can certainly have a privatised Channel 4, or you can have Channel 4 with its full public service remit. You cannot have both.

Channel 4's case against privatisation is too important to be hijacked by ideology and the special pleading of ITV. The only reason Channel 4 can deliver extended programme choice for viewers, pubic service competition for the BBC, and revenue competition for the ITV is that it is a statutory corporation with no shareholders.

When Channel 4 was created back in the 1981 Broadcasting Act it could easily have been just another commercial channel, in other words ITV2. The government saw that such a solution would have introduced the wrong sort of competition in programming. It would have been competition to be the same. McDonald's versus Burger King. It would have created competition for revenue but without adding any real choice for viewers. So instead the channel was charged with a special statutory remit to innovate and to complement ITV.

There is no doubt that Channel 4 has successfully delivered what was intended: it has added to viewer choice; it has added new competitive outlets for advertisers; it has found new and efficient ways of broadcasting; it has stimulated and developed the independent production sector. It provides the seed corn for British television and increasingly film production. Who could dispute that Channel 4 is now the nursery of talent? And we do it without a penny of public subsidy. It has been a huge public policy and public service success . . . I defy the Treasury to produce a justification for chucking this achievement down the drain . . . The idea bears all the hallmarks of desperation in the Treasury's family silver department.

To justify privatisation, a smokescreen has been thrown up suggesting that over recent years Channel 4 has been steadily altering its remit, that it has become more overtly commercial and has thus set itself up as a suitable candidate for privatisation . . . it is a charge that has been rejected in three successive performance reviews by the ITC. Channel 4's commercial success has not been built on a down-market rush to build audience share. It has been built on selling its airtime at its true value since the ITV monopoly ended in 1992. If Channel 4 had abandoned its remit, I promise you I wouldn't be sitting here with just an 11 per cent share.

Jeremy Isaacs knew what we know, that to deliver the whole of the remit you need a number of revenue driving programmes . . . No one would thank me today if Channel 4's share were only 3 to 5 per cent of viewing. It would not deliver competition for advertisers. It would not produce financial independence. And it would not sustain real additional choice for viewers. It would face either extinction or the need for massive subsidy. So let me be clear. I am proud that Channel 4 continues to enhance the quality of the remit and I am convinced that our share of viewing is adequate to sustain it.

There are those who say this happy state of affairs could continue undisturbed after privatisation. Not a chance. The remit works . . . because it is a shared objective between Parliament, the regulator and the Board of the channel. The whole purpose of the channel is to operate as efficiently as possible to deliver the maximum resources to that common objective on the screen.

Post privatisation, a second and irresistible dynamic would come into play: the need to maximise the return to shareholders. In that situation the remit, however explicitly defined, would represent the most you had to deliver to avoid regulatory sanction. That done, all efforts and efficiency would be directed at enhancing the bottom line. This dynamic sucks money off the screen and out of British production. Thus the remit would effectively be a battleground, not a shared objective . . . Trying to write a remit which would resist shareholder pressure is an impossible task. The very language of the present remit recognises the need to take risks, be creative and to deploy resources in a way which cannot be achieved at the same time as ensuring maximum profits . . . Does anyone honestly think that a bunch of hard-nosed shareholders would have signed the cheque to finance *Trainspotting*? Let us not ever discount one of the key virtues of the channel's present constitution – its independence. Once we are captured by shareholders we lose that independence.

The acid test for privatisation . . . is that there must be some demonstrable benefit for the consumer, in our case the viewers. Channel 4 plc simply fails this test. There is nothing in it for the viewer. To claim the remit would survive privatisation is either naïve or dishonest. It would not.

Michael Grade (1996) 'The Privatisation of Channel 4', Speech delivered at the Edinburgh Festival, 26 August.

FINANCING THE BBC

2.7 Peacock and the Licence Fee

The Conservative government established the Peacock Committee in 1985 to explore the possibility of replacing the licence fee with advertising revenues as the major source of financing (See 2.1). The government believed that such a reform would promote competition in broadcasting, choice for viewers and efficiency among broadcasters. While Prime Minister Thatcher dubbed the licence fee a regressive 'poll tax', Peacock found much too recommend its retention in the short run, although this surprised contemporary observers. The committee eventually recommended an indexed licence fee to finance the BBC with a move towards a system of subscription in the late 1990s.

Before addressing alternative ways of funding the BBC, we feel we must first say a word about the status quo. The licence fee has been the traditional source of finance for the BBC. It has always been argued that it helps to preserve the independence of the BBC, to maintain a direct relationship between the BBC and its audience and further that it embodies the principle that broadcasting, as a public service, should be universally available to all at equal cost . . . The evidence we received suggested that the present system:

(i) is regressive in that the licence fee is a kind of poll tax which all owners of TV sets must pay independent of wealth or income;
(ii) is potentially unfair in that, in theory, owners of TV sets might prefer to watch ITV only;
(iii) is expensive to administer and is therefore an inefficient use of resources;
(iv) appears to require excessive increases in the licence fee because the licence fee is increased only every three years;
(v) encourages evasion of payment of the licence fee because costs of detection are high and penalties for detection relatively low;
(vi) does not seek to define . . . the service which is to be paid for by the licence fee nor is any evaluation of the performance of the BBC in meeting its objectives undertaken;

(vii) implies a degree of political control because the level of the licence fee is set by the Home Secretary. It is unlikely that the licence fee will ever be set to a level which the BBC 'requires'. It was suggested that an advisory body, accountable to parliament, should be set up to take the matter out of direct political control . . .

(viii) means that in effect the ordinary licence payers are providing a subsidy for hotel proprietors and guests because of the present arrangement for hotels whereby proprietors pay a standard licence fee to cover their own accommodation and up to 15 guest rooms . . .

Nevertheless, a number of those submitting evidence felt that the licence fee had much to commend it. The licence fee system, they said:

(i) is a secure form of financing for the BBC;
(ii) gives a good deal of freedom from political control;
(iii) preserves the independence of the BBC from other influences;
(iv) maintains a direct relationship between the BBC and the consumers, and
(v) enables the BBC to produce programmes of high quality covering a wide range of subjects.

211. There are some problems about defining of the status quo. It is not simply sufficient to argue that the licence fee has served us well for 60 years. We must consider whether such a system is suitable for the new age of broadcasting which is already dawning.

243. The conclusion is that, paradoxically, the status quo . . . represents an unstable situation. If cable and satellite services develop to the extent that they begin to compete significantly for audiences then this will either have an impact on the BBC's programming policy (in order to maintain its audience share) or will make justification of the licence fee politically difficult (because of its declining audience share). If cable and satellite services do not develop the evidence is that ITV revenue will grow at a high rate. It seems doubtful if the aspirations of the BBC could be fulfilled without changes in the BBC's revenue structure. Given the government has ruled out the financing of the BBC from a direct grant, the licence fee would have to rise at the rate predicted in paragraph 219 to keep pace with the ITV companies (an increase of 33%).

Report of the Committee on Financing the BBC (1986) (Chair Professor Alan Peacock), London: HMSO, Cmnd 9824.

2.8 Paying for the BBC: The Options

The Department of National Heritage Green Paper *The Future of the BBC* (Cm 2098, 1992) was the first official discussion (post-Peacock) of the Corporation's finances. The pros and cons of the licence fee, direct taxation, advertising, subscription and a mixed financing system were each examined. The final judgement favoured the licence fee. Two years later, the White Paper *The Future of Broadcasting: Serving the Nation, Competing World-Wide* (Cm 2621, July 1994) endorsed this conclusion and promised a review of the licence fee in 2001 – a policy which the tabloid press promptly dubbed 'the space odyssey option'. The review would be conducted in the light of new technology and the possibility of subscription funding: the linking of the fee to the retail price index would be reviewed in 1996.

Two significant policy options for BBC funding were published by the think-tanks the Institute for Public Policy research (IPPR) and the Centre for Policy Studies (CPS). Interestingly, each suggested a policy which ran counter to what might have been anticipated. David Boulton, in his pamphlet *The Third Age of Broadcasting*, for the left-of-centre IPPR, argued that the licence fee should be abolished because it is a regressive tax, with high collection costs and unpopular with the public. He rejected the alternatives of advertising and subscription in favour of funding the BBC by a grant from government which would make a direct charge on the taxpayer, similar to the other public services of health and education.

Damien Green's pamphlet *A Better BBC: Public Service Broadcasting in the '90s*, published by the right-of-centre Centre for Policy Studies (CPS), examined the effectiveness of the three major sources of funding for the BBC: the licence fee, advertising or subscription. Green rejected the latter two and provided a fourth 'involving a combination of the licence fee paid not to the BBC but to a body which promotes quality television': A Public Service Broadcasting Authority. Green also offered radical proposals for changing the ways in which the BBC 'makes money from its own products' (Green, 1991: 26). These include selling its library of programmes to other global broadcasters and privatising Radio 1 and Radio 2.

Paying for the BBC – licence fee

6.6 The BBC services have been paid for from a licence fee since 1927 and, so far, no one has devised an obviously better system. The licence fee is readily understood. It guarantees the BBC a regular income and it preserves the arms length relationship between the broadcasters and the government.

6.8 But the licence fee is an oddity. All viewers are obliged to pay it irrespective of whether they watch or like many BBC programmes. Black and white television set owners pay less although they receive the same programmes. Rich and poor must pay the same. Payment is enforced through the criminal law but evasion is estimated at nearly 8%.

6.10 Continuing to fund some BBC services by the licence fee does not mean keeping the present system unaltered.

6.11 It would be possible to increase charges to those with more than one set or to have a lower fee for those least able to pay.

Paying for the BBC by taxation

6.12 The BBC provides services which benefit the public as a whole. Some people believe that the BBC should be paid for by those who can most afford to contribute to the well-being of the community and not by all households which use television regardless of their income. But if the BBC were financed from income tax, it would need an increase of nearly a penny in the pound on the standard rate to produce the amount which is at present raised from the licence fee. General VAT rates would have to be increased by 0.5% in order to produce the same revenue.

6.13 It is sometimes argued that the BBC could be funded through a levy on particular goods and services directly associated with television broadcasting, such as television sets, VCRs. But at least £300 would have to be added to the price of a television set to raise income equivalent to the licence fee.

6.14 The argument against funding the BBC . . . services from general taxation has been that it would make the BBC vulnerable to government or political pressure on the content of programmes

Advertising on BBC services

6.15 The possibility of advertising on BBC services was examined closely by the Peacock Committee on Financing the BBC, which reported in 1986 [see 2.2] . . . They concluded that BBC television should not take advertising. Most of them thought that Radios 1 and 2 could take advertising, but they should not remain BBC services.

6.16 More recent research has exposed further the difficulties of funding the BBC's services from advertising. For example, advertising revenue is unlikely to increase sufficiently to provide the additional £1,000 million which would be needed . . .

6.17 Sponsorship is another form of advertising limited to a statement in a programme that it is being financed by a particular organisation. This is less intrusive but unlikely to provide sufficient revenue to finance more than a small proportion of programmes. There is, too, a risk that organisations which pay for programmes are more likely to want to influence their content.

6.19 Introducing advertising might alter the range and quality of programmes.

6.20 Advertising on BBC services would change the prospects of others who benefit from advertising revenue, particularly other broadcasters and the press.

Subscription

6.22 The Peacock Committee concluded that in the longer term subscription should replace the licence fee as the main source of BBC finance. It could take several forms, ranging from a single fee for all BBC services to paying to watch individual programmes.

6.23 One advantage of subscription is that it could make a direct link between the providers and users of the service. Unlike the licence fee, subscription need not oblige television set owners to pay the same amount regardless of how many programmes or services they use . . . In 1987 a study commissioned by the Home Office recommended a gradual introduction of subscription television but not a wholesale immediate switch to existing services to subscription.

6.24 The BBC has already introduced some services for limited audiences which are broadcast during the night and financed by subscription.

Mixed financing

6.25 There is no reason why the BBC services should be financed exclusively by the licence fee or by any other means. Already the BBC obtains part of its income through BBC Enterprise, trading commercially and BBC World Service radio is funded by Government grant.

Value for money

6.27 Whatever the method of financing, the BBC needs to give value for money and to demonstrate that it is doing so. It needs to improve the efficiency of its activities each year, while maintaining the quality of its programmes.

6.28 The government has urged the BBC to improve its efficiency. The decision to hold licence fee increases below the levels of inflation . . . has encouraged the BBC to look for ways of reducing its costs and diverting funds from administration to programmes. The BBC initiatives 'Producer Choice' and 'Re-Shaping for the Future', and its scrutiny of overheads, are all steps in this direction.

6.30 Clear objectives are essential in achieving value for money. As the BBC moves towards the 21st century, it will need well-defined aims and duties if the public are to be able to judge whether it is efficient and effective.

Department of National Heritage (1992) *The Future of the BBC; A Consultation Document*, London: HMSO, Cm 2098.

2.9 Privatising the BBC?

In his 1993 essay *Sharper Visions: The BBC and the Communications Revolution,* Ian Hargreaves explored a number of possible alternatives to resolve the Corporation's financial difficulties including a licence superfee, a Public Service Broadcasting Council, a federal BBC, a 'dismembered' BBC (broken into smaller units such as television, national radio, local radio, etc.) and the possibility of metamorphosing the BBC into a publisher-broadcaster along the lines of Channel 4. Hargreaves rejects all these options since they fail to address the twin aims of broadcasting policy which he identifies: 'to improve services for consumers while creating the conditions in which the broadcasting industry can flourish in an international context.' He concludes that it is necessary to 'devise a plan to transfer the BBC to the private sector': Hargreaves acknowledges that the very suggestion might strike many observers as 'taboo' (p.38).

None of the ideas proposed considers the possibility the BBC might move towards a different funding base. And it is assumed that a publicly-funded BBC is unlikely either to be capable or to be allowed to compete on the international stage against private sector competitors . . . The BBC has already in recent months run into controversy with commercial rivals over a number of non-core ventures: its joint football contract with BSkyB, its 20% participation in the UK Gold advertising-funded satellite channel, the spread of World Service Television, and its cross-promotion of BBC magazines on television . . .

The Government has in recent years encouraged the BBC to seek ancillary money-making activities to supplement the licence fee, but it seems likely that as life becomes tougher for the BBC's commercial competitors, they will insist on further restrictions on the corporation . . .

All of these arguments point to the same conclusion: that a purely public sector corporation faces mounting self-contradictions in the international market place of modern broadcasting. Logic demands that we address the licence fee taboo and as a necessary corollary devise a plan to transfer the BBC to the private sector, so enabling it to compete vigorously, not only with the commercial broadcasters, but also against Mr. Murdoch and the international media conglomerates . . .

The key is not to imagine that it will be possible instantly to replace one form of funding wholly with another, but to devise the most attractive blend of funding alternatives for the BBC, which could easily vary by activity and be introduced in a phased way. It has often been pointed out that parts of the BBC, like Radios 1 and 2, would fit relatively easily into an advertising-funded mould . . . A case can also be made for some advertising on BBC1 and even BBC2, although there are probably greater attractions in exploring the possibilities of a subscription format for a relatively specialised channel like BBC2. There is no reason why a BBC of the future should not run a general entertainment channel, funded by advertising, a more specialised channel like BBC2 on subscriptions or with an advertising/public subsidy mix, along with a range of other services.

With the spread of satellite and cable infrastructure the BBC is in a uniquely strong position to offer new, revenue-raising services, many of which would enable it to use existing resources more efficiently. An obvious example would be to create a BBC television news channel making better use of an expensive and unique resource whose output is currently jammed into the congested 30 minutes news format. Given the cheapness and availability of satellite and eventually cable capacity, the BBC could easily offer events channels – a Wimbledon Channel, a Proms Channel, an Olympics Channel, a cricket channel, the possibilities are endless. The task would be to define core services and to encourage the BBC to innovate at the periphery by giving it the freedom to raise finance to do so . . .

It would be both feasible and desirable to maintain public funding for BBC services with a defined public service, non-commercial character, as well as for other broadcasters' public service activities, adjusting these over time. Radio 4 and Radio 3 might be defined as public service and funded accordingly . . .

A move from licence fee to advertising and subscription for the bulk of BBC revenue would allow the ITV companies time to adjust to extra competition and for the Treasury to gauge the right pace at which to wind down its levy on ITV profits. The fact that commercial broadcasters would fight tooth and nail against such a proposal does not make it wrong: the ITV companies tend to take a different view of the size of the advertising pot during debates about the BBC than they do when they are building optimistic scenarios to try to secure franchises from the Independent Television Commission . . .

It will also be argued that access to advertising will turn the BBC into an ITV lookalike, but this is not convincing if we are looking to a mix of funding which includes advertising, subscription, public subventions and income from other activities. Even with a funding base drawn exclusively from advertising, Channel Four is able to achieve a distinctive style . . .

Once it is accepted that there are realistic funding alternatives, it is possible to address in a new way the most fundamental question of all: who owns the BBC and what is it for? . . . One possibility is for the BBC simply to be floated on the stock exchange like British Telecom, British Gas or British Airways. This would undoubtedly bring advantages in terms of access to capital, freedom to manage, efficiency and innovation, as has been the experience in other privatisations. A straightforward float however would turn the BBC into a profit-maximising corporation, unanswerable to its institutional shareholders. There would be some risk that the unique qualities and character of the BBC would be lost . . . Conceivably the form of privatisation could be as a non-profit distributing trust, a kind of mutual association, constituted to execute the wishes of its members and granted certain fiscal and other privileges consistent with the public good it provides. In the world of media the experience of Reuters prior to its floatation on the stock exchange offers one possible model . . . Another example worthy of study is the Scott Trust which owns the *Guardian* . . .

Here then is a sharper vision of the BBC's future: a BBC liberated from political control, free to invest, to expand, to make alliances and to develop new services. Such a BBC would have a first rate chance to emerge as a major UK player in the international market place. (pp.36–43)

Ian Hargreaves (1993) *Sharper Visions: The BBC and the Communications Revolution*, London: Demos 49pp.

2.10 Producer Choice and Organisational Change at the BBC

John Birt's Response to his Critics

Policy is not solely the province of government. While politicians, think-tanks, interest groups and the government were exploring the adequacy of the licence fee and alternative funding mechanisms for the BBC, the Director-General John Birt was implementing a number of policy changes. By 1993, Birt's radical changes to the BBC's organisational and managerial structures, designed to deliver substantial cost efficiencies and savings, were opposed by critics within and outside the BBC. Michael Grade in his 1992 MacTaggart Lecture, for example, denounced the new style of management for its alleged stifling of creativity; the following year, from the same platform, Dennis Potter repeated the charge (see 1.8–9). Birt argued that the internal restructuring of BBC finances was vital to save the Corporation from going 'broke'. Producer Choice, one of the most significant innovations, moreover, generated more resources to make more creative programmes and would reinforce rather than undermine the BBC's 'craft-base'.

At the end of my term in this job I shall be judged not by whether the BBC is more efficient (though I trust it will be), nor by whether our financial controls are more effective (though I hope they will be). At the end of the day there is only one measure on which I or any other Director-General of the BBC must be judged. Did we deliver the very best, the most delightful, the most stimulating and surprising programmes? And that is what our reforms will achieve. So let me confront some of the black propaganda that has been obscuring what's actually happening in the BBC.

First, let me address those critics *outside* the BBC. They come in many forms: traditionalists; opportunists; society's hecklers, ever ready with a quote; and there's even the odd old BBC soldier, sniping at us with their muskets, still telling nostalgic tales of the golden days when no one bothered much about management. When all was creativity and romance. But either they are ignorant of, or they conveniently ignore, the changed universe in which the BBC now operates – changes not of our making.

Michael Checkland started a revolution when he challenged some of those old comfortable certainties. For he saw all too clearly that chaos lay ahead unless we took radical action. But our critics do not believe there was any need for the BBC to change.

They say:

- The BBC was perfectly efficient in the old days.
- The reforms are bringing no visible benefits of any kind to the BBC.
- The BBC is drowning under a tide of paper, and galloping bureaucracy.
- They say all the BBC has to do to ward off political predators is to make good programmes (but they are ostriches if they really believe that).
- If it ain't broke, don't fix it (but the truth is, we would have been broke if we'd carried on with those arcane financial systems).

Let me tackle the myth that the BBC was already efficient:

- In fact we had an unwieldy, almost Soviet-style command economy, where money was allocated from the top to every activity, to every programme department, to every maintenance workshop.
- The whole system demanded from programme makers the skills of supplicants at some Byzantine court, rather than straight business dealing, where all is open, clear and transparent.
- No-one knew what anything actually cost. We didn't really know, for instance, what individual programmes cost because studios, and all resources, were financed separately from programmes. So programme makers had no incentive to keep down costs that were not deducted from their own budgets.
- A lack of adequate financial information and control permeated the whole organisation.

Without a shadow of doubt, there was much waste in the old BBC. What we found in recent years when we examined ourselves carefully was often uncomfortable.

- We uncovered a tendency all over the BBC to command your own fleet, to invest in a full range of expensive facilities, and the people to staff them, whether they were necessary or not.
- As a result we owned facilities vastly in excess of even the peak of our need.
- We found one brand new radio studio that was actually only used for 3 per cent of the time.
- We found a graphics suite which was only used for a full working day for one day a fortnight.

For the first time ever we discovered what our overheads were really costing us – and it was a staggering £300 million a year. By concentrating on reducing these we will in due course make savings of £70 million every year. Millions of pounds were wasted through the years, frittered away on over-provisioned overheads, and equipment lying idle. Waste is money that should have been spent on programmes.

So there was no choice for us but Producer Choice. For the first time programme makers are now free to control their whole budget, and to spend it as they want. Suddenly they find themselves with more money and more power to help them make the best possible programmes. We can now see where the money is going, and why – also for the first time.

Over a period of years this change and reorganisation has delivered truly astounding results. Since 1990 we will have saved in all £180 million at today's prices. A small fortune has been redirected into programmes. Current savings are running at over £100 million a year. This remarkable success is nowhere reflected in the reporting of the progress of Producer Choice. So I want to take this opportunity to lay to rest some of the other myths.

Producer Choice has been caricatured as bureaucracy gone mad, with multitudes of business units exchanging contracts in a whirl of paper and computer messages. In fact, its introduction has been a remarkable success. Yes, of course there are teething troubles. This is the most radical and fundamental organisational change in the BBC's history. But now we know at last how much each of our departments costs to run and what the demand is for their services, I will be prompting mergers to reduce the number of business units and therefore the volume of trading within the BBC.

The next lie to nail is the one about the battalions of bureaucrats they say we've hired to operate Producer Choice. The truth is . . . while the overall workforce has decreased by 14 per cent in two years, the numbers in programme production have gone up by some 5 per cent. Let me repeat there are now *more* people in absolute numbers on the programme side, and far *fewer* engaged in support functions.

We have been accused, too, of undermining our only real asset, our talented employees. I am as against the contract culture that pushes valued people on to insecure six-month and one-year contracts as I am against the old jobs-for-life culture. These apparent short-term savings lead to worse not better programme making. There will always be a short-term need to employ genuinely freelance staff; but in a well-run department, programme heads should aim to have longer associations for the overwhelming majority of their creative staff.

And let me once again insist that Producer Choice has not and will not destroy the BBC's craft-base. We looked recently at the top twenty organisations in the UK providing broadcast facilities. The BBC is the biggest; indeed, wait for it, it is twice the size of the next nineteen added together. So we have a long way to go before our resource base can remotely be described as 'under threat'.

John Birt (1993) 'The BBC: Past and Present', Speech to the Radio Academy Festival on 13 July.

2.11 The Davies Report

The Case for a Digital Licence Supplement

In October 1998, the Secretary of State for Culture, Media and Sport announced a review of the licence fee and the future funding of the BBC (what eventually became the Independent Review Panel chaired by Gavyn Davies). The new funding arrangements must protect and guarantee the BBC's public service commitments but also allow the successful operation of the BBC in an increasingly competitive, multi-channel, digital broadcasting environment. Davies argued that during the 1990s the BBC's income had fallen relative to the private sector of broadcasting; a trend which was likely to continue across the next decade. To date the BBC had managed to develop digital services, despite this relative reduction in income, by achieving considerable savings and efficiencies. One cost of the latter may have been a 'dumbing down' in programming but public surveys reveal considerable audience contentment with programming. The Chairman's Foreword to *The Future Funding of the BBC* argued that 'self-help' would provide the

> major component of additional funding for the BBC and would be achieved through efficiencies and an expansion of commercial services. But the substantive recommendation was that while the licence fee should remain the Corporation's key source of income, a digital licence supplement should be levied on viewers who opted for digital television services. Davies suggested that such a supplement might offer some limited disincentive to rates of digital take-up among television audiences but argued that this represented the best possible funding option since it was desirable, fair and based on the principle that 'the digital user pays for the digital service'.

In principle, it would be possible to generate the necessary revenue by turning the BBC into something close to a commercial broadcaster, for example by raising revenue from advertising, sponsorship and subscription. But each of these courses of action would damage the BBC as a public service broadcaster, or set in train undesirable head-to-head competition for scarce revenue with private broadcasters, or both. We think that these options would be profoundly damaging for the broadcasting ecology in the UK.

This leaves two possible ways forward – an increase in the basic licence fee, or a digital licence supplement. We prefer either of these options to the 'status quo' of doing nothing. However, on balance, we think that a digital licence supplement has clear advantages over the basic licence fee, and fits in better with the British tradition of introducing new technologies in the broadcasting market.

A digital licence supplement would have compelling advantages:

- It would continue the established practice that people should pay more when there is a major change in the technical capabilities of their main receiver – analogous with the introduction of television, and later the colour licence fee;
- It would reduce resentment among those who have not adopted digital technology that 10% of their licence fee was being spent on something from which they do not benefit;
- It would provide buoyancy for BBC revenues as digital take-up increases; and
- once the initial decision was taken by government, it would remove the BBC licence fee from the arena of political controversy for many years to come.

Against these, some disadvantages have to be weighed:

- there would be concerns among manufacturers, the platform operators, Ondigital and BSkyB, and others that a higher licence fee for digital television might deter take-up of digital systems;
- it would add to the barriers to digital transfer faced by the poor;
- there may be enforcement difficulties, especially if many digital receivers were already in use before a digital supplement was introduced; and
- there would be uncertain effects on BBC revenue, dependent on the rate of digital penetration.

The fundamental argument against a digital licence supplement concerns the disincentive to digital take-up. It would be foolish to pretend that this does not exist but, at the level we consider appropriate, we do not believe that the damaging effect –

measured over a period of years – will be large. This is particularly the case as the BBC will be given a huge incentive to promote the rapid take-up of digital. We have examined evidence from all sides and would not contemplate recommending this course of action if the delay to digital take-up seemed likely to be large. A digital licence supplement will not kill the digital revolution any more than the colour licence killed colour television.

The specific package we propose is designed to avoid creating problems concerning analogue switchover by gradually phasing out the supplement by 2010. Therefore:

- A digital licence supplement of £1.99 a month would be introduced from April 2000. This would decline to 99p a month in April 2006, and would be planned to disappear altogether by 2010.
- This means that the total licence fee for digital subscribers would be fairly static at about £126–£128 per annum in nominal terms throughout the period up to 2006 (assuming the government hits its 2.5% per annum inflation target).
- The analogue licence fee would follow a path unchanged from the baseline – ie it would fall by 3.5% in real terms in the next two years, and thereafter it would be raised in line with inflation.
- The effect of this is that the analogue licence fee would rise gradually to meet the digital fee as the date of analogue switchover approached.

This option has enormous advantages:

- The average digital licence supplement charged from now to 2006 would be £1.57 per month, and people would know in advance that the supplement would drop to only 99p a month by the end of the period. We do not believe this would be a large disincentive to digital take-up.
- Parity between digital and analogue licence fees would be achieved in 2010. If the government wished to go for analogue switchover before that date, it would be easy to adjust either the analogue fee upwards or the digital licence supplement downwards, to achieve parity at an earlier date.
- Unlike the analogue option, this option does not increase the BBC's income in perpetuity, since the overall licence fee is the same when convergence occurs as it would be under the status quo or baseline option. (The easiest way to see this is to realise that the digital licence supplement eventually disappears altogether, while the analogue licence fee is uprated by exactly the same amount as in the baseline.)
- This means that the package does not preempt decisions about BBC funding which will need to take place at Charter review. At that time, the BBC will need to make out an entirely new case for extra funding. We see this as an advantage.
- The digital licence supplement declines through time. This has the disadvantage that the disincentive to digital take-up appears larger in the early years, but this pattern is unavoidable once we have decided to eliminate the supplement by 2010. There are already offsetting advantages to this pattern – it means that the higher charges fall on the early adopters (who presumably attach the most value to the new technology), and it means that the per head charge for digital services falls as the number of digital users increases, thus enabling the cost of the service to be spread over a higher number of users.

Despite these advantages, we recognise that there may be some people who would prefer simply to increase the analogue licence fee, so we set out an alternative analogue option which would raise the same amount of money for the BBC in the years up to 2006. This involves increasing the licence fee by £5 in both 2000 and 2001, instead of increasing it by only £1.60 in the two years, as intended under the five year settlement which ends in 2001.

On balance, the Panel prefers the digital option to the analogue option mainly because it better meets the principle than the digital user pays for the digital services. We see this as inherently fairer than loading all the costs of digital onto the analogue viewer.

However, we recognise that the digital option creates a disincentive for the take-up of the new technology. Although we do not believe this will be large, neither is it entirely negligible. The panel believes that if the government decides against the digital option, the analogue option is preferable to doing nothing.

The Future Funding of the BBC (1999) Report of the Independent Review Panel (Chair Gavyn Davies), Department of Culture, Media and Sport, 28 July, 210pp.

2.12 Commercial Television's Response to the Davies Report

The Davies Panel's suggestion of a digital licence supplement prompted a predictable opposition; not least from the commercial television companies. Writing in the *Guardian*, Clive Jones, Chief Executive of Carlton Television, alleged the supplement was a regressive tax which would obstruct digital take-up. The best way to fund the BBC in the digital multi-channel broadcasting system was to adopt another proposal discussed by Davies; namely a £5 increase in the analogue licence. This would generate greater revenues for the BBC and provide an incentive to digital take-up but it would not penalise those who had already invested in the new technology.

The publication earlier this month of the Davies report into the future funding of the BBC has triggered a loud outcry. The opposition of commercial broadcasters, including Carlton, to the proposed digital licence fee is discounted in some quarters. But evidence of public opposition is less easily explained away. Company switchboards, newspaper letter pages, even the BBC's own website have all been abuzz with ordinary licence fee payers expressing their overwhelming hostility to the proposed £24 digital tax.

This should not come as a surprise. The digital licence fee is a regressive tax – technologically and socially. As Sir John Birt told MPs before his Damascene conversion, it will be a tax on innovation. It will slow down the take-up of digital services and penalise those individual viewers who, with companies like ourselves, have invested in the technology already. And, like all flat rate taxes, those least able to pay will be hardest hit . . .

Some fundamental questions will remain even if the government rejects the digital tax. Most obviously how will public sector broadcasting be safeguarded in a digital age of multi-channel choice? The chances of a reasoned debate improved this week when the BBC finally caved in to months of pressure and published a report it commissioned from London Economics into the impact of a digital tax upon the take-up of digital television . . . The London Economics report backs all of the key claims of the campaign against the digital tax. Its main conclusion is that 'higher prices slow down take-up'. The transition to colour television was delayed by up to four years by the introduction of the colour licence. The impact of the digital tax threatens to be even more pronounced pushing the prospect of the final analogue switch off almost out of sight. The simple truth is that higher prices slow demand . . .

What of the argument that better funded BBC channels would boost demand? In fact, BBC digital services – accounting for one in 200 viewing hours – are simply not the spur to digital take-up. Multi-channel households watch less BBC than the average home. The digital licence fee really is a piece of Alice in Wonderland economics – those who watch the BBC least will be obliged to pay the most for it.

But while the case for the digital poll tax is pretty much impossible, supporters of the BBC like myself have to address the problem of how we can fund it adequately in the digital era.

Davies perhaps recognising opposition to his digital poll tax, offers his own alternative. His fallback proposal is the so-called 'analogue option' of a £5 increase in the basic licence fee next year and the year after that.

This would undoubtedly be fairer than the digital supplement. Eventually we will all benefit from digital programmes and services, so it seems fair that we all contribute to constructing the infrastructure required. Plus, of course the removal of a price differential between analogue and digital would allow take-up of digital services to continue apace.

Going for the analogue option would also mean a dual windfall to the BBC of a higher real licence fee and an extra £1 billion by 2006 – add in increases for inflation and privatisation receipts and that figure more than doubles. The analogue option poses the real question post Davies: does the BBC really need extra public money? After all just three years ago the BBC itself was quite categorically saying that it already had the 'lion's share' of funds required from the front loaded 1996 licence fee settlement and £233 millions from the sale of its transmission business. Davies justifies giving the BBC an extra £1 billion of public money on either of his options by balancing it with 'self help'. The BBC promises to find £520 million internally from increased commercial revenues and efficiency savings. It sounds impressive but the BBC figures just don't add up.

Let's take the efficiency savings. Over the last three years the BBC claims savings of £89 millions a year. With Sir Christopher Bland and Greg Dyke at the helm surely we should expect this run rate to be maintained? From 1998–2006 we could expect an efficiency return of around £800 millions. Davies lets the BBC off with a paltry £350 millions.

The same applies to commercial income. Last year the BBC promised the House of Commons select committee on culture, media and sport an increased commercial income well over £100 millions to 2006. The committee dismissed this figure as 'markedly ambitious'. It seems the Davies report is less ambitious still – he wants a mere £100 millions over eight years.

Close examination shows the Davies report has got the balance wrong. The report is more 'help yourself' than 'self help'. We could avoid the need for a divisive digital tax altogether by demanding greater value for money from the BBC. And don't forget that all this is on top of the gains to the BBC from an inflation-linked licence fee from 2002 to 2006. Other public utilities delivering new technologies and service improvements while regulated to keep price rises below inflation, must be rubbing their eyes in disbelief.

Finally to return to the commercial broadcasters, the *Guardian* and others put our opposition down to 'vested interest'. An interest in what? Our overwhelming commercial interest is in a smooth and rapid transition to digital. The government, equipment manufacturers, the *Guardian* and the general public share that vision.

The digital licence fee is an unfair tax on innovation for which the economic necessity is far from clear. If it would help digital take-up, we would still have a commercial interest in supporting it. It will hinder take-up, so we won't support it.

Ultimately I am confident that the government will not support the digital tax either because like the commercial broadcasters it supports the switch over to digital services, which will close the gap between the 'information rich' and the 'information poor'. If we want to see interactive television and the Internet brought together through the digital economy, we should be encouraging the switch over not hindering it.

Clive Jones, Chief Executive of Carlton Television (1999) 'A Tax Too Far', *Guardian*, 16 August, pp.8–9.

2.13 The BBC's Response to the Davies Review Panel

On 4 August 1999, the BBC responded to the Davies recommendations. The BBC welcomed the digital licence supplement but argued that by itself this would provide insufficient funding for the transition to digital services. The BBC also rejected the privatising of BBC Resources and BBC Worldwide as incompatible with the best interests of viewers. The policy document offered a detailed response to each of the Davies proposals.

BBC Director-General, Sir John Birt said:

> 'We are grateful for the panel's strong advocacy of the powerful role the BBC can play in the digital era ahead. Their report comprehensively sets out – and with considerable insight – the scale of the challenge the BBC faces in what it describes as the Fourth Broadcasting Revolution . . . But the panel

has not willed the means to achieve the ends it so clearly defines. The level of future funding they have recommended will not enable the BBC to offer its licence payers the substantial public service choice in the total digital era that the panel desires . . . Moreover, we are not convinced that some of the panel's specific proposals – for example, selling BBC Resources Ltd and a major stake in BBC Worldwide – are in the best interests of BBC licence payers.'

BBC view of the main licence fee panel recommendations

Recommendation	*BBC view*
BBC core revenue should increase by 2–2.5 per cent per annum in real terms up to 2006, roughly in line with GDP	'The BBC welcomes the Panel's support for buoyancy in its funding to enhance services for licence payers, since without growing revenues the BBC would be frozen out of the digital world. But in the face of the sheer scale and immediacy of the digital challenge, the funding level proposed will not enable the BBC to offer the full benefits of the digital age to licence payers.'
A digital licence supplement should be introduced from 1 April 2000 at a level of £1.99 a month, and that the supplement should fall to 99p a month in 2006.	'The BBC agrees with the Panel that the digital supplement option is the best means of providing buoyancy for the BBC, though raising the analogue fee is also a viable option. The BBC believes that either option would help fund an enhanced portfolio of digital services to attract free-to-air audiences to digital, but a digital supplement would be more equitable.'
An increase in the analogue fee of £5 in 2000 and 2001 is a preferable option to doing nothing, if the digital licence supplement is rejected.	'The BBC recognises that analogue switch-over raises significant issues in terms of television households who remain analogue-only as the switch-over date approaches. The Panel's proposal of converging licence fees is innovative. We, and no doubt the Government, will study it further to assess its implications for BBC services.'
There should be no introduction of advertising and sponsorship on the BBC's public services	'The BBC applauds the recognition that advertising and sponsorship methods of funding fundamentally restricts the ability of broadcasters to offer a wide range of public service programming.'
Sell a 49 per cent stake in BBC Worldwide *Sell 'the bulk' of BBC Resources Ltd*	'The BBC agrees with the Panel's underlying idea that we should make the best use of all our assets, both public and commercial, to provide the best value possible for licence payers. This should, where appropriate, involve partnerships with commercial companies who can provide both risk finance and business expertise.' 'We believe, however, that their specific recommendations in this area are not in fact in the best interests of licence payers.'

'The BBC notes that the Panel were not unanimous on these recommendations and will seek to convince Government of the most appropriate way forward for Worldwide and Resources Ltd.'

On BBC Worldwide:
'BBC Worldwide exists to exploit the BBC's programme assets and brands generated by licence payers over the years. As a wholly owned subsidiary, BBC Worldwide is able to ensure that its activities reflect values and expectations licence payers have of the BBC.'
'BBC Worldwide should work with a wide range of private sector partners across its businesses. We believe that these partnerships are better in driving value for licence payers in a way which is more consistent with BBC values than the Panel's proposal.'

On BBC Resources:
'BBC Resources is a valued part of the BBC, providing an unrivalled craft base for BBC programme makers. It also functions as a training ground for the BBC and the wider broadcasting industry.'
'The BBC does not believe that the recommendation on the sale of BBC Resources Ltd is in the interests of the licence payer.'

BBC (1999) *BBC Response to Licence Panel Fee Report*, BBC News Release, 4 August at http://www.bbc.co.uk/info/news/nes180.htm

2.14 The Select Committee on Culture, Media and Sport

Rejecting the Davies Proposals

On 20 December 1999, The Select Committee on Culture, Media and Sport published its report *Funding the BBC* which was highly critical of the BBC and rejected the Davies Committee recommendations for a digital licence supplement, the sale of BBC Resources and the sale of 49 per cent of BBC Worldwide. According to one national newspaper, the Committee chaired by Gerald Kaufman MP had 'unleashed a vitriolic onslaught against the Corporation' (*Guardian*, 21 December 1999: 2). The report criticised BBC *News 24*, arguing that its high costs of £53.9 million a year could not be met even if the proposed Davies supplement was introduced at the full rate of £23.88 a year given estimates of only 2.2 million digital subscribers. The report also criticised the BBC's claims for additional expenditure for new services and its use of funds to promote digital television. It recommended that: BBC Online should be transferred to BBC Worldwide (the commercial sector of the BBC); the BBC should lose its self-governing status with its commercial activities coming under the auspices of a new communications regulation commission; there should be no increase in the licence fee for 2000–2001 and 2001–2002 beyond those already agreed with government; pensioners over age 75 should receive a free colour television licence while – in line with the Davies proposal – registered blind people should receive a 50 per cent discount on licence fee. Labour MP John Maxton issued a dissenting paper suggesting that the majority report was 'anti-BBC' and constituted 'carping criticism' (*Guardian*, 21 December 1999: 2).

Our principal conclusions and recommendations are as follows:

(iii) This Committee admires the launching of BBC Online and the quality of the services provided . . . but . . . We recommend that BBC Online should be transferred to BBC Worldwide to enable it to expand its scope and service and take advantage of the commercial opportunities thereby created (paragraph 37).

(iv) It should be obligatory for the BBC, when introducing new services, to determine whether they are cost-effective bearing in mind the cost and the outcome. Judged against this criterion, we find it difficult to discern the justification for News 24 in view of its huge cost and small audience. The BBC has failed totally to explain why the costs of News 24 are so high in the context either of other news broadcasters or in the context of its total news budget. The case for News 24 has not been established by the BBC (paragraph 45).

(v) . . . We are bewildered and bemused by the BBC's figures for expenditure on digital promotion: on how it is composed; what exactly it has been spent on; and on how it is justified even though the *ex post facts* justification is that the BBC is funding 'a national success story' which consists almost entirely of subscribers who fund SkyDigital and Ondigital. This seems to be an obscure use of public money (paragraph 47).

(vi) The BBC has been a follower rather than a leader in the provision of digital channels. There are no grounds for accepting that this position will be reversed in future. The BBC has shown a disinclination to view its budget as a guide to the scope of its digital provision, preferring instead to advance an enormously ambitious vision. The BBC's claims for additional expenditure on new services are sketchy at best. The BBC has, in our view, singularly failed to make the case for a much expanded role in the digital era and consequently for additional external funding (paragraph 52).

(vii) Should the independent study of BBC projections which the Secretary of State for Culture, Media and Sport has now commissioned find that any BBC targets for efficiency savings are under-estimates, we recommend that any differential should be taken into account when assessing BBC claims of a funding shortfall, rather than being left for the BBC to spend on such unspecified services as it thinks fit (paragraph 58)

(viii) We reject the Davies Panel recommendation for a 49 per cent private sector share in BBC Worldwide at holding company level. We do, however, continue to believe that the BBC must prove its capacity for much greater increases in net cash flow from BBC Worldwide to the BBC in coming years under the current organisational arrangements (paragraph 62).

(ix) We recommend that the Secretary of State for Culture, Media and Sport rejects the recommendation of the Davies Panel that the bulk of BBC Resources be privatised (paragraph 68).

(x) The digital licence supplement would slow take-up of digital television and delay analogue switch-off. It would hamper the possibility of marginally free digital television being available to consumers and would accordingly bear most heavily on the most disadvantaged in society. In short, it would run directly counter to the objectives of public policy. Regardless of any decision on the funding requirements of the BBC, we recommend that the proposal of the Davies Review for a digital licence supplement should be rejected (paragraph 83).

(xi) The BBC has known the profile of its external income from 1997 to 2002 for several years: significant rises initially, followed by a relative decline. It was the duty of the BBC to cut its coat according to the cloth. The Secretary of State reaffirmed his commitment to the five year funding formula and explicitly excluded the matter from consideration by the Davies Panel earlier this year. We see no possible justification for the Secretary of State to resile from that position. We recommend that the level of the licence fee in 2000–01 and 2001–02 should be set in accordance with the settlement announced in 1996 by the previous Government and endorsed by the present Government (paragraph 89) . . .

(xix) We welcome the Secretary of State's remark that alternative means of governing and regulating the BBC might be examined as part of the consultation on broadcasting over the next year. The BBC's role and governance in coming years are highly contentious and inseparable from other broadcasting regulatory matters. They should be integral to the forthcoming review of broadcasting regulation. We recommend that the Secretary of State for Culture, Media and Sport should make an explicit statement that the BBC's future is a central subject matter of consultation prior to legislation early in the next Parliament and will not be hived off into a separate Charter Review in 2003–04 (paragraph 111).

(xx) The BBC's self-regulatory position separate from the rest of broadcasting is no longer sustainable. The case for a single regulator of the market as a whole which we made last year has been reinforced by the rapid development of the market. We reiterate our recommendation that regulation of the broadcast content and commercial activities of the BBC should be the duty of a Communications Regulation Commission (paragraph 113).

Culture, Media and Sport Committee (1999) *Funding the BBC*, Third Report, Vol. 1, London: The Stationery Office, 20 December, pp.xxxvi–xxxviii.

2.15 The Funding Review of the BBC

The Parliamentary Statement by the Secretary of State for Culture, Media and Sport Chris Smith

In July 1999, the Davies Review recommended a digital licence fee supplement to help to finance the BBC's development of digital services. The proposal was rejected by the BBC (which argued that it would deliver inadequate funding), by the commercial sector of digital broadcasting (which stressed the advantages it would provide to the BBC as well as the inertia effect of such a tax on rolling out digital services), and finally by the Select Committee on Culture, Media and Sport (because it would slow down the development of digital broadcasting, because the committee alleged the new digital services – especially *News 24* – were poor and because there was no independent evidence concerning the BBC's financial circumstances. In his statement, Chris Smith decided against a digital supplement, raised the level of the licence fee by 1.5 per cent above RPI, insisted on efficiency savings at the BBC, announced a new system for approving new BBC television services and declared his intention to institute new regulatory mechanisms to achieve transparency in BBC trading practices.

I want to leave the House in no doubt about the Government's commitment to public service broadcasting and to retaining the BBC at its heart. The BBC is the UK's most important cultural institution, and we have a duty to ensure that it can continue to play a central role in the nation's life. Specifically, the BBC should provide a strong and distinctive schedule of benchmark quality programmes on all its services and should drive the take-up of new digital and on-line services. A strong BBC is crucial in ensuring that everyone can have access to information, news, education and current affairs, using efficient modern methods, so that we can build a society for the 21st century on the solid foundations set down for us in the 20th.

It is to enable the BBC to deliver these priorities that I am prepared to offer it more support . . . to achieve this vision and to improve its services, the BBC needs to raise its game; it must become even more cost-effective and quality conscious. That is why we are not going to allow the BBC the massive injection of funds that it has sought from the licence fee – an increase reaching more than £700 million a year by 2006. We are setting it a number of challenges, in terms of sources of finance and in operations.

I shall now deal with the Government's decisions under four headings – finance, programming, transparency and licence fee concessions. They provide a balanced package of measures, which I hope can be widely welcomed.

We accept the judgment of the Davies panel that our vision for the BBC cannot be realised within the existing funding framework . . . The first place to look for new funding should be self-help by the BBC; new licence fee funding should be secondary. We are therefore providing for an increase in licence fee funding that will raise on average around £200 million per year between now and 2006. In addition, however, we are challenging the BBC to help itself by increased efficiency savings, and raising more revenue from its subsidiaries, to the tune of £490 million by 2006–07, over and above the £600 million which it itself estimated . . . We will leave it to the BBC how it meets the challenge, but we are leaving the BBC in no doubt that we expect it to achieve the figures set out here by efficiency savings, partnerships, joint ventures, reductions in bureaucracy and other means.

I have decided not to adopt the new mechanism of a digital supplement payable only by those households with digital television . . . Against my belief that digital television brings benefits to all, it would be wrong to signal that it is something special and only for the few. I am therefore going for the general licence fee option, and an increase of 1.5 per cent over the retail prices index in each year starting in April this year. That means an increase of 3p per week above inflation each year. On 1 April this year, the licence fee will therefore rise by £3.

The Davies panel proposed a package of reforms in the areas of transparency, fair trading and accountability. We support the thrust of the panel's recommendations. In particular, we intend to open up the process by which I approve new BBC proposals, and we shall also make the BBC's commitment to fair trading more transparent.

We are making it clear that we do not expect the licence fee to fund strands of the market, such as dedicated film and sport channels, to which the distinctive role of public service broadcasting has little extra to offer . . . We also propose to carry out a programme of reviews of all the current BBC digital services . . . We propose that a priority for such scrutiny should be News 24.

We shall open the BBC to more external scrutiny. It has, hitherto, been too much the judge and jury in its own cause. I am requiring independent scrutinies of the BBC's fair trading policies and its financial reporting, and I shall publish both scrutiny reports. In addition, I shall expect the BBC to have its regular fair trading and financial audits carried out by different auditors in future . . . Finally, we shall also be reviewing the public service role and governance of the BBC.

On concessions, we have already gone beyond the Davies panel's recommendation on assistance for pensioners . . . we are: introducing free television licences for the over-75s from 1 November; introducing half-price television licences for blind people from 1 April; setting new targets for subtitling for new BBC digital services; simplifying and making more equitable one of the key easy-payment schemes; and retaining the current accommodation for residential care concessionary scheme.

Our key aims throughout have been to ensure accountability, choice, quality, and value for money . . . I believe that the settlement will help to ensure the BBC's position and its role as our primary public service broadcaster into the new century. If we are serious about valuing the BBC at its best, about wanting to keep it at its best and about ensuring that we all have programmes of real quality to watch in the future, we must give it the support it needs. This statement will, I hope, give it precisely that.

Chris Smith (2000) Statement on BBC Funding, *Hansard*, 21 February, cols 1239–43.

PART THREE

Television Broadcasting Policy: Programmes

THE PUBLICATION OF THE PEACOCK REPORT and the subsequent White Paper *Broadcasting in the '90s* signalled the government's policy ambitions for a radical restructuring of British broadcasting ecology. The government wished to create 'a more competitive and open broadcasting market . . . without detriment to broadcasting standards and quality'. The implications of this policy ambition unravelled differently – and posed distinctive policy questions – in the commercial and public sectors of broadcasting. In the independent sector, government policy triggered an often-heated debate about programme quality, with critics alleging that a market-driven broadcasting system was incompatible with the provision of a diverse range of high-quality programmes. The policy issue which the expansive and increasingly competitive broadcasting system posed sharply for the BBC was to identify an appropriate role for a public service broadcaster in this new multi-channel environment and, in turn, to develop a relevant policy for programming.

Critics offered three arguments to support their suggestion that the restructuring of the commercial sector of broadcasting would generate a decline in programme quality and range. First, there would quite simply be less money available for commissioning, producing and broadcasting programmes. The newly established franchise auction had prompted overbidding for licences by some Channel 3 companies which diverted money away from programme budgets into the Treasury: one estimate calculated that in 1993, £360 million – a quarter of ITV's advertising and sponsorship revenues – went directly to the Treasury. The Broadcasting Act's (1990) requirement that Channel 4 should sell its own advertising, moreover, combined with increased competition for advertising revenues reflecting the establishment of Channel 5 and the rapidly expanding numbers of new cable and satellite channels, meant that Channel 3's share of relatively stable overall advertising expenditure might be expected to dip: a share already diminished by a sustained economic recession across the late 1980s and early 1990s.

Second, it was alleged that a market-driven broadcasting system offered programme makers few direct incentives to produce quality programmes; the motive forces in such a system impel in the direction of popular programmes. The broadcasting market favours low budget (i.e. minimum cost), high audience (i.e. maximum revenues) programme formats which maximise profits. Programme formats which accommodate this financial formula and which might be anticipated to flourish under the newly structured arrangements include programme repeats, compilation programmes (*All Right on the Night*), docu-soaps (*Shampoo, Pet Rescue*), game shows (*Can't Cook, Won't Cook, Countdown*) and quiz shows (*Who Wants To Be A Millionaire*?). Why bother, it was argued, to broadcast *La Traviata* when snooker attracts a larger audience? Critics suggested, moreover, that the impact of these market considerations might be particularly debilitating on news and current affairs programming since both are expensive to produce but, in audience terms, are a relative 'turn-off'.

Third, the ITC, the new regulatory body established by the 1990 Broadcasting Act, was charged with a legislative brief to regulate with a 'lighter touch' than its predecessor the IBA. Expressed broadly, there would be less 'quality control' in the British broadcasting system. Moreover, the desire to combine a competitive market system with quality product meant that the newly conceived regulatory brief was riddled with ambivalence and ambiguity. The Broadcasting Act 1990 makes it less than clear whether the role of the ITC is to ensure quality broadcasting or to oversee the provision of popular broadcasting for which sheer size of audience is the measure of a successful programme.

But advocates of the new market-based broadcasting system suggest there is no necessary tension between low programme budgets and quality programmes; indeed some spectacular television successes, such as the comedy series *Monty Python's Flying Circus*, began life as relatively low budget enterprises. In an extreme form, the pro-market argument has denied the very existence of 'quality' as some Platonic essence residing within and characterising particular programmes. There is no 'quality' in the abstract; the market provides the only litmus test. A quality programme is a popular programme evidenced by audience size and reach. Too frequently, the imputation of quality to particular programme formats has been used to legitimise the cultural preferences of narrow and traditional cultural elites (see Murdoch, 1.8). Markets in broadcasting, moreover, as elsewhere, represent the most cost-effective and efficient way of organising productive activity, allocating resources and maximising outputs, but the reality of British broadcasting has never reflected these extremes. British television has always attempted to combine majority audience taste with high-quality programmes while simultaneously incorporating sufficient programme diversity to satisfy the programming requirements of minority audiences.

The expansion of the television market with its increasingly multi-channel and competitive character has posed slightly different programme policy questions at the BBC. The anticipated decline in audience share for BBC services has long been acknowledged, and consequently the Corporation has been obliged to confront a complex policy question: What is the appropriate role for the key public service broadcaster in a multi-channel television environment? In terms of programming policy the question can be posed with sharper focus: Should the BBC try to compete for audiences for its programmes with the burgeoning commercial television services or should it try to shape a distinctive programme identity? The BBC needed to decide where it wished to locate itself and its programmes in the new television market.

The Green Paper *The Future of the BBC* suggested that the BBC might not be able to continue to broadcast the wide range of programming which had previously characterised its schedules; the multi-channel future signalled two options for a refocusing of BBC programming. First, the BBC might specialise in news, current affairs, arts, religious and scientific programmes, programmes for minorities and 'programmes which are unlikely to be broadcast by other organisations' (see 3.4); a programming policy promptly dubbed the 'Himalayan option'. Alternatively, the BBC could focus on programmes which capture and reflect 'the British way of life, history and culture' (see 3.4). The BBC's response was prompt and unequivocal. On 27 November 1992, two days after the publication of the White Paper, the BBC published *Extending Choice: The BBC's Role in the New Broadcasting Age* in which the Corporation rejected both options for the broadcast ghettos they promised to become. The BBC's preferred strategy was to offer a slightly narrower range of distinctive, high-quality programmes which commercial broadcasters would not provide (3.5). The Himalayan option was explicitly rejected with the assertion that the BBC 'is not planning to become a cultural ghetto or to retreat into minority areas and intends to continue to make programmes for everyone' (Birt, 1993). The BBC, moreover, is 'not interested in attracting large audiences for their own sake (*Extending Choice*, 1992: 8). A year later, the BBC confirmed this policy of providing a broad range of quality programming (*Responding to the Green Paper*, 1993: 36). Marmaduke Hussey, Chair of the BBC Board of Governors for the period of much of this policy debate, criticised John Birt very publicly in a House of Lords debate in March 1999, suggesting that the BBC should have strengthened its 'mainstream channels' rather than attempting to compete with its commercial competitors (3.7). Hussey's exclusion from these policy debates was confirmed in August 2000 when Greg Dyke, Birt's successor, announced his plans for the reshaping of BBC channels and the rescheduling of the BBC *Nine O'Clock News* at 10 p.m. Dyke's ambition was to maintain the BBC 'gold standard' of programme quality while acknowledging the competitive realities of the digital age (3.8). Dyke's critics denounced the plans as the 'dumbing down' of BBC programming.

The extracts in Part Three which explore television programming policy are grouped under three headings and address three particular questions. First, how have academics and broadcasters answered the question 'What is quality in television broadcasting?' Second, what should be the programme policy and strategy for a public service broadcaster like the BBC when confronting a multi-channel environment for television services? Finally, how have particular genres of programming fared in the new broadcasting ecology? More specifically, how persuasive have been critics' suggestions of a 'dumbing down' of programming in the context of news, current affairs and children's programming?

References

BBC (1993) *Responding to The Green Paper*, London: BBC.

Birt, J. (1993) *The BBC*, The Royal Television Society Fleming Memorial Lecture, London.

WHAT IS BROADCASTING QUALITY?

3.1 Broadcasting Quality

Snooker or *La Traviata*?

The Peacock Report's advocacy of deregulating broadcasting triggered a hotly contested debate about the impact that the more competitive market climate, which the report envisaged, might have on the range and quality of programmes. Simon Jenkins examined the issue of quality in broadcasting as the theme for the *Listener* Lecture at the Radio Festival in 1989. Addressing a group of radio broadcasters, his observations had obvious resonance for all broadcasters given the context of contemporary debates about the funding of broadcasting and possible consequences for programme quality. He began with a paradox. Quality is central to government broadcasting policy, yet the concept remains ill defined. Quality, he argues, has a necessary but ambiguous connection with audiences. Programmes may be judged high quality because they attract a large audience while others perceive quality in those programmes which attract only minority audiences. Quality is also closely connected with the professionalism of broadcasters, a crucial guardian of quality. But Jenkins concludes that the ultimate guarantor of broadcasting quality is an institutional structure which protects broadcasters from commercial and political pressures. He concludes that public subsidy of quality programmes which 'invest society with nobility and cohesion' is desirable.

The use and abuse of the phrase 'quality in broadcasting' have become endemic to the debate on the future of television . . . Yet nobody will offer an explanation of this clearly potent concept, nor explain its relationship with what is popularly taken as its antithesis – competitive broadcasting in a free market. No area of government policy is in so thorough an intellectual muddle.

Why should quality in broadcasting be a government concern? True, radio and television are inherently oligopolistic and some criteria must be found for allocating scarce frequencies. But why censor the airwaves for virtue? What is ethically wrong in allocating them on the basis of charitable or political donation, or by donation to the

Treasury (as the Government now proposes) . . . Yet this word 'quality' will not shut up and vanish. Even that bible of the new libertarianism, the Peacock report, spoke of 'enlarging opportunities for programme makers to offer alternative wares'. A policy objective, it said, should be 'the enhancing of consumer welfare' – again undefined.

So let us plunge in. Most would agree that quality has some relationship to public appeal, but an ambivalent one. Just as some would reject any naïve equation of quality with ability to amass big audiences, even big-spending 'ABC1s', so it cannot simply be equated with the inverse, with minority appeal. Our word is broad- not narrow-casting. The ability to win and hold an audience is intrinsic to any medium of communication. Broadcasting that turns its back on an audience defines itself out of existence, certainly out of justifiable cross-subsidy.

So what status do we accord the audience in the debate on quality? Those who work on successful and popular radio programmes are entitled to plead high standards . . . they certainly win awards. The broadcasting of Jimmy Young, or Brian Hayes is quality radio as is that of Brian Redhead, Sue MacGregor or Sue Lawley. This quality is rooted in the professionalism of the broadcaster, ideals of thoroughness, fairness, incorruptibility: as lauded in cult movies *Network Broadcast News* and *Good Morning Vietnam*, tales of producers and presenters fighting to uphold standards against pressures from devious bosses.

This aspect of quality is constant to all creative endeavour, including that supplied within the commercial sector. I must declare an interest here, as a minor participant in a current bid for a London classical music franchise. We would hope, as would our rivals, I am sure, that the nature and quality of our programming would attract enough listeners to obtain enough advertising revenue. It works in America and on the continent. I fondly believe it can work here. But market dependence will not produce radio for all tastes. Try as I regularly do to scan the richness of the American radio dial, the result is not self evidently a wider range of content than in Britain. There is a choice of what the IBA's Lord Thomson once called amiable rubbish, of popular music and instant news . . . There is to the best of my knowledge no modern drama produced under America's free market regime, no readings from classic novels and poetry, no Reith lectures . . . Convince me that a free market future . . . will give them to me and I will yield the floor. But for all my enthusiasm for markets, I do not believe for one moment that unsubsidised radio will supply them. The cost is too high and the audience too small . . .

The free marketeer says that if I really want a quality that advertising will not sustain, then I should pay a subscription or seek sponsors . . . Why should only some tastes enjoy public subsidy? If you are ready to pay the full-cost price for your snooker, why should I demand your taxes to pay for my *Traviata* or Radio 3?

I do not intend here to mix in this particular scrap, except to say that most of us do expect sophisticated societies to support the arts even where markets – and subscription is a market mechanism – are reluctant. We do so because we believe that products of the creative imagination invest our society with a nobility and cohesion with which snooker, for all its appeal, is not noticeably endowed. Put more bluntly, there are minority tastes which we either pay for collectively or do without – and we regard ourselves the poorer collectively if we have to do without.

Of course, to say that the market is not always an appropriate decision-taker in cultural matters leaves open the question of who or what is? . . . Wherein lies the guardianship of broadcasting quality? I am convinced the answer lies at two levels . . . The first obligation rests on the shoulders of the professional broadcaster. Whether in the commercial sector or the subsidised sector, quality reflects the desire of hard-working, committed, independent-minded, uncynical individuals to convey a serious message to a mass audience, straight and without guile. This is only half the story. To enable good broadcasting to flourish, it must operate in an environment protected from commercial or political pressure, from pressure to achieve quantitative rather than qualitative results . . . This means institutions strong enough to obtain resources, and managed so as not to waste them. The BBC's greatest weakness in recent years has been the quality not of its programmes but of its management. Overstaffing and poor cost control have left too little money for programmes. Thank goodness . . . it remains a remarkable repository of quality radio, remarkable not just nationally but internationally. Competition and pluralism are fine, but there are ghosts of excellence still flitting around Broadcasting House and I am too pragmatic to believe that snuffing them out will conjure up elsewhere ghosts likely to be their equal.

Simon Jenkins (1989), 'In Defence of Quality', *Listener* Lecture launching the Radio Academy's Festival in Cardiff and published in the *Listener*, 6 July, pp.4–6.

3.2 Quality in Broadcasting

An 'Essentially Contested Concept'

Mulgan argued that the debate about quality in broadcasting was often little more than a fig-leaf concealing political interests. For their part, liberal economists were more interested in markets, efficiency and freedom to buy, sell and publish. Similarly, advocates of quality in broadcasting used the concept to legitimate the narrow tastes and cultural prejudices of a small metropolitan elite to which Simon Jenkins (despite his avowed disposition in favour of markets) ultimately belongs (see 4.1). Mulgan claims it is not possible to define quality since it remains what philosophers delight in describing as an essentially contested concept: 'the word's richness and ambiguities should be seen as a virtue and not a problem' (p.7). But it is both possible and important to identify several criteria for judging television; Mulgan offers seven such criteria.

1. Producer quality and professionalism

In Britain the discourse of quality has traditionally been dominated by programme makers. Quality is seen in terms of production values, defined by the community of producers which includes the writers, directors and editors. It is concerned with technical issues of lighting, camera work, script and direction, the quality of acting the effectiveness with which ideas are conveyed or with which narrative is unravelled. It takes in its purest form the classic ingredients of quality drama (the very pinnacle of 'quality television'): expensive-looking productions (but without vulgar special effects), well known actors and actresses with theatrical pedigree and literary resonance in the subject matter.

2. Consumer quality and the market

Against producer sovereignty stands what is now the equally familiar claim for consumer sovereignty, usually propounded not by consumers themselves but by producers seeking entry to the marketplace . . . At the level of rhetoric at least, the centre of gravity has shifted from the producer to the consumer. Changing technologies have provided part of the push. The multiple channels of cable and DBS make television much more like other markets where consumers can regulate the quality and appropriateness of what is produced. Pay-per-view, pay channels, interactivity and the various technologies ranging from addressable converters to video-on-demand all promise the viewer much greater choice and control . . .

In relation to quality the 'consumer' argument comes in 57 varieties. The crudest (and most familiar) argues that the only useful notion of quality is that which identifies it with the preferences of viewers. The most popular programme is to all intents and purposes the best . . . Any alternative definition of quality, especially when it seeks to influence which programmes are made, automatically implies the imposition of one person's subjectivity over another, usually that of a metropolitan elite on to the population at large. The consumer argument is implicitly relativistic . . .

Those arguing the free market case for restructuring broadcasting have often accepted that certain kinds of programme should be insulated from market forces. In some cases there may even be an inherent value in producing particular programmes, whether or not people choose to watch them. Hence the argument made by Samuel Brittan and Alan Peacock, for a market system augmented by public funding of programme categories deemed worthwhile because of their quality, but unlikely to survive in the cut and thrust of the market place. This is the argument for an 'Arts Council of the Air'.

3. Quality and the medium: television's aesthetic

A third set of definitions covers various approaches to quality which start not with the producer or the viewer but with the intrinsic nature of the medium . . . They seek a televisual aesthetic, a set of rules of judgement similar to those which might be applied to a film or a book. Unlike the producer definitions of quality, these approaches seek a more objective and distanced aesthetic . . .

There are several possible starting points. Many people implicitly judge quality in terms of the durability and timelessness of what is produced. The best television is non-ephemeral, taking on some of the properties of literature or film: television is best in other words when it escapes from and transcends its instantaneous, transient nature . . . A diametrically opposed view sees quality in terms of television's ability to be true to its nature as a medium, a nature which is instant, superficial and, in the extreme view, a mere diversion or visual wallpaper. The best television is . . . the £500,000 advertisement and the pop video.

4. Television as ritual communication

Most theories of communication understand it as the passage of images or information from one place to another . . . An alternative view (James Carey) . . . sees communication as primarily ritualistic . . . it stresses the ways in which communication is bound up with sharing fellowship and participation. Meanings flow less from a particular programme or channel than from the whole system of communication, its historic cultural traditions and its political economy . . . Understood as a kind of ritual, the form of television is as important as its content . . .

Seeing television as primarily ritualistic lends a very different meaning to the word quality. Rather than having any intrinsic qualities, the quality of a particular piece of television is . . . its ability to define and bind a community. At certain times a particular programme will resonate in this ritual way, throwing ideas and phrases into everyday usage . . . These programmes will . . . serve to crystallize a community. Programmes ranging from a cup final to Live Aid, *Boys From the Black Stuff* to *Cathy Come Home* . . . become examples of the highest quality television not because of their art, or even the size of their audience, but because of their role within the history of the community they serve.

5. Television and the person

A related set of ideas about quality derive from different conceptions of the person, of what it means to be a good, mature, fully formed human being . . . The first strand of argument centres around citizenship and rights . . . Seen from this tradition, the good life is that of the active citizen, fully aware of the political and social life of the community and actively engaged with it. Television is seen as an 'informational commons' which citizens depend on to explain the workings of society and the experiences of others. It helps viewers to participate as fully formed social beings, better able to control their own destiny . . . Both the ritual and citizen approaches lead to similar conclusions – the one starting from the needs of the community, the other from the rights of the individual. Television is good when it creates the conditions for people to participate actively in a community; when it provides them with the truest possible information; when it encourages membership and activity rather than passivity and alienation; and when it serves as an invigorator of the democratic process rather than a medium for what Walter Lippmann called the 'manufacture of consent'.

6. The televisual ecology

Many commentators implicitly use ecological metaphors when they talk about television. They ask whether it is disruptive, polluting and corrupting . . . Clearly each of these metaphors is also an argument about quality. Better quality broadcasting, like better quality food or water, is non-polluting, and non-corrupting . . . The ecological metaphor remains very influential. The popular belief that television contributes to violence and immorality, or to sexism and racism, is still strong, even though an enormous amount of research has failed convincingly to impute any direct effects. Ecological metaphors are attractive because television can feel like an alien invader, even when it is placed in the cosy familiarity of the living room.

But their superficial appeal masks some unpleasant implications. For a start it must be agreed who is to say what is healthy and what is pathological . . . A second problem is the inherent difficulty of agreeing about when it is justified to restrict free speech.

7. Quality as diversity

The most fundamental factor that makes it hard to sustain an ecological metaphor is the absence of a broad enough consensus about what is good or bad, healthy or unhealthy. The lack of centre in a society that contains everything from charismatic Christians to militant Muslims, radical feminists to xenophobic racists helps to explain the crisis of the old forms of strong regulation that governed British broadcasting. It also gives us the seventh idea of quality, the idea of quality as diversity. Most people express the view that a broadcasting system of high quality must offer a wide range of programmes.

Geoff Mulgan (1990) 'Television's Holy Grail: Seven Types of Quality', in Geoff Mulgan (ed.) *The Question of Quality*, London: BFI, pp.4–32.

3.3 Defining Quality in Television

Views from the Broadcasting Research Unit

Shortly after the publication of the White Paper *Broadcasting in the '90s*, the independent research group the BRU invited distinguished television broadcasters, programme makers and academics to 'set down in not more than 2000 words' the 'essential elements in any definition of standards of quality'. The responses were published in the pamphlet *Quality in Television: Programmes, Programme-Makers, Systems*. The extract below begins with an abstract from the letter inviting contributions and concludes with some of the responses. The report rejected any simple equation of 'quality' with 'highbrow programmes' but argued that: diversity and range of programmes was crucial to defining quality in television; quality should not be confused with the merely 'popular'; market forces alone are insufficient to guarantee programme quality; and certain conditions are essential to generate quality in television.

Broadcasting 'standards' are currently attracting a lot of attention. The most striking instance of that interest is the establishment of the Broadcasting Standards Council . . .

the BSC's terms of reference illustrate the tendency to equate or almost equate 'standards' with the amount of sex, violence and bad language in programmes, with 'standards of taste and decency'.

Clearly, this is too narrow a definition. In our view, 'standards' should not refer only to levels of 'decency' (though they may have a part in some aspects of a full definition). 'Standards' should refer rather to the quality of programmes across the whole range of broadcasting, having regard to the different types of programmes and to different audiences.

In this perspective, a 'highbrow' programme may be of poor quality, whatever its own professions. So may a current affairs programme. A comedy or a sports programme may be each in their own ways of very high quality. An apparently worthy and high-minded programme may be intellectually shifty.

Yet to say that the test of 'quality' in programmes should begin by asking whether each is 'good of its kind' does not imply a totally relativist set of judgements which might lead to statements such as: 'Of course, most quiz shows are mindless . . . but as quiz shows go this is a corker and pulls in the viewers.'

Rather, though each programme will have to be judged in the first place by criteria peculiar to itself, these criteria are neither self-contained nor self-sufficient. Any kind of programme may be trivial, banal, patronising, tendentious, phoney, dishonest, evasive; such value-judgements are not to be eroded by appeals to the demands of particular types of programmes and to the assumed tastes of intended audiences. You will see that we are seeking to reach a definition of 'standards as quality' which is more broadly and firmly based than those commonly in use (BRU 1989: Preface).

Quality in broadcasting

Quality broadcasting offers a diversity of choices, a constantly widening range of subjects and of levels of approach; and should be judged first on its success in making such an overall provision. The timing of programmes is not decided by the wish to maximise the audience, above all; and all the time. It instead seeks to give opportunities, at good viewing times, to as many different tastes and interests as possible.

Quality programming does not pre-judge audiences by presumed height of brow. It assumes rather that we can all at some time and in some ways find our imaginations touched. So it seeks constantly to renew, not to repeat formulae; it explores, takes risks, pushes the boat out, extends the frontiers, takes itself and us by surprise as to what is possible in good television.

In all this it can be encouraged by the abundant evidence that most people are willing to try new kinds of programmes, do not want simple repetition of material already to their tastes. Even more interesting and telling: though millions watch *Dallas* and similar imported programmes, they express more appreciation of programmes from within their own culture and society.

On all the above grounds, quality broadcasting is not something which market forces, left alone, are able or anxious to guarantee.

Standards are indivisible, cover both the whole content of any programme that is broadcast, and the totality of all that is broadcast. Such an assertion does not need to claim that all programming can achieve high 'standards of quality'; such perfectibility is no more realisable in broadcast artefacts than it is in books, films, plays, or works of pictorial art. But the aspiration should and can remain a constant, as can the criteria for judging whether the aspiration has been fulfilled (p.1).

Where the White Paper falls short

The White Paper [*Broadcasting in the '90s*, HMSO, 1988] claims that, 'as viewers exercise greater choice there is no longer the same need for quality of service to be prescribed by legislation or regulatory fiat'. In contradiction to previous uses of the word 'quality' we now find it being used to mean, in effect, popularity. The market will decide what is good and what is not, there is no need for anybody to be concerned apart from the buyers and the sellers, it must be assumed that if something does not sell profitably it has no quality . . . Let it not be pretended that any ITV company has been exclusively concerned with programme excellence. Even if they had tried for this it would have been impossible. But a lot of the excellence they have achieved has followed from their partial, and enforced, attachment to the public service ethic. To cut this attachment may not damage 'quality of service' as the White Paper means it but it will reduce the possibility of standards as excellence (p.29).

The larger perspectives

Quality in television programmes is not a standard that can be codified and enforced. It is generated by a belief system, which in turn needs structural support. Among the necessary conditions are:

- Editorial freedom from the obligation to maximise ratings.
- Time, in the making of programmes.
- High levels of craft skill.
- Well-informed producers.
- Permission to take risks, and fail, without loss of income.
- Peer-group admiration for excellence.
- A sense of mission: the conviction among production staff that what they do should educate the nation, rather than anaesthetise it.

Conversely, quality is driven down by:

- The obligation to maximise ratings.
- Fear of failure, leading to reliance on copies of existing audience-pleasers.
- Shortage of time, leading to formula programme-making.
- Peer-group admiration for high ratings.
- No sense of mission: the awareness among production staff that they're only there for the money (p.31).

Broadcasting Research Unit (1989) *Quality in Television: Programmes, Programme-makers, Systems*, London: BRU, 32pp.

PROGRAMMING POLICY AND THE BBC

3.4 The Future of the BBC

Options for Programming

One of the most significant issues discussed in the Green Paper *The Future of the BBC* was the question of where the BBC should position itself and its programming in the increasingly competitive multi-channel television ecology ushered in by government policy and technological innovation. For its part, the BBC readily acknowledged that this changed broadcasting climate would inevitably prompt a decline in audience share. In reassessing its programming philosophy and strategy, the BBC had to decide whether it should attempt to compete for audiences with the burgeoning commercial sector or try to define and secure a distinctive programming identity. *The Future of the BBC* offered two options. First, the BBC could specialise in news, arts and science programming: i.e. identify and colonise the 'high ground' of broadcasting. Second, the BBC could focus on programmes of particular interests to British audiences. In its formal response to the Green Paper as well as in a series of key speeches by the Director-General the BBC rejected both options. In the Fleming Memorial lecture to the Royal Television Society in March 1993 John Birt rejected the Himalayan option and, sticking tightly to the geographical metaphor, affirmed the BBC's commitment to 'the green pastures of programmes which hold appeal to wide audiences' as well as to programmes of high quality.

4.4 At present, in the United Kingdom, the BBC broadcasts a wide range of programmes on its two television channels. The five national radio services are aimed at different audiences but together have a similarly wide range of programmes. Over 90% of the population watch some BBC television programmes and about 60% listen to BBC radio in the course of a week. The BBC provides these two television channels, the five national radio channels and local radio at the cost of about 22p a day, for each licensed household.

4.5 With the greater choice now available to viewers and listeners, the BBC could concentrate in future on providing news and current affairs, and programmes which are unlikely to be broadcast by other organisations. The BBC would broadcast few general entertainment programmes but more programmes for minority audiences, so increasing the overall diversity and choice of broadcast programmes for viewers and listeners. It could extend its coverage of the arts, of religion, science and industry. It could broadcast more programmes made in European countries. The BBC might be required to produce more programmes for minorities of all kinds including ethnic minorities and people with special interests, for children and elderly people, and programmes and services for those with disabilities. However, if the aim is to encourage people to widen their interests, this is less likely to be achieved by narrowing the range of programming and reducing the number of popular programmes, which attract more people to watch or listen to a programme.

4.6 There are other possibilities. The BBC could produce programmes of particular interest to United Kingdom audiences, which reflect the British way of life, history and culture, national political issues and the United Kingdom's evolving place in Europe and the wider world . . . The BBC services could include programmes made in other European countries about their views of European and world issues and showing how different countries approach similar problems. The BBC might be expected to ensure that national events were accessible to audiences throughout the United Kingdom and to encourage greater knowledge and understanding of the national culture and sporting heritage. In this way, the BBC would sustain a sense of national identity and extend diversity at a time when programmes are increasingly produced by organisations with multi-national interests for transmission in more than one country.

4.7 The BBC broadcasts many educational programmes on television and radio for schools and for those who have left school, including programmes for the Open University. It broadcasts programmes to encourage people to re-enter education and training, to help people learning foreign languages and those who have difficulty in reading . . . Overall, the BBC broadcasts educational programmes of all kinds for over 1,500 hours on its television services and over 700 hours on its network radio services. This output could be increased further. On the other hand with the greater availability of cassettes and other educational material, some of this output may no longer be necessary. There may be a need to review the BBC's role in providing radio and television programmes for schools to ensure they focus on clear curriculum needs and priorities and so give value for money.

4.8 As a public service broadcasting organisation, the BBC might be expected to continue to broadcast radio and television services for people in Scotland, Wales and Northern Ireland, reflecting their interests, activities and cultural heritage . . .

Department of National Heritage (1992) *The Future of the BBC*, London: HMSO, Cmnd 2098, pp.8–10.

3.5 BBC Programming Policy

Extending Choice by Pursuing 'Complementary Objectives'

The BBC policy document *Extending Choice* argued for different but complementary roles and objectives for the commercial and public sectors of broadcasting in the emerging television market of the late 1990s. This implied four key elements for the BBC's programming policy: the provision of in-depth news coverage to inform the national debate; support and stimulus for British entertainment and culture; the provision of educational programming; and programmes which serve as a communications link between Britain and the rest of the world. *Extending Choice* concludes that the 'BBC of the late 1990s should offer a range of distinctive, high quality programming services in each of the major genres' (p.24).

The substantial changes that are taking place in the broadcasting environment clearly justify a thorough reassessment of the BBC. That reassessment should ask whether there will be the need for a publicly funded broadcasting organisation such as the BBC in the broadcasting market of the mid-1990s – and if so what specific public purposes it should be required to meet . . . Commercially funded broadcasters and publicly funded broadcasters have different, but complementary objectives – and both have a role to play in ensuring a healthy and robust broadcasting system.

• *Commercially funded broadcasters* quite properly set their priorities for programming and services against the overriding need to make a profit and generate a return for their shareholders. That is their obligation as commercial organisations. Within the constraints of their contractual obligations to regulators, and their own concern for the public interest, these priorities require them to broadcast programmes that attract large or commercially attractive audiences; and to limit investment in programming to what the commercial market will afford.

• *Publicly funded broadcasters* in contrast, have a primary obligation to the public. They do not need to make a profit nor generate a return to shareholders. Their overriding public purpose is to extend choice by guaranteeing access for everyone in the country to programming services that are of unusually high quality and that are, or might be, at risk in the purely commercially funded sector of the market . . .

However the balance between the services supplied by publicly funded broadcasting and commercially funded broadcasting will change over time . . . In the past as a dominant provider, the BBC had an obligation to cover all audiences and broadcasting needs: in the future it will have an obligation to focus on performing a set of clearly defined roles that best complement the enlarged commercial sector . . . The BBC should pursue its primary roles through the distinctiveness and quality of its own output: through the way that it structures its programme schedules; and through the standards that it sets for itself and the whole industry. Over time, it should withdraw from programme areas and types in which it is no longer able or needed to make an original contribution.

What then are the defining characteristics of the BBC's public purpose?

Informing the national debate

Firstly, the BBC should aim to provide the comprehensive, in-depth and impartial news and information coverage across a range of broadcasting outlets that is needed to support a fair and informed national debate . . .

Expressing British culture and entertainment

Secondly, the BBC should support and stimulate the development and expression of British culture and entertainment. It should be a core role of the BBC to reflect the full and diverse range of culture and entertainment in modern British society . . .

Creating opportunities for education

Thirdly, the BBC should guarantee the provision of programming and services that create opportunities for education. A purely commercial market would be highly unlikely to cater adequately for the public's need and desire for programmes and services which help to educate them . . . We therefore believe that it should be a core role of the BBC to provide educative programmes in all services and genres.

Communicating between the UK and abroad

Fourthly, the BBC should also play a role as one of the primary means of communication between the UK and other counties. It should bring credit to the UK around the world and promote understanding of British culture and values.

The BBC is the only British broadcaster with the resources, experience and worldwide standing to deliver a coherent range of radio, television and other programme services to overseas audiences . . . It should be a core role of the BBC to provide programming services of value and distinction to overseas audiences as well as to reflect foreign cultures and perspectives in its services to the British audience.

This chapter . . . has argued that a publicly funded broadcaster such as the BBC is needed in order to guarantee universal access to some of the most important broadcasting services and benefits that are, or might be, at risk in a purely commercial broadcasting market. With this as its objective, the BBC of the 1990s should offer a range of distinctive, high quality programming services in each of the major genres.

We have considered the arguments of those who suggest that the BBC should focus on providing services that meet the minority needs of smaller audiences – needs that will clearly not be met in the commercial market. These people suggest that any programme or service which attracts a large audience could be adequately supplied by the commercial market – and should not therefore, be publicly funded. However, to go down this route would be to preclude the majority of licence payers from viewing and listening to programmes and services which they value and appreciate. It would be to force publicly funded broadcasting in the UK into the kind of 'cultural ghetto' which has so weakened the broadcasting system in the US, Australia and elsewhere. It would also be to limit unnecessarily the contribution that publicly funded broadcasting can make through the BBC to quality standards in broadcasting across the full range of programming.

The BBC should therefore maintain regular contact with all viewers and listeners and deliver programming which appeals to them . . . But it should do so in a way which places the greatest importance on developing services of distinction and quality rather than on attracting a large audience for its own sake. This is a creative challenge which the BBC, by virtue of its traditions, culture and aspirations is well placed to tackle. (pp.22–24)

BBC (1992) *Extending Choice: The BBC's Role in the New Broadcasting Age*, London: BBC Publications, 88pp.

3.6 *People and Programmes*

Continuity and Change in BBC Programming

People and Programmes reports the outcome of the BBC's comprehensive programme review – eighteen months of 'discussion, analysis and argument' – which builds on the programming principles elaborated in *Extending Choice*. The report's title, *People and Programmes*, underlines the significance of two communities to the programming success of the BBC: the audiences for BBC programmes and the creative programme makers. In a changing television market the success of the BBC's programming policy will require maintaining a 'strong bond' with both groups. *People and Programmes* also confirms the BBC's commitment to producing a wide range of high quality programmes for the twenty-first-century global television market.

The BBC's success depends on its relationship with two key groups of people: those who watch and listen to our programmes – the audience; and those who make our programmes – the creative talent. Without a strong bond of understanding with our audience, we run the risks of self-indulgence, elitism and, in the new age of broadcasting choice, irrelevance. Without a strong bond with our talent, we will find it impossible to meet the standards of quality and originality which our audiences rightly demand.

The BBC's ambition is to nurture these two relationships, not separately but together: to use our knowledge of our audience's needs to direct and inspire the talent;

and to share our confidence in our talent with the widest possible range of audiences. In the past, the BBC has for the most part succeeded in marrying the interests of audience and talent. It has reached out to almost every conceivable audience group, from the largest and most general to the smallest and most specialist, although very often over-reliant on its own judgement of audience need. As commissioner, scheduler, patron, collaborator, trainer and employer, it has gathered every kind of journalistic, artistic and broadcasting talent under its wing. But the world is changing.

Television and radio audiences are on the move. They already enjoy more choice than they used to and will soon enjoy far more. They are more discerning, more aware of their power and their rights as consumers of broadcasting, less willing to be patronised or talked down to, less ready to accept someone else's definition of what they should enjoy.

And the talent on which television and radio depends is changing too. In the UK and around the world, talented people of every kind – from the writers of comedy to film stars to great sporting institutions to individual programme-makers – are discovering that they too have new power in the marketplace. They are discovering that the new age of electronic information and entertainment has given them new choices which translate not just into more money at the negotiating table (though that is certainly proving to be the case), but also into greater freedom and greater creative control.

The effect of these changes is that the old calculations, the traditional relationship of BBC to audience and BBC to talent and the delicately maintained equilibrium between them, can no longer be taken for granted. Simply to continue working in existing ways and on existing assumptions risks failure to fulfil our remit.

That is why the BBC embarked on the comprehensive review of programmes which is summarised in this volume. This document springs from the principles set out in *Extending Choice* (published in 1992). It sets out a strategy for the future and the vision of the programmes and services which flow from it. It is about change, but also about continuity; about our strengths as programme makers and our weaknesses. It is about new ideas, new audiences to speak to, new subjects, new programmes.

Eighteen months of discussion, analysis and argument, the biggest audience research project ever undertaken by the BBC and substantial analysis of every programme area have stirred thinking and changed behaviour in every part of our radio and television producing areas, local, regional and national . . . Nor is this strategy intended to be set in stone. Creative imperatives change and so do audience needs; wherever necessary, we will adjust and adapt our plans to meet them. What will not change are our fundamental commitments: to quality, to originality, to range and diversity in every service we provide.

So the BBC faces a historic opportunity and major editorial challenges. This section is divided into seven parts, which deal with each of the major types of programme we offer:

- Arts, entertainment and drama, *including music, drama, comedy and entertainment, and coverage of the arts*
- The national debate, *covering news, current affairs, documentaries and features, and regional and local news and information*
- Knowledge building, *which includes science, history and other kinds of knowledge based factual programming, as well as formal and informal education*

- Religious programmes
- Leisure and sport
- Programmes for children and young people
- Programmes for ethnic minorities.

BBC (1995) *People and Programmes*, London: BBC, n.p.

3.7 People and Programmes not Policies and Processes

Hussey's Criticisms of Birt's Reforms

In the House of Lords' debate on public service broadcasting opened by Lord Bragg, Lord Hussey of North Bradley – previously Marmaduke Hussey, Chair of the BBC Board of Governors – was openly critical of many aspects of John Birt's reforms at the BBC including: the alleged over-bureaucratising of the BBC; the demand for an increase in the licence fee; the strategy for developing digital broadcasting, and the promotion of bi-media journalism. Hussey suggested that many BBC staff were demoralised by the reforms. Most significantly, Hussey distanced himself from Birt's programming philosophy and strategy, arguing for a focus on sustaining the quality of 'mainstream channels' rather than competing with commercial broadcasters and developing channels such as BBC *News 24*: a criticism echoed in the report of the Select Committee on Culture, Media and Sport (20 November 1999). His comments are valuable since they reveal, albeit retrospectively, the policy schisms within the BBC which were not evident at the time when policies were being promoted with apparent consensus.

The future of public service broadcasting lies first in the hands of parliament but also in the conduct of the BBC by its governors and managers. In my first week I was challenged to define my objectives. I replied that it was to leave the BBC complete with its channels and its licence fee in tact. At the time that was thought to be a very unlikely prospect. The general view was that we would lose several channels. In the event we retained them all and the licence fee and at the same time strengthened the power of the governors though you might not have noticed it.

There is a built in *frisson* between governors and management. The management want the plaudits of their fellow broadcasters, judged by the industry's benchmarks. The governors are concerned with independence, quality, high standards and the traditional ethos of a public service organisation . . .

The BBC is still a marvellous organisation. It still puts out great programmes on radio and television, but I do not think it has got its strategy right. We face the prospect of 200 or perhaps 500 competitive channels and the onset of digital. I firmly believe that the BBC's response should not be to expand its empire at the licence payers' expense but to concentrate on the mainstream channels and to invest in them . . .

Michael Checkland and John Birt, under pressure from the governors, made great administrative reforms, saved large sums of money, and radically improved efficiency, for which they both deserve great credit . . . There is still a lot of money about . . . If there is a shortage of money it is not difficult to see what should be done. There is too much bureaucracy, over bloated policy units and too much spent on expansion and management . . . The money should go on what the licence payer can hear and see, on those mainstream channels which won for the BBC its acknowledged reputation as the finest broadcaster in the world.

It is alleged that 'News 24' costs £30mn. That is an enormous amount of money, yet no one could find £4mn for the Test Match, now lost, together with the Cup Final, the Grand Prix and England at Twickenham. The BBC is a national broadcaster, where people expect to see and hear the big events. That should be the priority. It would be a great mistake to ask for a licence fee higher than the cost of living and might incur considerable resentment . . .

Equally, I do not agree with the amalgamation of radio and television. They are not the same. They are different art forms. I fear for the future of radio against the television monster. Much of it is very high standard supported by a dedicated and articulate audience. Anyone seriously interested in the news would listen to Radio Four's 'The World At One' or 'The World Tonight'. BBC television news is excellent but it has neither the time nor the space to give the coverage that radio does.

The BBC was founded by an engineer: an unusual engineer with moral and social vision. It has always been at the forefront of technology and must go digital both on radio and television. It gives much better reception. But digital broadcasting is not the message; it is only the messenger.

The moral, economic and intellectual organisation for a national broadcasting service funded by a poll tax lies in its absolute independence, the quality of its programmes, the breadth of its output and the manner in which it extends the choice of programmes for its audiences. If it does not do this it is a 'con'.

Currently the BBC is wading into a ratings battle with the toughest, roughest, richest companies in the broadcasting world. That is not a battle it will win. It does not have the money or the ruthless competitive streak that the opposition has.

The BBC is dedicated to setting higher standards for the industry and widening the people's choice and is staffed by men and women who share that motivation but many of who are now deeply depressed. The future of the BBC lies in the mind and skills of the programme makers whose budgets are now being dangerously squeezed . . .

If I may end on a personal note. I told the Prime Minister two years before I left the BBC that I would retire as soon as the Charter had been signed. I also made up my mind that I would take no decision in the last 6 months that might bind the hands of my successor, otherwise I would have taken a much stronger line on moving BBC radio and television into a large building which still doesn't work.

The future of public service broadcasting in the UK will flourish as long as the BBC remembers that people and programmes are much more important than policies and processes. That is what I have said to the BBC previously. I have made my views quite clear to the BBC, and it knows them, but never before have I stated them in public.

Lord Hussey of North Bradley's contribution to the debate on Public Service Broadcasting (1999) *Parliamentary Debates*, Lords Vol. 597, cols 1685–1687, 2 March.

3.8 Maintaining the 'Gold Standard'

Greg Dyke, BBC Programming and the Digital Television Marketplace

On 25 August 2000 Greg Dyke, Director-General of the BBC, used the prestigious MacTaggart Lecture at the Edinburgh Film Festival as a platform to launch his vision for a new BBC, which required melding the Reithian public service tradition with the realities of the digital television market in order to forestall the emergence of a 'digital underclass'. In the words of the *Guardian* leader the following day, 'the problem is for the BBC to be populist enough to win high ratings to justify a £2bn-a-year licence – raised mainly from poorer people – without betraying its Reithian mission to improve people's minds' (*Guardian*, 26 August 2000: 27). Dyke's vision embraced a number of concrete programming proposals. First, the BBC's *Nine O'Clock News* should shift to the 10 p.m. slot in the schedule to attract larger audiences. Second, two new children's channels will be created and the existing BBC television channels will have their programme contents revamped. Dyke suggested that BBC1 will remain the 'gold standard of mainstream television' but will become more focused on entertainment, drama and factual programmes. Some programmes currently at the margins of BBC1's schedule will be given a higher profile slot on BBC2. BBC2 will broadcast more specialised 'highbrow' programmes of a factual kind, BBC3 (a reworked version of the digital channel BBC Choice) will target a youth audience and promises to 'break the rules a bit' while BBC4 (currently the digital channel BBC Knowledge) will be 'unashamedly intellectual' and offer a televised amalgam of Radio 3 and Radio 4 with an emphasis on culture, music and the arts. During the daytime hours, the third and fourth networks will broadcast two new children's channels: the first for pre-school children, the second for children aged 6 to 13. BBC News 24 will comprise the seventh BBC television channel. Dyke acknowledged that his vision would require the agreement of the BBC Governors and the Culture Secretary Chris Smith before it could be implemented. While some broadcasters and politicians welcomed the new channel structure as a brave and necessary move to ensure the survival of the BBC in an age of digital television, others denounced Dyke's vision as a formula for dumbing down the BBC in order to win greater audiences in an increasingly competitive market. On 21 September 2000, following persistent pressure by the ITC, the ITV Network Centre announced that its was reinstating a nightly news bulletin at 10 p.m.: this move places the BBC in head-to-head competition for news audiences with the ITV network.

I believe the stark choice facing the BBC today is that we either change or we simply manage decline gracefully, and none of us joined the BBC to do that . . . I believe one of the problems of BBC television today is that too many of our services have been underfunded . . .

If we want to spend more money on our traditional services, and we do need to, there are certain consequences. First, we have to find the money, and second we have to limit our plans for new services to what we can afford.

I believe the potential for savings is significant. The BBC currently spends 24 per cent of its income on running the institution of the BBC. Our target is to reduce that figure to 15 per cent over the next three years which will give us an extra £200 million a year to spend on programmes and services . . .

I also believe we can increase our commercial income.

The second thing we have to do, if we want better funded services, is to limit our ambitions for expansion. We cannot possibly afford to have a tank on every lawn, or compete in every area of the market place . . .

In the year 2002–2003 we will be spending £480 million a year more on our programmes and services than we spent last year . . . This amounts to the biggest increase in programme expenditure in BBC history.

So what are we planning to do with the money?

We believe that in the age of digital television it will not be sufficient for the BBC to offer only two mixed genre channels which are somehow supposed to meet the needs of everyone. We need a more coherent portfolio of channels.

As we are inevitably constrained by money, this means we must limit the size of this portfolio. But there is another more important reason for limiting the number of channels we plan and that is the principle of universality. What universality means is making all our publicly funded services available in all homes.

We must avoid the emergence of a digital underclass, a world where some are information rich while others are information poor.

In order to achieve this principle of universality it means we are only going to offer a portfolio of channels now which, within a reasonable time will be available in every household in the land.

BBC1 and BBC2 will continue as the mainstays of BBC television for the foreseeable future. Getting these channels right for the future is the big challenge.

BBC1 needs to have a greater impact on people's lives. While this may mean that some of the old faithfuls disappear and others move from the fringe of BBC1 to peak time on BBC2, it does not mean we are banishing all current affairs, documentaries, religion and arts to other channels. Far from it. But programming in these genres, just as in drama and entertainment, needs to be more engaging, more exciting, more gripping if it is to be on BBC1.

Our aim is to make BBC1 the gold standard of mainstream television . . . More than half of the extra money to be spent on the BBC overall will go on improving and modernising BBC1 and BBC2 with most going to BBC1 . . .

In the long term we plan that BBC2 will increasingly focus on intelligent specialist programmes, our key leisure and lifestyle programmes, thoughtful analysis, creatively ambitious drama and comedy and specialist sports . . .

Now for the new channels. Imaginatively we've given them the working titles of BBC3 and BBC4. BBC3 will offer original British comedy, drama and music as well as providing arts, education and social action programmes delivered in a way likely to be attractive to the young audience . . . I suspect in developing BBC3 we will need to break a lot more rules before we're through. BBC3 will emerge out of BBC Choice but will have a significantly higher budget.

BBC4 will be very different. it will be unashamedly intellectual, a mixture of Radios 3 and 4 of television. It will be based around arts, challenging music, ideas and in-depth discussion. It will be serious in intent but unstuffy and contemporary . . . I am also very keen for us to deliver a rolling breakfast time business news on BBC4 . . . BBC4 will be developed out of BBC Knowledge. But again it will have a significantly higher budget. In all we plan to spend £130 million a year on BBC3 and BBC4.

Our fifth new channel will be News 24. It seems obvious to me that the world's biggest news gatherer, the BBC needs a 24-hour news service as part of its channel mix. We plan two new children's services to be played in the daytime on the channels occupied by BBC3 and BBC4 in the evenings. One will be for pre-school children and the second for children between 6 and 13 . . .

Together these channels will deliver the BBC's core aims. All will carry predominantly British original productions. All will make a contribution towards achieving our educational goals which I regard as one of the principal aims of my period as Director-General. All will include a broad news and current affairs agenda and all will carry challenging factual programmes. However, over time each channel will develop its own personality and will increasingly be aimed at particular target audiences.

In the digital era I believe the BBC's single most important role will be to make possible the production of great British programmes. Our channel strategy is a means of achieving this – a way of commissioning, producing and broadcasting original British programmes of all kinds on a mix of channels which will make sense to audiences in the digital age . . . This means creating inside the BBC an environment in which talented people can flourish.

Greg Dyke (2000) MacTaggart Memorial Lecture delivered at the Edinburgh International Film Festival, 25 August.

NEWS, CURRENT AFFAIRS AND CHILDREN'S PROGRAMMES

3.9 Changing News and Current Affairs Commitments at Granada

Since the mid-1990s, some academic observers and broadcasters have expressed a growing concern that the focus of news and current affairs programmes has shifted away from 'hard' news and the reporting of international stories to a 'softer', lighter, domestic news agenda in which 'human interest' stories have featured increasingly. In January 1999 the *Guardian* published a leaked document which contained Granada's successful bid for ITV's proposed flagship current affairs programme, provisionally titled *World in Action*. The document seemed to underline many of these expressed concerns. It revealed insights into Granada's perception of future directions in television news and current affairs, its ambitions to copy what it regarded as the successful formats of American programming and the substantial change in news values informing Granada's current affairs programmes since *World in Action* was first broadcast in the 1960s.

Extracted from Granada's *A Fresh Start for ITV Current Affairs*

A new audience is waking up to the appeal of factual programmes on television. Both in Britain and America it is clear that documentary specials, popular factual shows and docu-soaps are key weapons in a network's armoury. A new grammar of factual television has helped revolutionise the audience perception of such shows. Now it is time for current affairs to catch up.

A new hour-long series presents an opportunity to reinvent the genre, with one of the most exciting current affairs innovations of the past 20 years. Get it right and ITV will be an essential part of the zeitgeist reflecting and contributing to the era we live in, interpreting and revealing the facts we need to know. We believe Granada is uniquely placed to deliver such a series.

THE FORMAT: One of the problems of the traditional single-issue current affairs programme is that by and large the subject matter determines the size of the audience. If the viewers are not interested in the subject, they won't watch the programme. The benefit of a multi-item magazine is that viewers will be attracted by a consistent mix of light and shade.

Our research shows that our new approach is both appealing and innovative, and viewers perceive it as 'upbeat and lively'. The respondents 'undoubtedly felt that what they were being shown was a new way of presenting a current affairs programme'.

The researchers concluded that 'the programme appeared to be more accessible for the less committed current affairs viewers than some of the existing offerings'.

We believe this programme should nearly always be multi-item. It should also be live and presenter-led from a studio. The series should include a regular mix of the following:

- An original investigation
- The hidden angle on a major running news story
- An irreverent approach to a current controversy
- News-related 'reportage' (e.g. finding out what it's really like in a women's prison in the week of Deirdre's conviction in Coronation Street)
- News-related biography or human interest feature

We believe there is huge scope in this last category. Profiles could involve a celebrity, e.g. George Michael in the week of his arrest for 'lewd behaviour' or Judy Finnigan on her return to the TV screen following an extremely public hysterectomy. Alternatively, it could be a politician – Mo Mowlam in the week of the Ulster peace agreement, or John Prescott in the middle of his row with the 'neighbours from Hull'. Or we could even focus on an ordinary person in an extraordinary situation, e.g. a day in the life of a Lottery jackpot winner, or the parents caring for a teenage daughter with CJD.

We would seek interviews with the subjects themselves, but – with the politicians and celebrities at least we could still draw together illuminating 'unauthorised' biographies. In fact the weekly profiles in the Sunday broadsheets are often more fascinating when made up from quotes by 'friends' than from the subjects.

We are anxious to move away from the static desks and conventional look favoured by studio current affairs. In the way that the style of C5 News has made us think again about the look of news, we need to make current affairs less threatening to younger viewers.

THE TITLE: Whether [measured] by performance, image, heritage or perception, all agree on the value of World in Action. It's a value that has risen ever since the programme's launch. In the sixties it was bold and brash, with strong opinions and vivid imagery. By the seventies it was TV's premier investigative programme, exposing crime and corruption. In the eighties it concentrated on storytelling while its BBC rivals conducted a 'mission to explain'. And in the nineties it rediscovered a populist approach that delivered mass audiences.

A combination of scheduling and a worthier brief from the Network Centre has weakened that ratings position in the last couple of years. But, with fresh ITV leadership, and a new editor committed to a popular agenda, we are confident the audience will build again.

Whatever the recent history, the World In Action brand remains incredibly robust. Our audience research shows viewers immediately linking the name with authority, credibility and investigative skill.

NEW AGENDA FOR NEWS AND CURRENT AFFAIRS: We believe the time has come to once again think boldly, laterally and irreverently.

Thus . . .

When Lord Irvine says you can't find his £300-a-roll Pugin wallpaper at the DIY store, we would put it to the test. At least three – Fads, Do-it-All and Texas – told us they could run up a duplicate within a week. We take our own 'Master of the Rolls' – 'Big Ritchie' Aspinall from Liverpool's Garstang Wallpaper Centre – to do vox pops outside the Lord Chancellor's flat, asking passers-by if they can tell the difference between the Pugin version and his own. Finally we would approach his lordship himself for his own opinion on our taxpayer-friendly decor . . .

When New Labour celebrates a year in power we prove that Tony Blair's government is actually more grey and faceless than John Major's. Showing photographs to people in the street we see how many can identify such household names as Ron Davies and George Robertson. As a joke we put in a photo of a New Labour 'clone' (actually an actor) and ask people to tick off a name from a multiple choice list. (We conducted a pilot survey of 30 people in Salford which found numbers of people recognising the following: Blair (25); Cook & Prescott (16); Blunkett (14); Mowlam (10); Short (7); Beckett, Straw & Cunningham (3) . . .

It's stunts like these that will get programme talked about. Along with popular investigations and campaigns they'll give the series its character and mark us out from our rivals. Young viewers, in particular, regard current affairs programmes as solemn and boring. But we will change that perception. For, as long as our journalism is solid, we can be as cheeky and entertaining as we like.

We must be careful to avoid becoming a slave to the news agenda. If we are to be ruthlessly discriminating when commissioning our investigative output, the same populist criteria must apply when it comes to news. The main story of the week should not be an automatic choice as an item. If that were the case we would be like *Newsnight* or *Channel Four News*, providing extended reports on topics that often lack mass appeal.

LESSONS FROM AMERICA: Current affairs programmes are markedly more popular in the USA than in Britain. The long-running CBS 60 Minutes series remains the pack leader, though like all the major magazine programmes its ratings have been in decline since 1994. That said, it still usually makes the Top 10 and recently reclaimed number one spot thanks to an exclusive interview with yet another Clinton sex-accuser, Katherine Willey.

NBC's Dateline now airs four times a week although audiences are erratic. Meanwhile audiences for early-evening 'tabloid' programmes such as *Hard Copy* are way down on what they were five years ago: CBS has dropped its own tabloid series *West 57th* because of poor ratings.

American magazine shows – like US news programmes – are aggressively domestic, with minimal coverage of the world beyond their shores. They feature anything between three and six items with health, crime, human interest stories and personality profiles the most common fare. Says Andrew Heywood (CBS 48 Hours): 'Tabloid shows are there to get an audience and generate profits. We have to do that too, but we also need to set a standard for Public service.' Thus in a Clinton sex harassment story, the tabloids are only interested in the salacious detail. Current affairs magazines will include those details but also look at their implications for the Presidency.

PERSONAL JOURNALISM: The most successful current affairs magazines tend to avoid 'essays' or 'missions' to explain. Instead, they follow the advice of 60 minutes founder Don Hewitt: 'People always ask me for the formula for our success, and I tell them its simple – four words every kid in the world knows: "Tell me a story. Its that easy. In television, if you don't know how to communicate with words, you're in the wrong business."' Hewitt also believes that it should be real people – correspondents with names and faces – who tell the stories, rather than presenters narrating from studio, or remote 'voices from the sky'. When he began 60 Minutes he thought viewers would want to witness the adventures of his reporters as the stories they covered.

PRESENTATION: As mentioned earlier, the American series are the subject of expert packaging. ABC's *20/20* and *Dateline NBC* provide the best models. Their sets are well designed, perfectly-lit, the titles arresting without being pompous. The attention paid to the opening segments – before the first commercial break – is highly impressive. Professional trailmakers take the rushes from the segment producers to come up with one-minute teasers for each of the stories. These are then edited and post-produced almost to the standard of commercials. Throughout the shows great use is made of 'coming up' stings where again the strongest shot or the most emotional piece of sync is used in order to keep viewers watching for the next item.

CONCLUSIONS: We do believe the American approach to current affairs can be adapted here to a great degree. That means we should focus more on human emotion and drama, develop our storytelling skills, be less sniffy about seeking the journalistic angles on populist stories.

When it comes to presentation we have learned great lessons. We must 'be bolder about selling our product to the viewers, paying far more attention to promos, titles, design, graphics and post-production. We have the journalistic ability but we must now echo Hewitt and 'package the facts' like Hollywood 'packages fiction'.

SUMMARY: Our ambitions for the new *World In Acton* are extremely high. We believe this programme offers ITV a chance to reconnect its flagship current affairs programme with a mass audience and attract – perhaps for the first time – a new generation of young and upmarket viewers.

To achieve this we will need to tap into the everyday concerns and passions of our audience by delivering a programme mix that is informative, surprising and fun; we need to find an approach to current affairs that makes watching it a pleasure, rather than an obligation. Achieving this will be largely about the stories we choose and the mix in each and every programme.

'World in Action meets Yoof TV . . .' (1999) *Guardian*, 18 January, pp.6–7.

3.10 'Flashing Blue Light' Television

The ITC Annual Programme Review

The 1990 Broadcasting Act established the ITC as a bulwark of regulatory probity against the economic pressures, increasingly evident in the commercial sector of broadcasting, which critics argued would impact in a debilitating way on programme quality. A significant weapon in the ITC armoury has been its annual review of programmes broadcast by each of the Channel 3 licence holders to ensure that the television companies are meeting the programme promises made in their initial licence bids, as well as the ITC's specified minimums for such formats as news and current affairs, regional programming and children's programming. Prior to the publication of the first such review in 1994, David Glencross, then Chief Executive of the ITC, expressed concern that while 'factual programmes still have a considerable presence in peak-time across all four channels the mix has changed. There are many more programmes recollecting and reconstructing crime, vicarious exposure of disasters or near disasters and exploitations of the sex lives of the famous and not so famous . . . With a year's experience behind it the network needs a little more adventure . . . An occasional evening dip in the ratings does not spell the end of life as we know it' (Glencross, 1994: 8). Such criticisms have featured routinely in subsequent reviews.

In 1996, for example, the review said, 'the ITC identifies a noticeable shift in the overall balance towards more entertainment-led programmes. The network schedule contained . . . less documentary [see 3.11] and arts output: and the less obviously popular programming such as education, religion and arts was often in the margins of the schedule'. Glencross' successor Peter Rogers commented, 'We think the balance has shifted and is approaching or is at the limit of where it should be . . . We have nothing against cheap programming if it works well, but some of it is a bit tacky. The amount of police and crime shows is near its limit'. The extract from the 1998 performance review congratulated the network on its successes but remained critical of 'shortcomings in areas such as current affairs, comedy and arts'; the ITC also reminded of the need for programmes 'of innovation and quality' in the gap in the peak-time schedule created by evacuating *News at Ten*. In 1998, network current affairs programmes fell to a record low.

ITV showed a determination to refresh and revitalise its service in 1998. Past ITC criticism of limited diversity in peak-time was answered by increasing factual material and consequently reducing reliance on drama. Overall there was a marked and welcome improvement in the supply of documentaries, of entertainment and drama specifically for children, as well as of sport. However, shortcomings in areas such as current affairs, comedy and arts need to be addressed.

In 1999 and beyond opportunities for further diversity provided by the opening up of the weekday peak-time schedule, following rescheduling of the news bulletins, must be pursued vigorously. ITV has argued in the past that *News at Ten* has inhibited the post-9pm scheduling of documentaries, arts programmes, and comedy of the kind which has been successful on BBC One. Viewers have been led to expect benefits from the changes and the ITC will require that programmes of innovation and quality should appear, adding to diversity in the peak-time output.

Current affairs

Nineteen ninety eight was also a year of transition in ITV current affairs. Of the three long-running half-hour series, *The Big Story* did not reappear in 1998 and *3-D* returned for a final short run. With the new Granada hour-long current affairs magazine programme due to be introduced in the first half of 1999 [see Granada's programme plans 3.9], *World in Action* also came to the end of its long and generally distinguished existence, in its current form. Critics alleged that the programme, towards the end, adopted a lighter and more consumerist tone. There was some truth in this, with programmes about bad holiday hotels, and the content of dog food. However, there were also investigations of consumer issues with wider policy implications, such as bank charges and power utility mis-selling. And there were other programmes of which *World in Action* could have been proud at any point in its history, dealing with Britain's role in the legal systems of West Indian countries, and the violent Combat 18 organisation. The ITC will expect to see strong investigative work continuing in ITV's new programme.

Last year's ITC review commented on a disappointing level of high quality international current affairs coverage, which is a specific requirement of the Broadcasting Act 1990. There were some encouraging signs in 1998, with *World in Action* visiting Iraq among several other countries, Jonathan Dimbleby's return to Ethiopia after 25 years, and an excellent documentary on the aftermath of the Nairobi bombings, *True Terror*. Nevertheless, the ITC wishes to see the proportion of international material rise higher in 1999. *Westminster Women* and *New Labour in Focus: Tony Benn's Video Diaries* usefully supplemented the political coverage provided by *Dimbleby* on Sunday lunchtimes. The consumer programme *We Can Work It Out* was a welcome addition to the schedule, but the ITC will not allow it to count (in its existing format) towards ITV's current affairs requirement in future years. The ITC also felt that the science series *What Will They Think of Next?* would have been more appropriately classified as education than current affairs. Finally, the ITC had concerns about the quality of a one-off documentary on *Diana: Secrets Behind the Crash* which was widely criticised for fuelling conspiracy theories about the Princess's death.

The amount of current affairs in 1998 fell, compared with the unusually high levels achieved in the General Election year of 1997. Without *We Can Work It Out*, the average would have fallen to 1 hour 25 minutes weekly, the lowest network figure on record. The ITC will monitor this aspect of provision closely in 1999 and expects to see an improvement.

Factual programmes

ITV's factual output in 1998 showed evidence that the criticisms made of it last year by the ITC were being addressed. Documentary series and single documentaries shown between 6pm and 10.30pm more than doubled, to reach an average of 57 minutes weekly and 29 minutes weekly respectively. There were some notable successes, particularly among single documentaries, but material that was genuinely innovative in style, content or approach was limited.

Although the *Network First* banner, to designate ITV's serious documentary strand, disappeared in 1998, other programmes in the 10.40pm slot on Tuesdays more than adequately replaced it. with a more diverse range of material. A positive development was the increase in documentaries with an international focus such as *An Ethiopian Journey*.

The most significant increase in factual output was in popular factual series, many attracting large audiences. The search for the worst of human behaviour in the . . . . *From Hell* collection worked better in some programmes than others, but its popularity with viewers was consistently matched only by the enduring *Police Camera Action* series. *Vice: The Sex Trade* attracted a sizeable audience at 9pm but also a substantial volume of complaint on the grounds that it was scheduled much too early – two of its three editions breached the ITC's Programme Code for this reason. A 'docu-soap' series in the early part of the year, *Airline*, also rated particularly well. Overall, while appreciating the importance to the network of attracting audiences, the ITC would have liked to see rather more documentaries in the best ITV tradition – stimulating thoughts and sympathies, as well as passions.

ITV's daytime factual output mainly trod well-worn paths with *This Morning* celebrating 10 years on air in November, and little sign of the format wearing thin. Indeed, its consistency remains impressive. Last year's criticism, however, of a lack of imagination in the daytime factual schedule as a whole was not answered in 1998. *Vanessa* transformed seamlessly into *Trisha*, whose rapport with audiences was at once evident. Instead of an alternative to chat shows, criticised in 1997 as narrowing diversity, the Network ran for parts of the year *The Jerry Springer Show* which frequently focuses on the extremes of emotional difficulties in personal relationships. Generally editions were carefully selected for acceptability in daytime. However one particular programme, in which participants resorted to violence, occasioned an ITC Intervention.

ITC (1998) *Annual Reports and Accounts*, London: ITC, 29 March 1999

3.11 The Decline of Documentaries on ITV

In 1998, the Campaign for Quality Television produced a pamphlet cataloguing what it claimed was a substantial decline in serious documentary programming on ITV across a twenty-year period. A marked decline in the number of hours that documentaries are transmitted, has been accompanied by a 'creative' redefinition of the term *documentary* to include the 'lighter', more popular genre of docu-soaps and a tendency to reschedule documentary programming at the edge of

> peak time. Before the creation of the ITV Network Centre in 1993, the two main documentary programmes – Yorkshire's *First Tuesday* and Central's *Viewpoint* – complemented by a number of other regular documentary strands such as Granada's *Disappearing World* – routinely focused on serious domestic and international issues. In the early 1990s, 'ITV documentaries outstripped the BBC in providing a true window on the world and established an international reputation for highly professional film-making allied to meticulous research' (p.3). With the establishment of the Network Centre in 1993, all existing documentary strands were cancelled. A new ITV documentary series *Network First* was scheduled for 10.40 p.m. and, for two years, broadcast a wide range of high-quality, high-budget documentaries which attracted considerable audiences (despite the move out of peak time). The year 1995 witnessed cuts in the number of films commissioned as well as their budgets, combined with a narrowing of subject matter with a greater focus on crime and domestic reports. As a consequence audiences reduced dramatically. More recently documentary programming has been characterised by an emphasis on docu-soaps. This trend, the report concludes, is unlikely to be reversed unless the ITV Network Centre agrees to 'allocate discrete series of "serious documentaries" to individual companies' (p.17). But while docu-soaps will 'prove an important weapon in ITV's battle to regain its previous share of the audience . . . they will not satisfy its licence commitment to "serious documentaries"'.

This devaluing of . . . [documentaries] attracted direct criticism from the ITC in its annual report on ITV.

> *The most serious disappointment of the year was the greatly reduced number of Network First documentaries and a narrowing of the range of subject matter addressed by them.*
>
> *The channel's established documentary slot (10.40pm) carried only three Network First documentaries in the first four months of the year.*
>
> *The total number for the year was 18, about half that broadcast in 1995, and only one more than the number of occasions on which the slot was occupied by an acquired film or drama.*
>
> *There was a further overall reduction in the amount of documentary programming in peak time. Most seriously, overall documentary output fell short of the licence commitments of the majority of ITV companies.*

Faced with this damning report, ITV might have been expected to stop the rot in its 'serious documentaries'. The ITC, after all, is the statutory regulator with power to enforce compliance with licence commitments. But ITV simply ignored it. The 1997 schedules included precisely the same number of *Network First* documentaries (18) as in 1996. The Network Centre also repeated that year's pattern of interrupting the run of the series with seemingly-random non-*Network First* programming, and of deferring transmission of several of the *Network First* films it actually managed to commission until 1998.

Budgets were also reduced: domestic *Network Firsts* now attracted a maximum of £180,000 per film, international *Network Firsts* (an increasingly rare commodity) £190,000. At the same time the ITV companies themselves began taking a increased (20%) profit margin off the top of the budget for each film they produced.

The subject matter, too, reflected a narrowing of vision with an increase in the number of films about royalty or celebrities. And, for the first time since *Network First* replaced the highly successful *First Tuesday* and *Viewpoint* strands, the Network Centre failed to produce a promotional brochure for the series. The impression was very clearly of a series which was being left to die.

Perhaps unsurprisingly audience figures continued to slide. The average *Network First* audience figure for 1997 was 2.9 million – down by almost a million on the average for the inaugural series in 1994 . . .

New documentary commissioning

From the middle of 1997, ITV ceased to commission new *Network First* documentaries. Throughout much of 1997 the Network Centre actually 'closed its doors for business' (its own phrase). When it did re-open those doors, it was not to commission new 'serious documentaries'.

Instead the then factual programmes' head, Paul Corley, told production companies he was only interested in films or series which could successfully run at 9pm. 'Successfully' was clearly spelled out: audience figures of at least 10 million. This change of focus had been brought about by one programme: Carlton/Central's *Neighbours From Hell* – a clever re-packaging of a series of well-worn stories of feuding neighbours. The programme drew an audience of 11 million – as much as most glossy dramas for a fraction of the cost. The Network Centre immediately commissioned a series of follow up . . . *From Hell* films in the hope of repeating the success.

The *Neighbours From Hell* saga illustrates two dangerous trends in ITV. The first is its late awakening to the evidence that factual programmes can attract huge audiences. The BBC has for almost two years been proving this with so-called 'documentary soaps' such as *Airport*, *Driving School*, *Hotel* and a raft of vet or hospital-based programmes. Scheduled in the heart of peak, these observational series have drawn audiences of more than 8 million – and punched large holes in ITV's audience share for the slots they occupy. Simultaneously each BBC channel transmitted what ITV would classify as 'serious documentaries'. In essence it ran a balanced schedule of light and more heavyweight factual programmes.

The second trend is that once ITV realises it has failed to spot a successful formula, it overreacts on a grand scale. And so, from summer 1997, the sole factual programming interest of the Network Centre has been these cheap and cheerful documentary-soaps. We do not question the worth of such series, much less the audiences they draw. But ITV should not – nor be allowed to – rely on them as its sole documentary programming.

'Serious documentaries': the future

If the Network Centre does not move fast to repair the damage of the last two years, it will find itself locked into a spiral of ever-decreasing ideas, leading to ever-decreasing output. One solution would be for the Network Centre to allocate discrete series of 'serious documentaries' to individual companies – either from within the ITV network or the independent sector. This would have two major benefits. First it would introduce a breadth of vision to the commissioning process. By its very nature the centralised commissioning which accompanied the creation of the Network Centre meant a narrowing of subject matter to that which appealed to one central commissioning controller. Under the previous system there were at least three, frequently more, separate strands each with their own commissioning editor.

Secondly it would ease the commercial problem of individual companies and allow them to retain sufficient staff to develop the very best films. It would also allow companies to amortise budgets across a series of films, devoting higher budgets to the projects – typically lengthy investigations or overseas stories – which need them. This was precisely the system by which all the classic *First Tuesday* and *Viewpoint* documentaries were created.

One thing above all is clear: ITV needs to expand not contract its documentary programming. But it is not enough for ITV simply to increase quantity, without a corresponding expansion in the breadth of subject matter. The new head of programmes at the Network Centre, David Liddiment, has promised an increase in ITV's factual output. But crucially his public promise was to a new raft of 'factual but entertaining' programmes.

Documentary soaps will prove an important weapon in ITV's battle to regain its previous share of the audience. But they will not satisfy its licence commitment to serious documentaries. Nor will they satisfy the advertisers – for the very good reason that they will ultimately not satisfy a broad audience. Just as low-fibre 'fun foods' can never make a wholesome diet on their own, so low-fibre 'documentary-lite' shows can never deliver the balanced factual schedule which ITV and its audience wants.

Campaign for Quality Television (1998) *Serious Documentaries on ITV*, London: Campaign for Quality Television, 17pp.

3.12 Changing Trends in British Television Current Affairs

The suggestion that the focus and character of television current affairs might be changing – and for the worse – was given dramatic endorsement in 1999, when Steve Barnett and Emily Seymour published the findings of their study of drama and current affairs broadcasting across a twenty-year period. Based on a content analysis of current affairs programming since 1977 (two four-week periods of programming were sampled in 1977/78, 1987/88 and 1997/98), combined with in-depth interviews (thirty-four) with senior programme makers, editors and commissioners, their research provided a detailed empirical account of the rapid and considerable changes in current affairs programme contents as well as an explanation of some of the reasons underlying these changes.

One notable finding concerned the declining coverage of foreign affairs and the increasing reliance on a domestic agenda for current affairs. On ITV, for example, foreign affairs reporting, as a proportion of current affairs, had reduced from 26 per cent in the 1970s to 15 per cent in the 1980s and settled at 7 per cent in the 1990s. On a connected note, the expansive domestic agenda for current affairs has been increasingly dominated by programmes focused on policing and crime: as a programme category, this has doubled in the last ten years and is now the largest single component in television current affairs. Barnett and Seymour conclude that 'there is less peak-time current affairs on ITV than ever before' and there is 'a general trend towards "softer" issues, particularly crime, consumer moral/ethical themes' (p.11). The extract below derives from the executive summary of their findings.

Executive summary

There has been a significant decline over the last twenty years in foreign affairs coverage, which is now almost wholly confined to BBC2. Commercial television has effectively vacated political and economic current affairs, which is now covered almost exclusively by the BBC. Across all channels, there has been a very noticeable rise in coverage of police and crime issues and – to a lesser extent – consumer issues.

The drive for ratings in peak-time has greatly increased over the last ten years, and appears to be almost as dominant on the BBC and Channel Four as ITV. Especially on ITV, ratings targets or guarantees increasingly dictate programming decisions.

- In current affairs, this translates into more emphasis on the domestic, consumer and ratings-friendly subjects at the expense of covering foreign affairs, Northern Ireland or more complex political and economic issues. It also favours a more emotional and picture-led approach to current affairs at the expense of more analytical or investigative programmes. Some believe there is a growing tendency towards a more 'cynical' form of journalism, designed solely to amass large audiences. There is a deep-rooted sense of crisis about this television genre.

Over the last ten years, the downward pressure on budgets has become much more intense. Producers are – almost without exception – experiencing progressive budget cuts leading to an unprecedented squeeze on their programme costs.

- In current affairs, this has had a serious impact on the volume and quality of research, with particularly unhappy consequences for investigative journalism and subjects requiring long-distance travel. There is almost no room for 'speculative' investigations which may not produce tangible results, and consequently little prospect of ground-breaking programmes or anything which requires long-term commitment of time or money.

Reduced budgets have also increased the pressure on programme makers' working lives. Particularly in drama, many talked about the stress of punishing shooting schedules which imposed intolerably long working hours on directors and technicians, with a negative impact on professional standards and personal lives.

Though most still enjoy their jobs, they feel that goodwill has been stretched to its limit and the industry is becoming a less attractive place to work.

Short-term contracts and lack of job security means that training opportunities are fewer and less sustained . . . In current affairs, it means little or no training in traditional techniques of journalism and staff being required to work above their ability and experience. Research is therefore less thorough and mistakes are more likely.

Particularly in current affairs, there is considerably more emphasis being laid on measuring, interpreting, and responding to audience requirements. Programme makers recognise the need to avoid elitism and make subjects more accessible, but are worried that focus groups and other methods of audience research are eroding journalistic instinct.

There is resentment at the number of managers who involve themselves in the creative process, whether for compliance or budgetary reasons or to enhance ratings potential. This adds to programme makers' sensor of caution. The commissioning process, however, is now perceived to be concentrated in too few hands with inhibiting consequences for diversity and innovation.

New technology is mostly seen as offering the benefits of cheaper and more flexible working methods, although there is some anxiety that it might simply be exploited by broadcasters as a means of reducing costs without raising or even maintaining standards.

There is a growing pressure, particularly on expensive current affairs projects, to look for international co-funding . . . it is acknowledged that overseas funding involves compromises on content and creative treatment that may not suit the domestic British audience.

Within the BBC, there is concern that current affairs has lost its sense of direction and that internal structural changes have weakened its creative potential. There is a sense in both genres that the BBC has lost its corporate self-confidence.

Throughout the industry, structural changes and rationalisation have weakened collegiate practices and increased programme makers' sense of isolation. In current affairs, the loss of 'brand name' programmes with no long-term investment in replacements has made serious journalistic endeavour much more difficult.

Steven Barnett and Emily Seymour (1999) *'A Shrinking Iceberg Travelling South . . .' Changing Trends in British television: A Case Study of Drama and Current Affairs*, London: Campaign for Quality Television, September.

3.13 *News at Ten*

Markets versus Interfering Politicians

Richard Eyre's November 1999 lecture at Leeds outlined the 'new approach at ITV' since his arrival as head of the ITV Network Centre. He detailed the 'fundamental restructuring of ITV' and spoke of 'the need to refresh a relationship that was in danger of falling into decline'. ITV's mantra was 'programmes that would "get connected" with people'. A crucial factor in this broad restructuring was the need to shift *News at Ten* which he justified on market grounds: 'You can't ignore a daily exodus of a quarter of your audience at 10 O'Clock.' Politicians who attempt to re-establish *News at Ten* in its old slot in the schedule, Eyre suggests, are interfering paternalists. But despite these protestations, on 21 September 2000 (almost twelve months after Eyre's move to become Chief Executive of Pearson Plc) the ITV Network Centre announced its intention to reinstate a nightly news bulletin at 10.00pm. The move represented an unhappy compromise for ITV following substantial falls in audience for ITV news, requests for a return to the 10.00pm slot by politicians and the Select Committee on Broadcasting and determined pressure from the ITC which insisted on legal redress if the ITV companies failed to meet their franchise commitments to live broadcasting of news in a nightly 10.00pm slot.

Structurally I believe we now have an ITV that is very much more versatile than two years ago. And it's working. By the end of last week, week 42, ITV's share of the peak time audience had grown from 37.9% last year to 38.9%. We are on target to . . . achieve something that has not been pulled off by any broadcaster anywhere in the world – turning around the decline – flying in the face of the market forces that anticipated our decline.

The . . . vision for the future of ITV has helped frame some very tough decisions, like the move of the *News at Ten*. By no means a simple decision to tackle the conservatism of the British public, inviting them to engage with a new schedule shape after 32 years with the old one. But if you're serious about growth, you can't ignore a daily exodus of over a quarter of your audience at 10 o'clock, because you want to curry favour with a few politicians.

Coming out of the most watched half-hour in British television, 9.30 to 10.00pm, 27% of viewers were switching off ITV. 37% of people under 35 . . . and I honestly think now as I thought then, that any Chief Executive of any broadcasting company that failed to address defection of viewers on such a scale would have to be switched off himself.

You see ITV's economy is a simple one. If we lose audience, we lose revenue; if we lose revenue we lose the means to invest in programmes; and reduced programme investment begets, guess what – reduced audience levels. Two years ago this vicious circle was a real threat to ITV. Had it begun you could forget even the current scale of investment in news by ITV, not far short of £2 million a day, an additional £1 million devoted to ITN's coverage of Kosovo alone.

It is naive of politicians to insist on bringing back *News at Ten* and imagine business as usual in ITV's economy. Now that we've stopped the decline and had a year of audience growth, you can't just pop the *News at Ten* back and hope for the best.

Digital Television is an important part of this government's agenda. I believe the Secretary of State has played an important role in ushering in an exciting position where Britain leads the world. But you can't say you think it's good for Britain to embrace a technology that enables hundreds of new channels in the UK and insist for political reasons, that ITV return to a schedule that is the legacy of a two-channel market. It's like opening the floodgates and manacling ITV to the bottom of the pool.

What we see here from the Secretary of State and the Chairman of the DCMS Select Committee is party politics, political interference dressed up in the haughty clothing of knowing what's best for viewers. A million people a night switch off ITV at ten o'clock and Gerald Kaufman weighs in to tell them they really ought to know better. They'll *have* the *News at Ten* because that's what's best for them . . .

Of course, politicians are entitled to have a view about the news but if their concern is about an informed electorate, I can reassure them that broadly the number of people watching television news in the UK has not changed. ITV has lost some news viewers – as it has every year since the arrival of multi channel. It's not something I take lightly, but our agenda was about the performance of the whole schedule, not just the news. Because had the whole schedule continued to perform as it was, our peak-time share in 1999 would not have been 39% but 35% – and the pressure on programme budgets including our investment in news coverage for 2000 would have already been acute.

But this has nothing to do with any such high flown objective as an informed electorate. If it did, simple comparison of the number of news viewers then and now would make the issue go away. No, this has more to do with the fact that New Labour's legendary news managers find the move of the news inconvenient. That is why the timetable on the Government's demand is the reinstatement of the *News at Ten* before the next election. Interesting isn't it?

But look, it is not appropriate for any democratic government to believe it can manipulate the schedule of a free broadcaster, especially as it relates to the broadcasting of news.

To be clear, we have no intention of moving the news back to 10 o'clock. People don't want films and dramas interrupted by the news any more. Apparently they *do* want the fantastic range and diversity of new programmes on offer from ITV at 10 o'clock. That's why a million more people are now watching ITV every night at 10. More people in total, more upmarket people, more younger people, more people with university educations. This isn't dumbing down, this is recognising that the viewer is king, that the viewer has a choice, and that a commercial television network that thinks it can thrive with any other agenda than staying connected to the interests and imaginations of that viewer will not survive.

For ITV to continue to stand for something unique and distinctive, both with viewers and with advertisers, it cannot live in the past. The reassuring familiarity of a schedule shape stable for 32 years was a hole beneath the water line that would certainly have been the sinking of ITV had we not dealt with it. I know the politicians don't care about that – but their constituents do.

Richard Eyre (1999) 'Television at the Turn of the Century', CAM/TAS Lecture, 22 November, at Trinity and All Saints University College, Leeds. Eyre was Head of the ITV Network Centre at the time of the lecture although he had just announced his move to the post of Chief Executive, Pearson Television.

3.14 The Americanisation of Children's Television?

Media scholars Jay Blumler and Daniel Biltereyst's survey of children's television programmes broadcast by thirty-nine public service broadcasters in seventeen countries revealed considerable changes. The range and diversity of programming was reducing with an increasing reliance on imported programmes (especially from the USA) and a tendency towards decline in factual programmes accompanied by an increase in animation. Most significantly from a 'policy standpoint' was 'how the broadcaster was financed' with proportions of broadcasters' revenues deriving from advertising and sponsorship correlating positively with a tendency to broadcast more children's programmes, to use less domestically produced programmes and to rely on US imports and animation. Blumler and Biltereyst offer a number of policy prescriptions to halt these trends.

Executive summary

1 European public broadcasters have endeavoured to serve children as all-round developing personalities and future citizens for many years. This meant that they should devote a significant part of their output to children; that such programming should span a broad range of genres, including drama, information, animation and other entertainment; and that they should take account of differences in children's stages of development, offering programmes suited specifically to toddlers as well as children at school and adolescents. In stark contrast, children's programmes in the more market-oriented system of US commercial television have been dominated by entertainment (mainly animated) and geared to the interests of advertisers and toy manufacturers.

2 But today European public television is only one force in a multi-channel framework. Numerous private channels offer different programming menus, competition is keen, budgets are tight, and regulation has receded. Specialist services for children are available day-long in several internationally distributed cable and satellite channels. This study asks whether and how the provision for children of Europe's public broadcasters has been affected by these developments. Do the traditional public service values still apply to it? Or is European public television for children conforming more closely to the US model?

3 In the autumn of 1996, the children's programming departments of all public broadcasters who belong to the European Broadcasting Union were surveyed by post with questions about their policies and provision for the previous year. Twenty-five organisations providing children's programmes on 39 channels in 17 different countries responded. Their replies were co-ordinated with two other sources of data:

(i) from a comparable survey of children's programming in 1991 and 1993;
(ii) with information about the modes of finance and market conditions of the departments' parent broadcasters, available from a Yearbook of the European Audiovisual Observatory.

4 Overall, the findings were mixed. In some respects, public providers of children's television appear to be standing their ground and fighting the good fight for their values. But, in other major respects, their programme output is demonstrably changing. On the one hand, a picture emerges of a programming sector that is impressively supported by fine traditions, dedicated personnel, and much service-inspired production. On the other hand, gripped by the tides of multi-channel expansion, competition, commercialisation and internationalisation, it is drifting away from some of its crucial standards. The forces propelling such drift will not abate in the future. It is therefore urgent that policies be pursued for halting the drift.

5 It is not that a public service philosophy of children's television has been jettisoned. Many responding departments eloquently underlined their crucial public duty and social responsibility towards children when outlining their goals and objectives. Nor had they lost status inside their own broadcasting organisations. They have been trying to adjust to the competition from other television stations. And, strikingly, almost all were hopeful about their future prospects, drawing confidence from the distinctiveness and social value of a principled broadcasting service for children.

6 Nevertheless, the survey shows that the programming offered children by Europe's public broadcasters is being significantly transformed in key respects:

- Much more of it is being provided than in the past – an average increase of 28% in children's output since 1991.
- Much less of the programming is domestically produced and more is imported – an average fall per station from 203 hours of domestic production in 1991 to 177 hours in 1995.
- More of the imported children's programmes came from the United States than from anywhere else, exceeding imports from all the other European countries combined.
- The range of programme types was also narrower than expected. Although programme profiles differed greatly, only about a half of the departments seemed to be providing a fully diversified schedule. In the whole sample, twice as many hours were devoted to animation than to either factual or dramatic programmes.
- Broadcasters who provided an above-average amount of children's programming depended more heavily than the others on animation to fill their schedules.

- Broadcasters who imported an above-average number of children's programmes also depended more heavily than the others on animation and provided fewer factual and dramatic programmes.
- The provision of more children's television is thus a two-edged sword: although it gives children more to view, it diminishes diversity both in genre (more animation) and in origins (more US imports).

7 Hence, a degree of Americanization does seem to be seeping into European public programming for children. Although some features of the full-blown US model are still absent from the European public television scene (e.g. fixed ratings criteria for all children's programmes and near-*carte blanche* for advertisers to target children), certain North American patterns glimmer through many departments' approaches to children: in the intensification of scheduling strategies to build loyalty and habit among young viewers; in reduced diversity and higher proportions of animation; in a growing dependency on US imports. In a few cases, these trends have arguably opened a gap between departments' professed policies and their actual provision.

8 Despite being swept by common trends, European public service television is not a homogeneous category. On almost all matters covered by the survey, there were big differences among the responding organisations – e.g. in the amount of children's programming provided; how it is scheduled; the ages catered for; the range of programming offered; reliance on domestic production; the countries from which imports are drawn.

9 Three distinctions between departments explained many of these differences. One was the *cultural region* in which the broadcaster was located. Those in Nordic Europe conformed most 'purely' to the traditional public service model, while some of the Romance-language stations have almost adopted a commercial model. The *size of the country* served by the broadcaster was also important. With tighter budgets, departments in small countries offered less programming for children, less of it domestically made. Public broadcasters in the larger countries of Britain, France and Germany were better off in children's programming volume as well as amount and share of domestic production, but they also faced keener competition in their markets. Most important from a policy standpoint, however, was *how the broadcaster was financed*. Broadcasters with higher levels of income from advertising and sponsorship tended to show more children's programmes, less domestic material, more US imports and more animation.

10 What are the policy implications? The authors propose the following:

(i) to recognise what is happening, since inattention can only favour more erosion and drift;
(ii) inside public broadcasting organisations, to set concrete targets for programme range and domestic production and to allocate sufficient budgets for children's departments to meet extra scheduling demands without resorting to floods of cheap imports;
(iii) resistance by national policy-makers to any further commercialisation of public broadcasting finance;

(iv) vigilance by civic groups to put pressure on decision-makers in broadcasting, government, and parliaments;
(v) action by European institutions – the European Union, the Council of Europe and the European Broadcasting Union – to support more co-production, cross-border programme exchanges by public service broadcasters, and the firm regulation of television advertising aimed at children;
(vi) full recognition and support by the European Union for the special role of public service broadcasting in the rapidly changing audiovisual environment and the future development of an information society for all;
(vii) Regular monitoring of trends in children's television and release of the results for public discussion.

(pp.5–7)

Jay G. Blumler and Daniel Biltereyst (1998) *The Integrity and Erosion of Public Television For Children: A Pan-European Survey*, London: Broadcasting Standards Commission, 16 February 1998. Research sponsored by the Center for Media Education (Washington DC), the Broadcasting Standards Commission (UK), the European Institute for the Media, and the European Broadcasting Union.

PART FOUR

Television Broadcasting Policy: Regulation

FROM ITS INCEPTION British television broadcasting, founded on the tradition of public service, has been subject to regulation. Such regulation has combined two distinctive but overlapping concerns. First, there has been a concern to regulate programme content. The preoccupation here has been to guarantee programmes' compliance with popular standards of 'taste and decency'. While critics have suggested this is an elusive concept, almost impossible to define with any precision or consensus, regulators have typically assumed their brief is to guard against the gratuitous use of bad language in programming, to offer guidelines and police the presentations of violence in factual (news and current affairs) and creative (drama) programming, and to caution broadcasters to be sensitive and thoughtful in their portrayals of sexual activity in programmes. But as the programme codes of regulatory bodies such as the BBC (4.1 and 4.2), the ITC (4.2) and the Broadcasting Standards Commission (BSC) (4.2 and 4.5) reveal, regulatory concerns are much broader and embrace the need to secure impartiality and fairness in political programmes, sensitivity in portraying children, people with disabilities, members of ethnic minority communities and the need to avoid offence against religious viewpoints. Some of these regulatory requirements enjoy statutory reinforcement. The Representation of the People Act 1969, for example, imposes clear rules and requirements for impartiality on broadcasters during the period immediately prior to a general election.

Certain constituent audiences are judged to be especially vulnerable to programme content and consequently in need of particular consideration by regulators. Children are typically offered as candidates here and, despite the time-shifting possibilities offered by video recorders, the insistence of regulators on the need for broadcasters to strictly observe the 9 o'clock watershed derives much of its force from considerations of children's supposed susceptibility to television messages.

A second concern has been to regulate what are usually termed 'economic issues' arising from broadcasting. The focus here has been to sustain or create a competitive market for broadcasting services, to regulate to prevent monopoly concentrations of media ownership and, especially in the period post-Peacock, to regulate the growing phenomenon of cross-media ownership by media conglomerates. This regulatory concern has not been motivated by an opposition to monopoly *per se*, but the belief that broadcasting monopolies, as in other industrial sectors, might operate in ways which are not always conducive to the public interest. More specifically, in television broadcasting the concern of regulators has been that monopoly structures of ownership might reduce the range and quality of goods and services on offer to consumers; i.e. the range and quality of programmes. This illustrates neatly how the two regulatory foci of programme content and economic issues are perceived to be closely connected by some observers.

These regulatory functions are allocated to different institutions in the public and commercial sectors of broadcasting. At the BBC (see 4.1) the Board of Governors' regulatory responsibilities are set down in the Royal Charter, the Agreement with the Secretary of State for Culture, Media and Sport, which describes the services and standards expected of the BBC and the BBC's Statement of Promises to Viewers and Listeners, which prescribes the BBC's commitments to its audiences. The ITC regulates television services on Channels 3, 4 and 5 as well as cable and domestic satellite services (see 4.2). The BSC Code of Standards, first issued in 1997, applies across all television services (4.2 and 4.5).

Developments in broadcasting technology have often provided the impetus for regulatory change. In the mid-1980s, for example, the emergence of cable and satellite technologies created the prospect of a multi-channel television ecology and prompted considerable developments in regulatory structures. The ITC, a new regulatory body, was established to oversee the emergent and more competitive multi-channel environment with a 'lighter touch'. Again during the late 1990s, the development of digital services, a burgeoning of new television channels and the prospect of media convergence triggered a reappraisal of structures and systems of regulation. One suggestion in the Green Paper *Regulating Communications*, for example, was that media convergence might signal regulation convergence and, following the report of the Select Committee on Culture and Media, that the existing overlapping regulatory bodies might be replaced by a single regulator (see 4.10).

Regulatory trends across the period since the Peacock Report are interesting, not least for the apparent paradox they present to students of media organisation. The broad policy trend since the mid-1980s has been towards the sustained deregulation of media markets. The Peacock Report, the 1988 White Paper *Broadcasting in the '90s* and the Broadcasting Act 1990 each placed the consumer (viewer) at the heart of broadcasting and suggested structures for the development of broadcasting which they intended should oblige broadcasters and producers to give premium priority to the programming wishes of sovereign consumers. There were similar policy prescriptions advocating the introduction of a system of auction for Channel 3 licences, a changed financial base for Channel 4 which made it a competitor for advertising revenues with Channel 3, the introduction of a new terrestrial channel (Channel 5) and encouragement for the development of new satellite and cable services. Each of these measures contributed to the development of an increasingly deregulated and highly competitive market place for television services. The Broadcasting Act 1996 added to this deregulatory impetus by relaxing the rules governing media ownership, while the White Paper *A New Future for Communications* removed the restrictions on the ownership of the two London franchises, paving the way for the emergence of a single owner of the Channel 3 network (4.11).

But this deregulation of the economic structures of media markets has been accompanied, until very recently, by a proliferation of organisations concerned to regulate programme content. The Broadcasting Standards Council, established in May 1988 and Chaired by William Rees-Mogg, was given a specific brief to monitor portrayals of sexual and violent behaviour in programming. The Council joined the regulatory ranks of the Broadcasting Complaints Commission, which since 1981 has adjudicated on individual complaints about unfair treatment and invasion of privacy, as well as the IBA and the BBC Board of Governors: the BCC and BSC received statutory recognition in the Broadcasting Act 1990. This profusion of bodies, with areas of responsibility which occasionally overlapped but typically generated contradictory judgements concerning what constituted 'taste and decency', increasingly attracted opprobrium from broadcasters, politicians and the general public. Regulation smacked of the 'Nanny State' at a time when the mood politically – and among policy makers in television broadcasting – favoured free markets and consumer choice. The Broadcasting Act 1996 amalgamated the BSC and BCC into a new single body: the Broadcasting Standards Commission. But by 1998 when the Department of Culture, Media and Sport published *Regulating Communications*, responsibility for regulating different aspects of media operations and structures was still distributed among a wide range of organisations including the BBC, BSC, ITC, OFTEL, OFT and the DTI. Perhaps not surprisingly, Chris Smith, Secretary of State for Culture, Media and Sport, in a speech to the Royal Television Society in September 1999, announced that part of his 'vision' for digital broadcasting was 'a future where broadcasting regulation is based in the first instance on competition law' and where it would prove possible to 'rationalise the various regulators to avoid duplication and confusion'(see 4.16). On 12 December 2000, the White Paper *A New Future for Communications* announced the realisation of this 'vision' by proposing the creation of a single, powerful new regulatory body OFCOM, which would incorporate its predecessors and, for the first time, exercise some regulatory functions over the BBC (4.6 and 4.18).

The extracts in this section are grouped under three headings examining, in turn: the various regulatory institutions and codes of practice designed to regulate programme content; a number of oppositional contributions to the debate on the desirability of regulating patterns of media ownership, and finally, issues with regulatory salience arising from the development of digital broadcasting technologies.

PROGRAMME CONTENT

4.1 Regulating the BBC

The Governors, the Public and Accountability

The BBC is regulated by a Board of Governors which is appointed by the government and entrusted to defend the independence of the BBC from outside pressures, both political and economic. But they also serve as 'trustees to the public to ensure that the BBC's programme services maintain standards of excellence, offer value for money and reflect the needs of the audience' (*Future of the BBC*, 2nd Report, 1993, Vol. 1, p.xvii). The Board appoints the Director-General who in turn recruits a senior management team; the latter's responsibility is for the day-to-day running of the BBC and the production and broadcasting of programmes. The governors have a distinct role. They oversee the managers, ensuring that programming conforms to Charter specifications and represents the public interest (*The Future of the BBC*, Cmnd 2098, 1992, p.38). The Governors' role is clearly set out in the most recent Charter. 'It shall be the function of the Governors' it states,

> to exercise the powers and discharge the duties of the Corporation in accordance with this our Charter and in particular . . . approve clear objectives and promises for the Corporation's services, programmes and other activities and monitor how far the Corporation has attained such objectives and met its pledges to its audiences . . . and determine the strategy of the Corporation in respect of the Home services in the manner which they consider best calculated to ensure that the Corporation's services, programmes and other activities reflect the needs and interests of the public.
>
> (BBC Royal Charter, 1996, Article 7 (1))

Governing Today's BBC was an attempt by the BBC to clarify the Governors' role and distinguish it from the activities of managers.

The BBC's unique public obligations are defined in three main documents:

- *the Royal Charter* outlines the BBC's purpose and defines its constitution
- *the Agreement* between the BBC and the Secretary of State for Culture, Media and Sport accompanies the Charter and describes the services and standards expected of the BBC
- *the BBC's Statement of Promises to Viewers and Listeners* which is required under the terms of the Charter and Agreement sets out in detail the BBC's commitment to its audiences.

In addition, the BBC is subject to a number of statutory obligations, such as the requirement to publish findings of the Broadcasting Standards Commission as directed and to commission 25% of non-news television programmes from independent producers.

The Royal Charter

The BBC has been established and governed by successive Royal Charters since 1926.

The current Charter, granted in May 1996 for a ten year term ending on 31 December 2006, sets out the role of the Governors with greater precision than previous Charters have done. It firmly establishes the Governors as regulators of the BBC and trustees for the public interest.

The Charter outlines a number of specific functions. The Governors must:

- determine strategy for the licence fee-funded services broadcast to United Kingdom audiences to reflect the needs and interests of the public
- determine the strategy of the World Service in respect of broadcasts to overseas audiences in languages approved by the Foreign Office
- determine strategy for the BBC's commercial services and ensure that these are funded, operated and accounted for separately from the public services
- approve objectives and promises for BBC services, and monitor how well these are met
- ensure that BBC activities are carried out in accordance with:
    - any agreement made with the government, e.g. conditions imposed for new services
    - the BBC's fair trading commitments
    - the highest standards of probity and propriety
    - the need to provide value for money
- consult National Broadcasting Councils about services in Scotland, Wales and Northern Ireland and give due consideration to the Councils' views
- ensure that comments and complaints by viewers of, and listeners to, the licence fee-funded services are properly considered
- ensure that the BBC fulfils its legal and contractual obligations particularly in relation to impartiality and standards of taste and decency and that it complies with any directions given by the Broadcasting Standards Commission

- maintain an Audit Committee
- appoint the Director-General and, with him, appoint the rest of the Board of Management and certain other key managers.

National Broadcasting Councils

The 1996 Charter also establishes a clear role for the three National Broadcasting Councils chaired respectively by the National Governor for Scotland, Wales or Northern Ireland. These Councils are to be consulted by the Governors about services for relevant audiences.

In particular, it is the duty of the Councils to:

- keep in touch with public opinion
- offer advice to Governors on the extent to which BBC objectives reflect the needs of audiences and the extent to which those objectives are met
- offer advice on those objectives which relate specifically to Scotland, Wales or Northern Ireland, on the way the budget for local programmes genres is allocated and on any proposal to make significant changes to the local resource base
- offer advice on the contribution to network programming from Scotland, Wales or Northern Ireland.

Annual Report

The Charter requires the BBC to publish an Annual Report which includes the Corporation's audited accounts. The Chairman must submit this to the Secretary of State for presentation to Parliament.

The Agreement

The Agreement between the Secretary of State for Culture, Media and Sport and the BBC recognises the BBC's independence in relation to the content and scheduling of its programmes and the management of its affairs, but specifies the services and standards required of the BBC.

The BBC undertakes to maintain high general standards in programming and to offer a wide range of programmes providing information, education and entertainment in the licence fee-funded services. This includes programmes that stimulate and reflect the UK's diverse cultural activity; comprehensive, authoritative and impartial coverage of news; and high standard, original programmes for children and young people.

The Agreement also requires the BBC to make an annual Statement of Promises available to all licence payers, and to consult the public before making any material changes to the nature of the licence fee-funded services.

On programme standards, the BBC agrees to cover a wide range of subjects, to serve the tastes and needs of different audiences, not to offend against good taste and decency, to treat controversial subjects with due accuracy and impartiality and to draw up a code giving guidance to programme makers on impartiality.

The BBC is required by the Agreement to publish objectives for the licence fee-funded services and to report in detail on the BBC's performance in the Annual Report. This must show:

- how far programme standards and objectives have been met
- how audiences have been consulted
- how complaints have been handled
- how far the BBC has complied with statutory and regulatory requirements
- an analysis of the hours and costs of different types of programmes and of programmes made in different parts of the UK
- how far BBC services represent value for money
- the BBC's financial performance.

In the World Service, the Agreement requires the BBC to broadcast programmes in languages approved by the Foreign and Commonwealth Office, to consult with the FCO over long-term objectives and to maintain high programme standards.

The Statement of Promises to Viewers and Listeners

In addition to the Royal Charter and Agreement, a third document sets out the BBC's obligations to the public. This is the Statement of Promises to Viewers and Listeners, published by the BBC for the first time in the autumn of 1996 after wide public consultation, and revised each year. It represents a firm commitment by the BBC to its audiences. The Statement sets out in detail:

- what the BBC will provide on its television and radio channels and its national, regional and local services
- the standards of fairness, accuracy and impartiality for which the BBC aims
- how the BBC aims to provide value for money
- how the BBC aims to make its services more accessible to disabled viewers and listeners
- how the BBC aims to be accountable and responsive to its audiences
- specific promises relating to programme genres and issues that particularly concern audiences.

BBC (1997) *Governing Today's BBC: Broadcasting, the Public Interest and Accountability*, London: BBC, December.

4.2 The BBC's *Producers' Guidelines*, the ITC Programme Code and the BSC's Code of Conduct

Producers' Guidelines

In 1993 the BBC published an updated edition of *Producers' Guidelines*, a 'code of practice' or 'handbook' for programme makers, which was distributed to all editorial staff. In the introduction, John Birt claimed that the *Guidelines* embodied 'the editorial and ethical principles which drive the BBC'. In 1997, the latest version of the *Guidelines*, containing thirty-seven sections, offered broadcasters advice on the scheduling of sensitive material, upholding standards of accuracy, impartiality and depth of inquiry, as well as sensitivity in reporting traumatic events, the inclusion of children in programming and the reporting of Northern Ireland.

BBC *Producers' Guidelines* (1997) London: BBC, also available at bbc.co.uk

The ITC Programme Code

The ITC was charged by the Broadcasting Act 1990 with regulating commercially funded television services with a 'lighter touch'. Unlike its predecessor the Independent Broadcasting Authority (IBA), the ITC does not enjoy the opportunity to approve programme schedules in advance. But the 1990 Act empowers the ITC to award Channel 3 licences only to those contractors who meet a fairly stiff set of programming requirements: the 'quality threshold' (see 4.3 below). Regulation of content is therefore 'built in' to the structure of Channel 3 broadcasting and the need to 'leap' this quality threshold in combination with the ITC *Programme Code* and the Commission's appraisal of each of the Channel 3 services (see number for annual review in programme quality), which is published in its *Annual Performance Review*, establishes a comprehensive system of regulation. The Programme Code includes guidelines for broadcasters concerning subjects such as taste and decency, including sexual portrayal, violence, privacy, impartiality and advice for broadcasters to avoid giving undue prominence to commercial products in programming (product placement). The ITC has a wide range of powers to enforce the Code. Cases involving a minor breach are resolved via discussion between the service provider and regulator, but more serious breaches may involve a formal warning, an on-screen correction or apology or the imposition of a fine. In the most extreme cases, the ITC can shorten the term of a licence or even 'pull the plug'. The ITC also regulates with a broader remit to ensure quality and diversity are maintained on Channels 3, 4 and

5 and the Public Teletext Service and that, taken as a whole, television services appeal to a range of tastes and interests.

ITC website http://www.itc.org.uk

The BSC's Code of Conduct

The Broadcasting Act 1996 established the Broadcasting Standards Commission (BSComm) and required it to draft, implement and consider complaints arising from a code of practice for broadcasters (Broadcasting Act 1996, Sects 106–130). The Code on Fairness and Privacy was published in November 1997 but effective from 1 January 1998. The Code on Standards was largely derived from the Code of the former Broadcasting Standards Council but updated, following consultation with broadcasters and other interested parties. Revisions were also made to reflect and incorporate research findings, trends identified, the consideration of complaints and the Commission's Roadshows.

BSC *Codes of Conduct* available at http://www.bsc

4.3 Beechers Brook, Regulation and the Broadcasting Act 1990

Regulation of television services in the commercial sector, since the Broadcasting Act 1990, has been the responsibility of the ITC. The Act changed the relationship between the regulator of the independent television sector and the commercial television companies. The Act specified that the ITC could award a franchise only to companies which agreed to comply with certain programming requirements which were very clearly specified in the Act: the ITC would conduct an annual review to ensure companies' continuing compliance with these requirements. The programming conditions, which were judged to be much more demanding than had been anticipated, were designed to placate contemporary concerns that a competitive market in broadcasting might prompt a reduction in quality and range of programming: they were described by the then Minister responsible for broadcasting as a 'veritable Beechers Brook' of regulation.

16. (1) Where a person has made an application for a Channel 3 licence in accordance with section 15, the Commission shall not proceed to consider whether to award him the licence on the basis of his cash bid in accordance with section 17 unless it appears to them –

(a) that his proposed service would comply with the requirements specified in subsection (2) or (3) below (as the case may be), and
(b) that he would be able to maintain that service throughout the period for which the licence would be in force . . .

(2) Where the service to be provided under the licence is a regional Channel 3 service, the requirements referred to in subsection (1)(a) are –

(a) that a sufficient amount of time is given in the programmes included in the service to news programmes and current affairs programmes which (in each case) are of high quality and deal with both national and international matters, and that such news programmes are broadcast at intervals throughout the period for which the service is provided and, in particular, at peak viewing times;
(b) that a sufficient amount of time is given in the programmes included in the service to programmes (other than news and current affairs programmes) which are of high quality;
(c) that a sufficient amount of time is given in the programmes so included –
    (i) to a suitable range of regional programmes, that is to say, programmes (including news programmes) which are of particular interest to persons living within the area for which the service is provided, and
    (ii) if the service is to include the provision of such programmes as are mentioned in section 14(3), to a suitable range of programmes for each of the different parts of that area or (as the case may be) for each of the different communities living within it, being in each case a range of programmes (including news programmes) which are of particular interest to persons living within the relevant part of that area or (as the case may be) the relevant community,

    and that any news programmes so included in accordance with sub-paragraph (i) or (ii) are of high quality;
(d) that a suitable proportion of the regional programmes included in the service in accordance with paragraph (c) are made within the area for which it is to be provided;
(e) that a sufficient amount of time is given in the programmes included in the service to religious programmes and programmes intended for children;
(f) that (taken as a whole) the programmes so included are calculated to appeal to a wide variety of tastes and interests;
(g) that a proper proportion of the matter included in those programmes is of European origin; and
(h) that in each year not less than 25 per cent of the total amount of time allocated to the broadcasting of qualifying programmes in the service is allocated to the broadcasting of a range and diversity of independent productions.

(3) Where the service to be provided under the licence is a national Channel 3 service, the requirements referred to in subsection (1)(a) are such (if any) of the requirements specified in subsection (2) as the Commission may determine to be appropriate having regard to the nature of that service.

Broadcasting Act 1990, London: HMSO.

4.4 Regulating for Regional Programming

The Campaign for Quality Television argued that one of the great strengths of the independent television sector has been the development of original regional programming. Television companies' commitment to producing programmes within the region, exploring facets of regional culture and life, has been a major factor in generating programme diversity. These programmes have diminished, however, since the Broadcasting Act 1990. The CQT suggests that ITV companies should no longer be required to make regional programmes but should be levied to finance the production of such programmes from other providers.

The public service element of ITV expressed most clearly in the quality and positioning of its news, documentaries, current affairs, arts and religious programming, has been a matter of decline and controversy since the passage of the 1990 Broadcasting Act. But, partly because of its inter-relationship with other channels, partly because of its own intrinsic worth, it is important that the licensees be required to meet those commitments and to do so more positively. With the prospect of reductions in their licence payments and company amalgamations producing dramatic cost cutting, the companies are comfortably placed to meet such an enhanced requirement, particularly if the nature of the competition they face from other commercial broadcasters were made more equal, as suggested earlier in the paper.

In one area of the [ITV] companies' public service obligations, however, we propose a more radical solution. The *Campaign* believes that one of the most important innovations in British television brought about by the creation of an Independent Television sector has been the development of regional programming on a scale which the BBC has not attempted to match. The existence of a number of well equipped regional studio centres led to the production of numerous major programmes exploiting regional themes and talent for national audiences, enriching the programme mix on ITV and making contributions also to Channel 4. There has, however, been growing concern, since the passage of the 1990 Act, that the ITV companies have fulfilled their regional programming responsibilities with growing reluctance. Their lack of enthusiasm may be attributed to the low financial returns derived from relatively expensive regional programmes and also to the amalgamation of companies leading to their centralisation in London.

Paradoxically, the decline in regional programming has gathered momentum at a time when, nationally, the Government has been promoting ideas of devolution and greater diversity. The Campaign believes that any acceleration in the decline would lead to a diminution in the range of material currently offered by British television to its audiences. It would be accelerated still further if ITV were put in the hands of a single company whose overwhelming superiority in the field of advertising has hitherto been seen as a decisive argument against its creation. While there is now greater competition for advertising revenue in British television than before, the scale of a single company would allow it to dominate the field for a long period to come.

One solution, already canvassed in the Press and discussed privately among the ITV companies, is that the requirement to produce regional programmes should be removed, saving production costs and freeing programme slots for more lucrative forms of programming. In return companies would be levied to fund the provision of regional programming from alternative sources.

Future possibilities can be identified for introducing such a change, the earliest of them occurring before the end of 1998 when digital broadcasting runs in parallel with analogue. Although the time scale makes this possibility highly remote, there may be available up to twenty digital channels with restricted coverage while all the main channels will begin to duplicate their services through the six newly created digital multiplexes. The second opportunity arises when, say, ten years ahead, the sale of digital receivers allows analogue transmissions to be terminated, releasing a great deal of spectrum for an untold number of channels. Another opportunity comes whenever the moment for analogue switch-off occurs. Part of the analogue spectrum could be reserved by the Government for a regional service, of a new, more diverse, kind, catering for more homogeneous communities than is currently possible. Evidence of the public's interest in more localised broadcasting can be found in the closer relationships existing between the smaller ITV companies and their audiences, the popularity of local radio, and the increasing take-up of Restricted Service Licences.

The Campaign believes that only with regulatory support of one kind or another can the future of regional programming, an important element in public service broadcasting, be safeguarded.

The Campaign for Quality Television (1998) *The Purposes of Broadcasting*, London: CQT, pp.21–25.

4.5 The Broadcasting Standards Commission

As well as the BBC Governors and the ITC, two further regulatory bodies, with a brief which embraced both the commercial and public sectors, received statutory recognition in the Broadcasting Act 1990. The Broadcasting Complaints Commission (BCC) was initially established in 1981 to receive and consider complaints from individuals who believed they had been treated unfairly or suffered unwarranted intrusion of their privacy in a broadcast programme (Broadcasting Act 1990, Sects 142–150). The Broadcasting Standards Council (BSC), established controversially under the Chairmanship of Lord Rees-Mogg in May 1988, was to construct a code of conduct for broadcasters which offered guidance concerning portrayals of sex and violence and matters of taste and decency. Many broadcasters resented what they judged to be an unnecessary intrusion into their professional practice. The remit of these four television watchdogs occasionally overlapped, although they did not always concur in their judgements. The 1994 White Paper *The Future of the BBC: Serving the Nation, Competing World Wide* suggested a new organisation to replace the BCC and

BSC. The Broadcasting Act 1996 established the Broadcasting Standards Commission (BSComm) and gave the new Commission a statutory remit to draft, implement and consider complaints arising from a code of practice for broadcasters (Broadcasting Act 1996, sects 106–130).

107. (1) It shall be the duty of the Broadcasting Standards Commission to draw up, and from time to time review, a code giving guidance as to principles to be observed, and practices to be followed, in connection with the avoidance of –

(a) unjust or unfair treatment in programmes to which this section applies, or
(b) unwarranted infringement of privacy in, or in connection with the obtaining of material included in, such programmes.

(2) It shall be the duty of each broadcasting or regulatory body, when drawing up or revising any code relating to principles and practice in connection with programmes, or in connection with the obtaining of material to be included in programmes, to reflect the general effect of so much of the code referred to in subsection (1) (as for the time being in force) as is relevant to the programmes in question.

108. (1) It shall be the duty of the Broadcasting Standards Commission to draw up, and from time to time review, a code giving guidance as to –

(a) practices to be followed in connection with the portrayal of violence in programmes to which this section applies,
(b) practices to be followed in connection with the portrayal of sexual conduct in such programmes, and
(c) standards of taste and decency for such programmes generally.

109. (1) It shall be the duty of the BSC to monitor programmes to which section 108 applies with a view to enabling the BSC to make reports on the portrayal of violence and sexual conduct, and the standards of taste and decency attained by, such programmes generally . . .

110. (10) Subject to the provisions of this part, it shall be the duty of the BSC to consider and adjudicate on complaints which are made to them in accordance with sections 111 and 114 . . .

111. (1) A fairness complaint may be made by an individual or by a body of persons . . . but . . . shall not be considered by the BSC unless made by the person affected or by a person authorised by him to make the complaint for him.

112. The BSC shall appoint a committee, consisting of members of the BSC to discharge the functions of the BSC in relation to the consideration of fairness complaints . . .

114. (1) A fairness complaint or a standards complaint must be in writing . . .

116. (1) . . . every standards complaints made to the BSC shall be considered by them with or without a hearing or, if they think fit, at a hearing (and any such hearing shall be held in private unless the BSC decide otherwise).

The Broadcasting Act 1996, London: HMSO.

4.6 Regulating Public Service Broadcasting in the Digital Age

The White Paper *A New Future For Communications* argued for a continuing 'key' role for public service broadcasting in the multi-channel digital age, but suggested the need for changes in the way that public service broadcasting is regulated (see PSB). The White Paper proposed a new three-tier structure of regulation with a minimum or basic tier for all television services 'topped up' with further regulatory requirements for public service broadcasters at the other two levels or tiers. Widely anticipated changes to the regulatory role of the BBC Governors were not realised in the White Paper.

5.4.1 The reasons for public service broadcasting remain the same, but the challenges it faces are new. We need a different way of regulating public service broadcasting to achieve those goals . . .

5.4.3 The Government . . . accepts that the detailed, prescriptive requirements – often dubbed 'box ticking' – which are contained in present licences may inhibit creative innovation, and thus harm both the public interest and the commercial success of companies.

5.5.1 Our aim is to make the current system of broadcasting regulation clear and consistent by identifying three tiers of regulation. Each tier of obligation requires a different type of regulation.

5.5.2 A basic level of obligations will continue to apply to all broadcasters, including the impartiality and accuracy of news, ensuring fairness and the protection of privacy, preventing harmful content and giving access to programming for those with disabilities; and all broadcasters will continue to be subject to the Competition Act regime. For public service broadcasters, and for commercial terrestrial radio, there will continue to be additional requirements. While the level of public service sought from different broadcasters will, as now, vary between them, we want to achieve greater fairness in their regulation. At the same time we want to increase the extent to which they can regulate themselves in line with general public duties.

5.6 First tier

5.6.1 In the first tier, all broadcasters would be subject to:

- any relevant underpinning codes establishing negative minimum content standards set by OFCOM;
- rules on advertising and sponsorship;
- the provision of fair, impartial and accurate news;
- EC quotas (which apply to all television broadcasters) such as those on European and independent production . . .
- any other industry-wide requirements that exist or might be introduced

5.6.4 OFCOM would develop overarching codes applying these first tier minimum standards to services it licenses. These would also apply to the BBC, although regulation of the impartiality requirements would, in the case of the BBC, remain with the Board of Governors . . .

5.6.6 The second and third tiers would apply to all the public service broadcasters. Given their universal accessibility, and their access to terrestrial spectrum, and the licence fee in the case of the BBC, these public service broadcasters will be required by statute, or Charter in the case of the BBC, to provide a range of high quality public broadcast services. Thus the particular remits of BBC, S4C, ITV, Channel 4 and Channel 5 will be given expression in these tiers.

5.6.7 We are not proposing to change the BBC's role and remit. We are maintaining the link between the legal responsibility and authority of the BBC Governors for delivering the BBC's remit and will preserve their following core responsibilities inside the BBC:

- interpreting the Charter and setting the strategy to deliver the BBC's remit and responsibilities;
- upholding and protecting the BBC's political and editorial independence;
- assessing the BBC's performance against remit and objectives;
- calling management to account.

5.6.8 We will also maintain Channel 4 as a public service broadcaster with a remit which provides both complementarity and competition to the BBC and the ITV companies. We reject proposals to privatise Channel 4 and will maintain Channel 4's present structure of a non-profit making statutory corporation, but we will review the Channel's remit both to make it more positive and also to ensure that it continues to provide distinctive and innovative programming in the future.

5.6.9 The ITV companies have significant public service obligations and the Government agrees with most consultation responses, including from the ITV companies themselves, that they should continue to have a key role in delivering public service broadcasting. We consider this should persist up to, and beyond, digital switchover, but with less prescriptive regulation. Obligations will focus on the core requirements: a strong regional focus including regional production and commissioning, a diverse, high quality schedule including news and current affairs and original production, educational programmes, children's programmes, religious programmes and coverage of arts, science and international issues.

5.6.10 We acknowledge that, as digital television develops, it is possible that the competitive pressure on ITV's advertising revenue may increase and reduce its ability to deliver all the current public service broadcasting obligations in the same way as at present. The new regulatory framework will leave flexibility to review the means of delivering public service obligations after digital switchover.

5.6.11 Channel 5's public service broadcasting obligations are lighter. Unlike ITV and Channel 4, Channel 5 does not have universal terrestrial coverage. There is also increasing choice of more popular programming from cable and satellite platforms. We propose, therefore, to review all public service broadcasting requirements on Channel 5, with the aim of making the channel a far stronger competitor to the other public service broadcasting channels.

5.7 Second tier

5.7.1 In the second tier, OFCOM will be responsible for ensuring the delivery of those public service obligations which are easily quantifiable and measurable. Our preliminary thinking is that these will be confined to compliance with quotas for independent productions and original productions, targets for regional productions and regional programming and the fact of the availability of news and current affairs in peak time. The BBC is not currently subject to a requirement to provide news and current affairs in peak time, but the agreement between the Government and the BBC is to be changed to introduce such a requirement for the first time.

5.7.2 The level of requirements regulated at this level will not be the same for all – for example, Channel 5 will not be expected to comply with the requirements for regional production. The requirements to be regulated at each level for each of these broadcasters will be set out in statute.

5.8 Third tier

5.8.1 The general qualitative public service remit of broadcasters is less easy to quantify, without tipping back into box-ticking. We will maintain those high level obligations as statutory or, in the case of the BBC, Charter requirements, but give the public service broadcasters an opportunity to demonstrate that they can be better delivered and monitored through self-regulation.

5.8.2 . . . The BBC, S4C, Channel 4, ITV and Channel 5 will continue to be required to produce a mixed and high quality range of programmes, variously including educational material, children's programmes, religious programmes and coverage of arts, science and international issues. The BBC is also required to ensure that the Home Services contain programmes that stimulate, support and reflect, in factual programmes, drama, comedy, music and the visual and performing arts and the diversity of cultural activity in the UK.

5.8.3 However, it will principally be for the boards of each of the broadcasters to ensure that these remits are delivered. There will be a requirement for the public service broadcasters to develop statements of programme policy and self-regulatory mechanisms in order to give confidence that this new system will be effective. These statements, setting out in some detail the way in which broadcasters' remits will be implemented, will need to be updated each year.

5.8.4 Each broadcaster will be required to report annually on how they have delivered their programme statements, and to set out how they intend to operate for the year ahead.

DTI and DCMS (2000) *A New Future For Communications* London: HMSO, Cm 5010, Sections 5.4.1–5.8.4.

MEDIA OWNERSHIP

4.7 A Bill to Regulate for Media Diversity

Historically the regulation of television has involved not only the contents of programmes, especially where they might offend standards of public taste and decency, but also the economic structures of media ownership where the latter might impact on the quality of programmes. Chris Mullin's Private Members Bill argued for new regulatory measures to control the increasing concentration of media ownership and the trend towards cross-media ownership. Both, he believed, were eroding the editorial independence of news media, producing a 'marked decline in standards' with a reduction in the provision of news and current affairs, and the 'trivialisation' of British culture. The Bill proposed regulation to guarantee diversity of media ownership, quality and pluralism in media output and a level competitive playing field both for commercial terrestrial and satellite broadcasters.

Mr. Chris Mullin (Sunderland, South):

I beg to move,

That leave be given to bring in a Bill to regulate the ownership of the media.

My Bill will reverse the growing trend towards monopoly ownership of the most of what we see on our television screens and read in our newspapers. The purpose of the Bill is to protect our culture and democracy from the barbarism of the unregulated market. I hope that it will appeal to democrats of all political persuasions. I am glad to say that it has attracted support from hon. Members on both sides of the House.

Although our television has always been carefully regulated, it has long been the situation that many of our national and regional newspapers are controlled by unscrupulous megalomaniacs. Now, the same people are taking control of our television. Rupert Murdoch, who owns five national newspapers, also has what is effectively a controlling interest in satellite television, which, we are told, will be in one home in two by the end of the century. Michael Green, of Carlton, has acquired Central Television, and with it a 36 per cent stake in Independent Television News and a similar stake in Independent Radio News. Granada Television, headed by a ruthless profiteer, Mr Gerry Robinson, has acquired London Weekend Television and with it a 36 per cent stake in ITN, all in defiance of section 32 of the Broadcasting Act 1990, which says that no shareholding in ITN may exceed 20 per cent, precisely with a view to preserving its independence.

Every day, the frontiers that regulate the independence and quality of our television are pushed back a little further. The Government are under enormous pressure to remove what restrictions remain and to let the market rip. And not only the government. Seeing the possibility of a Labour victory at the next election, a massive bout of free-lunching has been unleashed by the vested interests concerned, and its purpose is to persuade my right hon. and hon. Friends charged with responsibility in these matters that big is beautiful, that the triumph of the market is inevitable and that it will not diminish the quality of the product. One of the purposes of the Bill is to stiffen the resolve of my hon. Friends.

The rise of Messrs. Murdoch, Green, Robinson and others has already led to a marked decline in standards. Documentaries such as *This Week* have disappeared. *World in Action*, one of the last refuges for inquiring journalism has been under heavy pressure. Even ITN's *News at Ten* is not safe as the new masters press for its removal to a more obscure slot, to make way for an unending diet of bland American movies. Already there has been an obvious decline in quality at ITN, a reluctance to invest in foreign reporting, and an increasing tendency to conduct long and pointless live interviews between an anchorman in Grays Inn road and a correspondent rarely more than two or three miles away. The other day on ITN there was a lengthy item on Kermit the frog.

There is talk of new technology bringing in 20, 30 or 40 channels. It is said that we will have more choice, but in fact we will have less. We are headed down the American road – 40 channels with nothing worth watching on any of them and our culture colonised by American junk television. Our domestic television production capacity will be wiped out, just as our film industry has been. Indeed, it is already happening. Industry is being remorselessly casualised. Since the Broadcasting Act, the number of full-time jobs in commercial television has halved. Who will provide the training for future generations of television film makers when the present generation is gone? Or are the new masters just intending to poach from the BBC?

What I fear most is not political bias, but the steady growth of junk journalism – the trivialisation and demeaning of everything that is important in our lives, and its consequent effect on our culture, a flat refusal to address what is going on in the world in favour of an endless diet of crime, game shows and soap operas, and the unadulterated hate that is already a feature of our most loathsome tabloid newspapers. In the long run, there is danger – I put it no higher – that, with an increasing concentration of ownership and progressive abandonment of standards, television will become fertile ground for demagogues, offering simple solutions to complex problems. One has only to look at the rise of the religious right in America, or to Italy – governed until recently by a man who owns three major television stations – for a clue as to where the future may lie.

My Bill has three principal purposes. First, it seeks to enforce diversity of newspaper and television ownership in the belief that healthy competition rather than monopoly is the best way to ensure the survival of our democracy.

Secondly, the Bill seeks to provide for a minimum level of quality in the firm belief that that is the best way to protect our television from the rise of junk culture.

Thirdly, the Bill seeks to create a level playing field between commercial and satellite television. At the moment satellite television is exempt from many of the regulations that apply to terrestrial television.

I shall list some of the specific measures contained in the Bill. First, there is a requirement that no national newspaper proprietor shall be permitted to own more than one daily or one Sunday newspaper. Surplus assets must be placed on the market within 12 months of the Bill being enacted.

Secondly, no one who is not a citizen of the European Community shall in future be permitted to own more than 20 per cent of any company owning British national or regional newspapers or British terrestrial or satellite television. That provision is based on similar regulations that already apply in the United States.

Thirdly, no company which has a controlling interest in a British national newspaper shall be permitted to own a stake of more than 20 per cent in a British television company, terrestrial or satellite.

Fourthly, no company that has a controlling interest in either terrestrial or satellite television broadcasting to the United Kingdom shall be permitted to own more than 20 per cent of a British national newspaper.

Fifthly, a given percentage of the output of any television company, satellite or terrestrial, broadcasting to the United Kingdom, shall be produced within the EC. That will extend to satellite television a provision which is already enforced on terrestrial stations.

Sixthly, no company shall be permitted to own more than 20 per cent of ITN, IRN or any other national broadcast news service and that any surplus should be disposed of within 12 months of the Act coming into force.

Seventhly, no company with a controlling interest in any local television or radio station or in any local newspaper shall be permitted to own more than 20 per cent of any other media outlet covering the same catchment area.

Eighthly, no company shall be allowed to own more than 20 per cent of the encryption system for satellite television and any surplus shall be placed on the market within 12 months. Hon. Members will be aware that at present Mr Murdoch has a monopoly of the encryption system which prevents anyone else from gaining access to the satellite market.

Ninthly, substantial regional commercial television production facilities must be maintained in at least the six largest population centres outside London.

Tenthly, a training levy will be imposed on any television company employing more than 100 people which does not spend a given percentage of its income on training.

Those measures should appeal to civilised people of all political persuasions. They are, as I have said, designed to protect our democracy and culture from the barbarism of the unregulated market. In many respects they merely enshrine or build upon regulations that already exist. Overall they will have the effect of introducing competition into areas where fair competition is being progressively stifled or eliminated.

We should not be afraid of regulation. Our broadcasting system has been carefully regulated throughout its existence and, as a result, it is widely admired around the world. I am anxious that it should remain so and that is the purpose of the Bill. I commend it to the House.

Hansard (1995) 11 January, cols 153–155.

4.8 Media Ownership

The Government's View

During the early 1990s, politicians like Chris Mullin (4.7) and interest groups such as the Campaign for Press and Broadcasting Freedom (4.9), were arguing that the growing concentration of media ownership and cross-media control by conglomerate owners were diminishing programme diversity and restricting viewers' choices. By contrast, commercial broadcasters and some Conservative politicians were suggesting that the only policy to secure the survival of UK television in an increasingly global market was to deregulate further the domestic television market place and encourage mergers guided by the broad (but often implicit) assumption that 'big is beautiful'. In May 1995 the Department of National Heritage published the Green Paper *Media Ownership: The Government's Proposals* (Cm 2872), which offered a two-stage approach to liberalising media ownership in a way which sustained media diversity but allowed British companies to flourish in conditions of rapid technological and market change. The first stage changed regulatory rules for radio ownership and was to be completed within a month. The second phase was to be the subject of legislation (The Broadcasting Act 1996) which would: allow newspapers with less than 20 per cent of the market to own two terrestrial television channels; forbid any single company from owning more than 10 per cent of the total media market or 20 per cent of any media sector; create an independent regulator to govern media ownership; plan for longer term changes to media regulation using a new measure of the total media market calculated either by measuring audience, circulation or revenue. The ITC will regulate future mergers between television and newspaper companies balancing three public interest criteria. The Commission will seek to promote diversity; maintain an economically viable industry, and ensure competition.

The Government's proposals

6.1 The Government believes that the existing structure of media ownership regulation, relying as it does on prohibitions which reinforce the traditional segmentation of the media market, is insufficiently flexible to allow media companies to exploit to the full the opportunities offered by the new technologies, particularly in view of the expansion of media services which will follow the introduction of digital broadcasting. The Government recognises that these technologies are making the traditional segmentation of the market increasingly anachronistic and that media businesses need to be able to regard the provision of media services as a single activity. This Government therefore believes that media ownership regulation needs to evolve to reflect these changes in the shape of the industry. The Government also believes, however, that the substitution of the existing structure by an entire new framework of rules that looks across the media market place as a whole, must be based on a full consultation process and widespread acceptance that the new structure is effective and fair.

6.2 The Government has decided to take its proposals forward in two stages . . .

6.3 Both stages involve some measurement of market share in the different media sectors. Public service broadcasters will be included in market share calculations, so that the complete market is addressed, but will be excluded from regulation because the Government already has direct control over their ownership. Joint ventures between public service broadcasters and private companies will, however, be included.

A new regulatory structure: the longer term proposal for consultation

6.6 The proposed new approach would build upon the Government's experience of regulating the concentration of market power elsewhere in the economy. It would:

- establish an independent regulator with specific powers to govern media ownership;
- define media markets and establish their overall size through the measurement of audience or revenue share;
- express the value of shares in one media sector in terms of shares in another. The weightings used could be based upon the relative influence or market power of different media;
- determine thresholds of ownership in the national, sectoral and regional/local media markets beyond which acquisitions would have to be referred to the media regulator; and
- provide a set of public interest criteria against which the regulator would have to assess existing holdings above the thresholds, as well as any proposals for merger or acquisition which brought holdings above them.

Summary

2. . . . the Government believes that a number of changes should now be made in order to preserve the diversity of the broadcast and press media in the UK, whilst introducing greater flexibility in ownership to reflect the needs and aspirations of the industry, against a background of accelerating technological change, including the introduction of digital broadcasting.

3. The Government has decided:

- that there is a continuing case for specific regulations governing media ownership, beyond those which are applied by the general competition law; but
- that there is a need to liberalise the existing ownership regulations both within and across different media sectors.

4. At the earliest legislative opportunity, the Government will enact primary legislation which will, inter alia:

- allow newspaper groups with less than 20% of national newspaper circulation to apply to control television broadcasters constituting up to 15% of the total television market (defined by audience share including public sector broadcasters), subject to a limit of two Channel 3/5 licences; and to apply to control radio licences constituting up to 15% of the radio points system;
- give to the relevant regulator the power to disallow such control where it is not in the public interest;
- prevent the development of local media monopolies by disallowing such newspaper groups to apply to control any regional Channel 3 licence or local radio licence in areas where the newspaper group has more than 30% of regional or local newspaper circulation;
- abolish the rules limiting ownership between terrestrial television, satellite, and cable broadcasters, except for those broadcasters which are already in more than 20% ownership by a newspaper with more than 20% national circulation;
- remove the 50% limit on combined Channel 3 holdings in ITN; and
- remove the numerical limit on the number of local radio licences which may be jointly held (while retaining the existing points system).

In the meantime, the Government intends to enact immediate secondary legislation which will:

- increase the limit on the number of local radio licences which may be jointly held from 20 to 35 . . .
- double the circulation threshold for newspaper referrals to the MMC.

6. The Government recognises that in the longer term, as the number of broadcasters increases and increasing technological convergence occurs, a more integrated system of ownership control may be desirable. This paper also therefore sets out a proposal for a system which would:

- define the total media market;
- reflect the different levels of influence of different media;
- set thresholds beyond which it would be for an independent regulator to determine whether acquisitions or holdings were in the public interest;
- provide the regulator with powers to prevent acquisitions or require divestment;
- set out the public interest criteria against which the regulator would act.

Department of National Heritage (1995) *Media Ownership: The Government's Proposals*, London: HMSO, Cm 2872, May.

4.9 Shaping the Democratic Vision

Campaign for Press and Broadcasting Freedom and Reforming Regulation

The Campaign for Press and Broadcasting Freedom responded to the growing concentration of media ownership and cross-media ownership, witnessed during the 1980s and 1990s, by asserting the need for 'positive regulation' to sustain and encourage diversity in programming: monopoly, the CPBF argued, is inimical to diversity of broadcast opinion which, in turn, is debilitating for democratic polities. The Campaign proposed a new Media Commission to regulate *all* media and with a brief to conduct media-relevant research.

The case for regulation

We consider that the best way to promote diversity of the press, broadcasting and telecommunications sectors is through accountable, positive regulation.

A body of law already exists which purports to regulate the press to promote accountability and diversity. The problem is that much of it is ineffective. For example the Monopoly and Mergers Commission (MMC) has signally failed to counter monopolisation . . . Existing laws need to be reformed, and new ones introduced to promote accountability and diversity.

In broadcasting and telecommunications the task is to halt the spread of deregulation and to re-regulate. But this must not be in the old style of allowing the electronic media to be run by unelected people. We must inject electoral accountability into the regulation of electronic media.

However it is also true that the range of regulatory bodies in existence is often confusing and ineffective in delivering standards and accountability. in proposing new regulatory bodies we believe new forms of election are needed, which avoid the political patronage and quangos developed in the Conservative years, and involve people with interests and experience who represent our diverse society. At the same time as the number of regulatory bodies are reduced, those that we propose would have clear and positive roles, with the resources to be effective.

As the pattern of ownership becomes increasingly complex we propose the establishment of one regulatory body covering the press, radio, television, cable, satellite, the Internet, and telecommunications. This body would have the facilities to research policy issues, and patterns of media ownership.

At the same time, viewers, readers and listeners need a separate body which can ensure that their interests, including the right of reply, are given a single coherent and effective voice.

Ownership

Conservative governments have allowed and encouraged the growth of large media combines. In particular News International has, in the last seventeen years, been allowed to build a media empire spanning print and satellite broadcasting, and to also control the means of distributing media products. In 1995 the government announced a package of measures designed to make it easier for major companies to own large slices of individual media across different sectors. A Labour amendment to the Broadcasting Bill proposed increasing to 25 per cent the market share allowed by a newspaper group seeking to buy an ITV company. This would allow Mirror Group Newspapers (MGN) to build up its television holdings, and the amendment by Labour seemed to be motivated by political expediency rather than principles. MGN already owns two of Scotland's strongest newspaper titles, the *Daily Record* and *Sunday Mail*, and is developing its cable TV service. If it was allowed to acquire Scottish Television a strong regional monopoly would be created which would not only concern groups like the CPBF on issues like diversity and plurality. Advertisers and media buyers also fear the prospect of 'conditional selling' and a 'take it or leave it' basis for setting the costs of advertising. It was this issue which actually led the MMC to recommend *against* the take-over by Northcliffe Newspapers of the Nottingham Post group. It would have created a regional press monopoly in the East Midlands and the prospect of advertising rates increasing by 20 per cent. The government overturned the MMC report, however, and in December 1994 the take-over went ahead.

There are vital issues here. Responsible democracies have long recognised the need to ensure that the printed word and the visual image, in the interest of diversity of opinion, should not be unduly monopolised. The case for limiting media ownership is based on democratic, cultural and social concerns: it is about encouraging wider participation and reversing, not promoting, concentration of media power into fewer and fewer hands.

Now such principles have been abandoned. The consequences of the proposed changes will be to allow the power of a few individuals who run large companies to grow unchecked. The need to promote diversity of ownership and to check the power of cross media concentrations is urgent. In suggesting these policies we are acutely aware of the failures of the MMC to prevent the present concentrations of press ownership at a national and regional level. Our proposals below for a statutory body, the Media Commission, are based on learning the lessons from the record of ineffectiveness, and establishing clear principles which will ensure that media diversity is not ignored.

We recommend:

- An immediate review of the ownership regulations by an incoming Labour government.
- The imposition of effective controls to limit the spread of cross media ownership and to ensure pluralism of ownership.
- The use of a levy on media advertising revenue to fund new forms of media ownership and new enterprises.
- The establishment of a Media Commission to monitor cross media ownership, and

to enforce the new regulations. This body would have a key role in researching all aspects of media activity.

Campaign for Press and Broadcasting Freedom (1996) *21st Century Media: Shaping the Democratic Vision*, London: CPBF, June.

4.10 The Need to Regulate the Market in Television Broadcasting

The Campaign for Quality Television argued that the market cannot be relied upon to fulfil all the purposes of broadcasting in a democracy and suggested that advocacy of an unregulated market for television is a dangerous policy which will result in trends towards monopoly ownership and fragmented audiences. Like the CPBF, the Campaign for Quality television argues that audiences enjoy a right to certain kinds of information which the unregulated television market will not deliver; that information, moreover, is crucial to the effective working of democracy.

The economic disincentive to produce diverse programmes for minority audiences (which are often substantial), is only likely to increase in the next broadcasting age of digitalisation. Anyone venturing into the large-scale development of digital services faces very high costs, the return on which remains problematical. Investment in programmes will be minimal with a premium on programme formats capable of reversioning.

The likely shape of the emerging market – and its consequences for quality of programming – is set out in detail by Andrew Graham and Gavyn Davies (1997) in *Broadcasting, Society and Policy in the Multimedia Age*. Their arguments, with which the Campaign substantially agrees, are as follows:

- The new technology creates strong pressure towards a broadcasting industry in which audiences are fragmented while ownership is concentrated. The high fixed costs of high quality content and the relatively low costs of editing or changing and the trivial cost of reproduction are the natural creators of monopolies.
- High quality material can still be produced while costing very little per unit, provided that it reaches large numbers of people (exploiting economies of scale) and/or provided that it is used in a great variety of different formats (exploiting economies of scope), but the exploitation of these economies of scale and of scope implies concentration of ownership and a narrowing of the range of programmes. Hence the trade-off between quality and choice which was noted earlier.
- Thus, while one source of monopoly, spectrum scarcity, has gone, it has been replaced with another – the natural monopoly of economics of scale and scope on the one hand plus the natural scarcity of talent on the other.

- The need to insure against market failure is uppermost in the minds of companies accountable to shareholders and their considerations, particularly when competing for revenue in a different country, with very different values, are necessarily different from those of locally based, publicly accountable, broadcasters. While not discounting international appreciation of the best drama and comedy programmes produced in North America, the identity of individual national communities should be reflected in work drawing on local experience and characters.
- Some strands of programming, such as education, do not earn their bread in commercial terms, but they enrich the individual and, through them, society. They fit the economists' description of a 'merit food', that is, a 'food' of which the consumers, if left to choose, avail themselves less than would serve their long term interests. While the expansion of the broadcasting market may provide opportunities for some of these strands to be produced commercially, others are unlikely ever to be produced and the production of yet others will be dependent on the changing fortunes of the market. The degree of risk is likely to intensify the more familiar pressures which dictate the capacity of commercial services to extend their range of programming into areas where the level of return on their investment cannot be assured.
- Citizens need, as a right, core information which the market could not necessarily be depended upon to supply. A community has views about society which cannot be captured in its buying and selling. Collective and individual capacities for imagination and achievement are affected by the 'company we keep' of which broadcasting is a part. The communications system we support as a society will be an important influence on the social values and concerns of the communities of the twenty first century. It is therefore particularly important that there exists a substantial element of indigenous control over the selection of significant parts of the programming available to both national and local audiences.
- It is a basic principle of democratic society that votes should not be bought and sold. Democracy depends upon the creation and sustenance of 'common knowledge' (what everyone knows everyone knows) which is not well guarded by commercial markets lacking any incentive to invest. Solutions, to be agreed, must be based on a common understanding of a situation. The common knowledge fostered by a commercial agenda differs in certain respects from the common knowledge which is a precondition for resolving many co-ordination problems for the citizens of democratic societies.
- The 'comparative advantage' of British broadcasting follows extensive investment over many years in talent of all kinds, artistic as well as scientific and technical. It would be profligate to abandon that tradition, particularly at a stage when, whatever might be claimed for it, the performance of an enlarged market can be no more than a matter for speculation, most crucially over its ability to fund the degree of digitalisation under contemplation.

In summary, in the Campaign's view the probable domination of the next broadcasting era by a small number of private monopolies must be the cause of great anxiety and a sufficient argument in itself for public policy intervention in broadcasting. But there are further powerful arguments, listed above, in favour of the direct intervention that society as a whole, just as much as the individual viewer, cannot do without.

The communications system which our society supports will be an important influence on the social values and concerns of the communities of the twenty first century. Broadcasting deals in the values of society, diverse as much as they are uniform, whether revealed in the conversation of two or three people, in the reflections of an individual or the passions of a dramatist. Broadcasting, too, replays our social history back to us, reflecting the great episodes of our national life, commemorative or tragic and sustains the work of contemporary artists of every kind.

By all these means, broadcasting at its most complete provides one of the most readily accessible ways of communication within society. As a forum for freedom of expression and in providing information, education and entertainment, broadcasting meets the needs of a democratic society, with the advantage of doing so directly in people's homes and relatively cheaply.

In calling for public policy intervention in broadcasting, the Campaign agrees both with the problem and the solution as defined by Graham and Davies.

> What public policy therefore requires is a positive force which would act as a counterweight to the concentration of ownership, deliver national coverage to counteract the fragmentation of the audiences, provide a centre of excellence, be large enough to influence the market, and so act as the guarantor of quality and widen choice both now and in the future by complementing the market through the pursuit of public service purposes.

As we have seen, from the mid-fifties a positive force, ensuring quality and diversity existed in British broadcasting, taking the form of the two separate kinds of governance, applying respectively to the BBC and the regulators of commercial broadcasting.

Within the ITV companies, at least until 1993, critical masses of production talent have been maintained to support high standards in a diverse range of programming. However, the ability of the commercial sector to contribute to the diversity and range of programming which has characterised the successful operations of past years depended heavily on the relative financial security it enjoyed, now diminished in the competitive situation of the 1990s. It is, in fact, no longer competition on an equal footing, with ITV companies and Channel 4 being bound by public service obligations not imposed on other commercial broadcasters.

To summarise, we believe that the existing regulatory structure, already circumscribed in the new circumstances of broadcasting, will be wholly inadequate to meet the needs of audiences and of our society at the start of the Information Age in the next century.

(pp.10–16)

Reference

Graham, A. and Davies, G. (1997) *Broadcasting, Society and Policy in the Multimedia Age*, London: University of London Press.

Campaign for Quality Television (1998) *The Purposes of Broadcasting*, London: CQT, 26pp.

4.11 Relaxing the Rules

Media Ownership and *A New Future for Communications*

The White Paper *A New Future For Communications* made significant changes to the rules governing ownership of television licences in the commercial sector of broadcasting. The White Paper argued that such changes were necessary because current regulatory controls were inhibiting the development of commercial television as a competitor in the global television market. First, it removed the restriction prohibiting ownership of licences which in combination delivered 15 per cent or more of total audience share. Second, it lifted the restriction on any single company owning both ITV licences in the London area. Third, the White Paper invited comments on reforms to the rules governing cross-media ownership. Contemporary observers argued that the rather vague language in which this invitation was couched – which seemed more typical of a Green Paper – reflected the government's belief in the need to be cautious not to offend key media interests in the run-up to a general election. Finally, the rules governing the ownership of the 'nominated news provider' were changed. The government believed that these changes would pave the way for further consolidation within Channel 3 (probably a merger between Granada and Carlton), leading to a single ITV company.

4.6.1 The Broadcasting Acts currently prevent anyone from holding two or more licences to provide television services which attract 15% or more of the total TV audience share. Many consultation responses, including that from the ITC, argued that the rule is more restrictive than is now necessary for striking a reasonable balance between a dynamic market and plurality of ownership, given the increasing range of alternative services now available. The rule is a potential barrier to ITV companies seeking to consolidate their holdings through mergers. For a summary of the recent Competition Commission report on the proposed mergers of Granada, UNM [United News and Media] and Carlton, see http://www.mmc.gov.uk/441.htm/

4.6.2 It is possible that there will be further moves towards such greater consolidation of the ITV network. These moves could have the benefit of streamlining the strategic decision making process within ITV, and promoting the international standing of ITV companies. Any proposed mergers would, however, be subject to examination under the merger provisions of the Fair Trading Act in order to assess the impact on the UK market with a view to safeguarding the interests of consumers and market players such as advertisers. We do not wish to put additional barriers in the way of the ITV companies, and will therefore develop a new system for ensuring plurality in television services. At its simplest, this might be achieved by retaining the prohibition on joint ownership of ITV and Channel 5, thus ensuring a minimum of at least four broadcasters providing free to air analogue television services (including BBC and Channel 4).

4.6.3 Where there is more than one regional ITV service being provided for the same area, the Broadcasting Acts also prohibit the same person owning more than one of the licences for that area. This restriction currently prevents any one person or company from holding both of the London ITV licences, and therefore from dominating the London TV advertising market. The competition authorities are best placed to consider the potential impacts on any such markets. So we propose to revoke this rule.

- We invite comments on the reform of the cross-media ownership rules.

4.8.1 The cross-media ownership rules set out in the Broadcasting Acts prevent any one company acquiring excessive influence across the media as a whole. This is done primarily by a rule which prevents owners of newspapers with a national market share of 20% or more from controlling a licence to provide, or having an interest of more than 20% in, a regional or national ITV service, Channel 5, or a national or local radio service. There are also rules which preserve plurality at a local and regional level by limiting the interests a local newspaper owner may have in the TV and radio services for the same area.

4.8.2 The legislation, which appears in the Broadcasting Act 1990, as amended by the 1996 Act, evolved following an extensive consultation in 1995 [*Media Ownership: The Government's Proposals*, Cm 2872: see 4.8] on a new approach to measuring and regulating media ownership. The consultation document set out proposals which would: define the total media market; reflect the different levels of influence of different media; set thresholds beyond which it would be for an independent regulator to determine whether acquisitions or holdings were in the public interest; provide the regulator with powers to prevent acquisitions or require divestment; and set out the public interest criteria against which the regulator would act.

4.8.3 Following consultation, the Government ruled that there were too many difficulties with this model for it to be introduced at that time, not least the problem of measuring shares in individual media and how those shares would be aggregated across different media markets . . .

4.8.4 Since 1996, media markets have changed to a significant degree, and the time is now right to review the Broadcasting Acts regime.

4.8.5 Many have called for the current cross-media ownership rules to be revoked, arguing that limits on cross-media investments are now unnecessary. Plurality concerns may diminish as more people gain access to the range of services now available on digital TV and radio and the Internet. For the time being, however, most people continue to rely on terrestrial TV, radio and newspapers. Cross-media consolidations which are desirable on economic grounds may tend to reduce the plurality of viewpoints and sources of information available.

4.8.7 . . . a number of . . . models have been proposed for regulating cross-media ownership. Some models concentrate on overall 'share of voice'; others involve cumulative sector-specific limits. There are various ideas about what such limits should be based on (audience share, audience reach and company turnover are just a few suggestions) or indeed whether there are other ways of achieving plurality objectives. These are just a few issues which need to be explored in establishing a system to reflect fully the new complexities of the industry.

4.8.8 In the light of this discussion, we invite comments on how we might reform the cross-media regime for the changing market conditions, whilst continuing to ensure a plurality of services to consumers and citizens

4.10 The ITV nominated news provider

- We will retain the nominated news provider system for ITV, but introduce a clause to allow the Government, on advice from OFCOM, to revoke it.
- We will consider relaxing the 20 per cent limit on ownership of the nominated news provider.

4.10.1 The nominated news provider system for the ITV network ensures that high quality national and international news is carried across all ITV regions at peak time by a single news provider. By requiring ITV to select a news provider from providers nominated for that purpose by the ITC, the current rules guarantee a nation-wide competitor to the BBC's news services. This competition serves to underpin the impartiality of both services, and guarantees plurality for viewers. We want to preserve these benefits. Television is a particularly important source of information and opinion and viewers have a high awareness of its impartiality. But we expect that the market will eventually ensure that the BBC has sufficient competition for the nominated news provider system no longer to be necessary. We will therefore introduce a clause to allow the Government to revoke it, on the basis of advice from OFCOM, should conditions allow.

4.10.2 At present the Broadcasting Acts prevent any one company from owning more than 20% of the ITV nominated news provider. This ensures that the news provider can act independently of the commercial interests of any one major shareholder. Modern market conditions, however, may mean that ITV's news provider will want the freedom to encourage further investment in its news services. We will therefore consider relaxing the 20% limit on ownership of the nominated news provider.

DTI and DCMS (2000) *A New Future For Communications*, London: HMSO, Cm 5010, Sections 4.8–4.10.

CONVERGENCE IN THE DIGITAL AGE

4.12 Regulating Communications
An Evolutionary Approach

The Green Paper *Regulating Communications: Approaching Convergence in the Digital Age* was concerned to examine the implications of expanding digital services and convergence in delivery systems for the existing regulatory structures of broadcasting. The government believed that the problems arising from the already complex and often overlapping system of broadcast regulation, overseen by a number of bodies – some with responsibility for content and others concerned with economic and competition issues – seemed likely to be exacerbated as a consequence of the expansion of digital services, unless organisations' regulatory remits were clarified. Contra many commercial sector broadcasters and others in the industry who favoured radical change, the government opted for an 'evolutionary path'. This policy posture placed the government in opposition to the House of Commons Culture and Media Select Committee; in a report published a month before the Green Paper, the Committee proposed radical changes including a suggestion to amalgamate the functions of the ITC, Oftel and the Office of Fair Trading into a single regulator. But the government argued that there were obvious difficulties in defining regulatory structures in advance of any developed market for digital services, especially when it seemed likely that rates of consumer take-up of services would be highly variable.

Our information age and convergence

. . . Our system of regulation faces new challenges as delivery systems adopt a common technology and assume common capabilities. Some new services fall within the remit of more than one regulator, creating a risk of excessive and/or inconsistent regulation. Where an identical service is transmitted over different delivery systems, it may be subject to different regulatory regimes. The development of new services, and their wide availability, must not be jeopardised by such regulatory overlaps and anomalies.

Despite these potentially far-reaching changes, the public policy objectives which underpin regulation will remain largely the same. The Government will attach particular importance to:

- serving the consumer interest
- supporting universal access to services at affordable cost
- securing effective competition and, through this and other means, the competitiveness of industry is a whole
- Promoting quality, plurality, diversity and choice in services
- encouraging investment in services and infrastructure
- providing economically efficient management of scarce resources.

The pace of change

The pace of change is not uniform. The practices of some have been – and may well continue for some time to be – little affected, whereas others are being rapidly transformed. The debate on convergence often therefore polarises, with policy-makers sometimes asked to choose between two visions:

- a radically new regulatory structure is needed to avoid barriers to competitiveness because convergence is with us
- the status quo will suffice because mass markets have not yet converged to a significant extent.

The Government considers this a false choice. The fact that technologies are converging does not mean that the markets which employ them become indistinguishable. Virtually all broadcast entertainment and information services are still consumed on radios and televisions. It may be some time before most households have digital television, offering hundreds of channels and interactive services, or computers capable of receiving good quality audio-visual material via the Internet. Even then, consumers may not readily regard their TVs, radios and computers as interchangeable for all purposes.

From the providers' perspective, digital technology is already widely deployed before services are presented to the consumer. So convergence is already bringing significant opportunities to:

- gain economies of scope and scale across different areas of the business (e.g. production and distribution)
- gain value by extending services from one medium to another as their technical capabilities become increasingly interchangeable
- undertake alliances, mergers and significant investment to exploit these strategic opportunities . . .

It therefore seems likely that a spectrum of distinct elements of provision, reflecting established patterns of consumption, will persist for some considerable time to come. At one end of this spectrum there is likely to be a segment which looks much like the universal broadcast television as consumers know it today. At the other, there is likely to be a segment with many of the characteristics of the Internet.

The challenge to regulation

This Green Paper sets out the Government's approach to the regulatory issues which arise from convergence. Rather than making a false choice between tearing up our regulatory structures or sticking to the status quo, we will follow an evolutionary path. We will work with the regulators to ensure that they co-operate to manage overlaps and anomalies. Where those problems cannot be solved by regulators operating within the current legislative framework, we will, if necessary, amend the legislation on a case-by-case basis in advance of possible wider change.

The first requirement is to provide greater coherence in economic regulation across all digital delivery media and all parts of the converging value chain. Foundations for this are already being put in place with the new Competition Bill, complemented by appropriate sector specific regulation, and the existing merger control provisions of the Fair Trading Act. The regulators and competition authorities (OFTEL, ITC, OFT and DTI) are committed to working together closely on matters affecting the converging sectors, and have announced the establishment of a co-ordinating group. That group will seek to identify at an early stage the regulatory issues which arise from new ventures, and to ensure that regulatory responsibilities are clear and handled in a coherent way.

Secondly, it is essential to reassess the present regulatory distinctions based solely on the method of delivery to the consumer, and to take steps to provide greater consistency in the regulation of similar material delivered via different mechanisms. However, different segments of consumer demand will continue to merit different regulatory instruments, so long as consumers' expectations differ between them. The Government should not, for example, necessarily attempt to extend existing detailed regulation of broadcasting to new on-demand subscription services. Effective self-regulation will have an important role, with 'backstop' enforcement provisions as appropriate.

Public service broadcasting will remain important as a benchmark of quality and as a guarantee of plurality, diversity and impartiality across the whole range of programming. There can be no certainty that the market will provide the necessary incentives to meet consumer expectations in these respects, and there will be a continuing need to ensure that they are secured through other means.

The key issues for consultation

The adequacy of structures for the present

The Government believes we should proceed in an evolutionary way:

- in economic regulation, building on the Competition Bill powers and progressively withdrawing from additional regulation down to the minimum needed to deal with such issues as bottleneck control, interoperability and universal access
- in cultural and related regulation, evolving to regulation based on categories of service which reflect differing consumer expectations.

Work is in hand to augment the current framework, making it more appropriate for the future:

- we are enacting the Competition Bill, which will provide tough new competition powers across the whole economy, including the converging sectors
- we are progressively lifting the restrictions which prevent telecommunications operators from carrying broadcast entertainment nationwide
- we are planning a Secure Electronic Commerce Bill to provide the basis, for the commercial use of encryption and a legal basis for digital signatures
- the principal regulators – OFT, OFTEL and ITC – have announced plans for closer collaboration.

What changes to regulatory aims and methods are likely to be necessary in the medium term?

As new services become more significant, changes to regulatory aims and methods will be needed. Making changes early in the process might help to ensure a regime appropriate to the digital future at an early stage. It could give the UK 'first mover' advantages. However, it is impossible to be sure how the markets will develop. We risk developing a system of regulation around a prediction of what the digital world will look like which, if it turns out to be mistaken, will leave the regulatory system obsolete.

What are the implications for the regulatory structure?

Commitment to a particular institutional model would be premature. However, greater co-ordination will be increasingly necessary, and there may come a point when the present structure is unable to provide the necessary degree of integration of the decision-making processes. A number of models are possible for the eventual structure of regulation, for example:

- separate regulators for infrastructure and for content-providing industry
- separate regulators for economic and competition issues on the one hand and for cultural and content issues on the other
- either of these or other possible models, subject to a co-ordinating body spanning both areas of regulation (including perhaps a wider range of content/cultural regulatory bodies) to ensure coherence and consistency
- single, fully integrated regulator whose internal organisation might be split along the lines suggested in the first two points.

(pp.2–6)

DTI and DCMS (1998) *Regulating Communications: Approaching Convergence in the Digital Age*, London: HMSO, Cm 4022, July, 65pp.

4.13 Regulation in the Digital Television Age

The Campaign for Quality Television, responding to *Regulating Communications*, argued that there is a need to replace the existing and diverse regulatory bodies with two new independent regulators – one for 'carriage' (to deal with issues of media ownership and competitiveness) and another for 'content' (focusing on the licensing of commercial broadcasters, research and consumer complaints) – with a brief to cover all broadcasters.

There are three main options for future broadcasting regulation:

- The continuance of the present system, with a proliferation of regulators.
- The establishment of a single regulator to govern all broadcasting, but with a real risk of concentrating on technology and finance at the expense of content.
- The creation of two separate regulators, one for carriage and the other for content. The content regulator would be responsible for licensing, complaints, standards and research, with a remit to promote public service broadcasting.

The Campaign for Quality Television strongly supports the last of the options set out above, the establishment of two regulators. There are, however, two essential requirements to safeguard programme quality: a strong public service presence and the constitution of the regulatory bodies themselves.

The task of constituting the strong public service presence which we consider fundamental lies primarily, but far from solely, with the BBC and not, we argue, with the BBC as now constituted.

At the moment, the BBC is preoccupied with the need to promote its commercial activities and to present itself in commercial trappings in, for example, its too frequent use of terminology and the espousal of values more appropriate to the world of business than to a public service institution. As a consequence, the public interest has been insufficiently distinguished from the requirements of the market. While the competitive successes of the BBC's schedules have been clearly registered, they have often lacked the distinctive quality which divides a publicly funded service from one which is sustained commercially. The availability of funding for programmes off the proceeds of its commercial activities, while easing financial constraints, carries with it the perpetual danger of permeating editorial judgements with commercial considerations affecting choice of material, its treatment and casting. This situation is, we believe, unlikely to be remedied as long as the Governors are liable to have their attention distracted from their main task by the demands of their commercial responsibilities. These, with straightforward indications of success and failure, may often appear more alluring than the difficult issues presented by the protection of the public interest.

We set out later our proposals for restructuring the BBC to restore its public service commitment, by placing its commercial activities under a separate agency, under the BBC umbrella. With regard to the public service obligations of the ITV companies, we propose that the new content regulator should ensure that the new satellite and cable companies share a measure of the same obligations. We consider this essential if the ability of the terrestrial companies to discharge their obligations is not to be destabilised. We recognise the financial difficulties under which new cable and satellite companies must operate in their initial years, but, as their survival becomes assured and their profit levels rise, we consider that the regulator should institute a graduated scheme under which these companies would incur increasing public service obligations. Where, for example, a single owner operates a number of channels, some might have public service obligations imposed on them while others, possibly niche channels, might not. The intention would be to bring about a more equitable sharing of competitive pressures than can exist in the absence of a level playing field.

We also propose that the ITV companies should be relieved of their responsibilities for regional programming, but should contribute to the funding of such programmes through a new mechanism. This proposal is also set out below in more detail.

Two new regulatory bodies

The second essential requirement is that the two new bodies, for carriage and content respectively, should be specially constituted for their roles and not simply amalgams of existing regulators which are demonstrably underequipped for the new demands facing them. The new structures must be capable of handling a complex period of transition whose duration and extent are unknown. We acknowledge that responsibilities for carriage and content cannot be entirely distinct: the choice of licensees, for example, requires the application of economic and competitive criteria as well as judgements of a potential licensee's programme-making capacities. Nevertheless, we believe that plurality of regulation is a virtue sufficiently important to justify the occasional difficulties in jurisdiction which may initially arise.

(i) The carriage regulator

The principal concern of the first regulator should be with questions of access to the full range of communications platforms. These would include ownership, competition, and dominance of gateways, in order to secure the service of the public interest in all these matters as the basis for the specific programme and other services which would be the responsibility of the content regulator.

(ii) The content regulator

The duties falling on the content regulator should include the licensing of all commercial broadcasting services, the conduct of research, and the handling of complaints. Performance of the complaints function should preserve the principle of independent lay oversight and appointments to the new body should reflect this principle in both the number of appointments and the range of interests represented. The new body would have the responsibility each year of advising the Secretary of State on how the broadcasting industry as a whole was promoting the public interest, as we have defined it earlier in this paper, in its varied services. In the future, the substantial returns enjoyed by the commercial companies in their monopoly period will either have disappeared under the pressure of competition or will have been transferred to the cable and satellite sector. We argue now for a better balance of public service broadcasting across all channels. We also urge effective monitoring since, as circumstances change, public service responsibilities may need to be weighted differently. Both the definition of the public interest and its interpretation in judgements made on individual programmes are strong arguments for instituting the body as a Commission rather than entrusting these responsibilities to a single individual (pp.15–18).

Campaign for Quality Television (1998) *The Purpose of Broadcasting*, London: CQT, 26pp. Contributors to the report include Anthony Smith, Liz Forgan, Colin Shaw, Andrew Graham, Jane Leighton and Ray Fitzwalter.

4.14 The ITC and the Future of Regulation

In a speech to the Royal Television Society in January 1999, Sir Robin Biggam, who chairs the ITC, identified the changing regulatory role of the Commission: the move to regulation with a 'lighter touch' and a growing focus on satellite and cable broadcasters rather than ITV licensees. Biggam argued for a review of overlap between existing regulators and suggested the need for consideration of a new government department to be responsible for the possible convergence of broadcasting and telecommunications.

From a hands on broadcaster/regulator we have had to move to a light touch regulator, relying heavily on the broadcasters to adhere to our published codes. The old emphasis on ITV licensees is declining and much more of the activity is taken up with satellite and cable licensees, while competition and economic issues now absorb a significant proportion of the time of the ITC. On a day to day basis we are dealing with a number of key economic issues such as the terms on which programmes or channels are made available. Almost all relate to content and demonstrate the indivisibility of content, licensing and economic regulation as we move into the digital age . . .

The current system of a tightly regulated commercial sector and a self-regulated BBC needs a critical review. It is certainly difficult to see the markedly different systems surviving into the digital era when there will be much greater pressure on all free to air broadcasters as they fight to hold share of a reducing market. The complexity of the BSC position – which can adjudicate on all content complaints – both radio and television – but has no regulatory power will also need to be considered and resolved . . .

Before considering the future form broadcasting should take, government needs to determine its own structure. We have heard talk of an OFCOM type structure, with telecomms and broadcasting under a single regulatory body. There is no fundamental difficulty in consolidating regulation when markets are recognised as converging and governmental responsibility rests with a single department. This has been demonstrated recently by the move of gas and electricity under a single regulatory body but responsibility within government is entirely within DTI. Do the same criteria exist with regard to telecommunications and broadcasting? The external market has no problem in differentiating between media and telecomms businesses. One is all about culture, programming, rights and distribution, the other about infrastructure and carriage. Within Government responsibility is totally clear with DCMS having broadcasting while DTI has responsibility for telecommunications. Unless government is prepared to combine its responsibilities into a single or new department under one secretary of state, then the possibility of combining the currently separate regulation under an umbrella organisation cannot be considered as a serious proposition. The sooner government clarifies this issue, the sooner we can all give serious thought to the key broadcasting issues.

Sir Robin Biggam (1999) 'The Future of Regulation', Speech to the Royal Television Society at the Grosvenor House Hotel, London, 21 January.

4.15 The BBC Response to Regulating Communications

The BBC response to the Green Paper on regulation in the digital age of media convergence was broadly supportive although it identified the need for a single strong regulator of media infrastructure to resolve potential problems resulting from the anticipated greater concentration of media ownership, as well as the need to regulate to guarantee interoperability to allow consumers the widest possible access to services via a single delivery system.

Convergence and consumer take-up

- Digital technology is bringing together three previously distinct industries – broadcasting, computing and telecommunications. But whilst the rate of technological convergence is breathtaking, so far the rate of consumer take up for new converged services has been relatively slow. Compelling content offered with greater convenience, either free to air or at competitive prices, will be essential if consumers are to take advantage of the new technological possibilities. The BBC will be a key player in driving the take-up of new digital TV services, and is already playing an active role in the provision of on-line content and in developing interactive services.

Regulatory challenge

- Regulation is not the only obstacle to convergence, but regulation will have to adapt to ensure that the pursuance of public policy goals recognises changes in technology and above all in consumer behaviour. The future regulatory challenge will be to create a balanced framework for the media which guarantees effective competition, maintains a strong European production base for the EU to compete in world markets, and aids democratic debate, whilst giving expression to Europe's rich diversity of cultures.

Infrastructure, competition & standards

- Ensuring fair access to infrastructure for consumers and service providers will require greater vigilance in the digital era. Spectrum scarcity is being replaced by new and more complex gateways. The Green Paper rightly draws attention to the problems that could be presented by the interaction of conditional access systems . . . Attention must also be given to emerging gateway functions – such as the management of memory in the set top box – which currently fall outside the scope of any regulation. Economies of scale and scope in the era of convergence will increase concentration of ownership. These trends suggest that member states will need to develop single, strong regulators of communications *infrastructure*.
- Interoperability will be key to the development of a competitive environment, where service providers can reach the widest number of consumers, and consumers can receive the widest possible number of services through a single delivery system. There is a risk that some may abuse their control of proprietary standards to prevent interoperability, or to permit it on terms which enable them to dominate the market and/or prevent entry. Common open standards offer one route to interoperability – and the BBC is encouraged by attempts to reach agreement on a common API in the DVB. In the absence of open and common standards, an alternative route is to ensure that proprietary standards are made available on fair, reasonable and non-discriminatory terms to third parties. This requirement must apply to *all* the software concerned (see above). This is an area where the EU could play a vital role.

Content

- Content regulation is quite different to infrastructure regulation. It serves a whole spectrum of social and cultural purposes – from proactive regulation to promote access, diversity and quality, to negative regulation to prevent the obviously harmful. Convergence does not alter these objectives, although it may change the ways in which they might be best achieved. In contrast to infrastructure regulation the regulation of content requires different and specific skills and is much more likely to be culturally specific.

Public service broadcasting

- A new regulatory paradigm may arise, where as traditional methods of negative regulation decline in importance and effectiveness, public policy goals are increasingly achieved through positive intervention in the market, through, among other things, support for public service broadcasters. With this approach there will be a premium on achieving public service objectives through organisations with public service values at their centre

BBC Response to *Regulating Communications: Approaching Convergence in the Information Age* http://europa.eu.int/ISPO/convergencegp/bbc.htm

4.16 The Regulation of Television in the Digital Age

In a lecture to the Royal television Society at Cambridge in September 1999, Chris Smith, the Secretary of State for Culture, Media and Sport, set out his vision for the future of digital television. He promised that the interests of viewers – judged by the key tests of 'availability' and 'affordability' – would be paramount in deciding the pace of the switch-over from analogue to digital television services. Smith anticipated a start date of 2006 with the process complete by 2010. He announced broadcasting legislation in the coming parliamentary session to merge existing regulatory bodies and to 'lighten' existing requirements on broadcasters. This statement seemed to represent something of a diversion from the 'evolutionary path' he intended to tread in *Regulating Communications*. But Smith affirmed his support for public service broadcasting and rejected Richard Eyre's suggestion that it might be supplanted by public interest broadcasting.

On the eve of the millennium, it seems to me appropriate to dream dreams, to think daring thoughts . . . I want to set out a vision of the future, together with some practical steps that will help to take us there . . .

Everybody here knows there's a revolution taking place in the world of broadcasting and communications: a transformation in compression, picture quality, interactivity, conditional access. In a word, there's a revolution going on in TV technology; and Britain is at the forefront of the change. I want to keep us there, and press home our global advantage. But it's not technology that will decide the ultimate success or failure of the digital revolution – it will be the range and quality of services, the ease with which viewers are able to navigate round the digital world and – of course – it will be price. The government wants to see this process unfold quickly and smoothly. But the heart of my message is this: It's your job to make the digital revolution happen. It's my job to make sure that it happens in the interests of the consumer.

My vision

Broadcasters too have an essential part to play in leading people through into the digital age; the sense of trust and familiarity viewers have for television has been built up through long association.

There's no doubt that digital television has the potential to harness the best of the old – the familiar strengths of television in entertainment, information and education – with the most exciting of the new: greater choice and individualised schedules, interactivity, home shopping, home banking, e-mail, Internet access. All this can be delivered with improved picture and sound quality, wide-screen format, and a massive increase in the number of channels. But digital television also represents a qualitative change . . . it means the end of television as broadcasting and the beginning of electronic communication as a seamless web which transcends the old distinctions between TV, computer and phone. It has the potential to create a world where all sections of society have access to information, news, education and current affairs, erasing the difference between the knowledge-rich and the knowledge-poor.

And there's a further dimension too. The UK is now a world leader in digital television and digital technology. With the huge increase in global communication, entertainment and learning, that has potentially momentous consequences for some of your companies and for the national economy . . . We are all in a game where the stakes – and the rewards – are very high. It is also essential that we have the necessary flow of skilled people to stay at the cutting edge of change.

What should government do?

First, we can remove barriers to investment and expansion. I can imagine a future where broadcasting regulation is based in the first instance on competition law with a reduced set of distinctive media rules added only where strictly necessary . . . I believe that we must be ready to contemplate a more radical approach, including major legislation early in the next Parliament.

The main issues for this next piece of legislation might be how to achieve deregulated but distinctive content regulation; how to rationalise the various regulators to avoid duplication and confusion; what the role of public service broadcasters should be in the longer term.

Secondly, I am clear that the ethos of broadcasting as a public service must remain at the heart of the system. Richard Eyre recently argued in his MacTaggart Lecture that the traditional definition of public service was dead – or soon would be (see 1.11 above). Richard, I do not agree. Of course what 'public service' means is changing. But it needs a redefinition rather than a requiem. And that doesn't mean abandoning the concept altogether and putting 'public interest' in its place. Despite the increase of choice which digital television brings, I believe that we will continue to need public service broadcasters including Channels 3 and 4, as well as the BBC – to sustain a diversity of viewpoints and to act as a quality benchmark.

Thirdly, and finally, the government has a role in setting out clear criteria for any move towards digital switch-over . . . although industry is very much driving the digital switch-over. I want to set out two crucial tests that must be met before the analogue signal is fully switched to digital: availability and affordability. First, the key test must be that everyone who currently receives free-to-air analogue channels should be able, after switch-over, to receive these same channels digitally. But I'd like to go further than this basic condition, if possible. I want viewers to be able to enjoy new additional services, including in particular basic Internet access.

Second, switching to digital must be an affordable option for the vast majority of people. Consumers must not face unacceptable switching costs when moving to digital services, either for televisions or for VCRs.

How quickly can this be achieved?

Full switch-over will take place when – and only when – these two tests of availability and affordability are met. I believe this could start to happen as early as 2006 and be completed by 2010. But that depends very much on how the broadcasters, manufacturers and consumers behave over the next seven years. I want today to set you all a challenge: work together to bring consumers attractive services and affordable equipment so that the whole country can and will make the switch to digital and achieve this ambitious and exciting target.

Future consultation and review

I have attempted to be as clear as I possibly can on the government's view of the principles, criteria and a plausible timetable. Let me make it clear that the government wants the digital revolution to succeed . . . But there are enormous uncertainties. We have to make assumptions against market realities but we need regularly to check those assumptions against market realities, and to measure progress against the two key tests I have set out. I propose to do this through a series of two yearly reviews, kicked off by formal consultation of the BBC, ITC, industry and consumer groups before the end of 2001. This will mean the key industry players are involved at every stage.

None of this will happen however without the confidence and support of viewers. So I also want to set up a Viewers' Panel which will assess the evidence provided by industry, broadcasters and government at each review stage both to perform a reality check on it and offer independent advice to government on the issues which matter most to the public.

Conclusion

I hope you'll agree that the approach I have outlined here today to steer the UK broadcasting industry into the next millennium is the right way to instil clarity and confidence into a dynamic and exciting new industry. I want to steer a path which is bold and forward-looking but realistic, clear but flexible, challenging but reassuring. I hope you will support me in this vision.

Chris Smith, Secretary of State for Culture, Media and Sport (1999) Lecture delivered to the Royal Television Society, Cambridge, 17 September. Department of Culture, Media and Sport.

4.17 Regulating the Gateways to Digitopia

Towards the end of his tenure as Director-General of the BBC, John Birt decided to seize his 'last chance to take the gloves off' and 'to share . . . some deep and passionate convictions' about the possible dangers of the digital age for programme diversity. He argued that the growing power of gateway controllers would limit viewers' choice, and that government should regulate to protect consumers and promote choice.

Gateway dominance

The first difficulty is that the digital age may be marked by dominance, rather than by plurality and diversity. The producer, rather than the consumer, may be in the driving seat. This is because of the emerging power of those who will control the gateways to digitopia – the gateway to your computer screen, to your TV screen, to the server in your school or to the memory store in your set-top box.

The power of the gateway controllers could become more and more important – ordering and marshalling, if not barring, your choices of programmes, holidays and myriad financial and other services. Already the BBC's digital choices are scattered across Sky's Electronic Programme Guide, its front-page menu. Already it stops us – and other service providers – setting out the whole array of our services clearly for our licence payers.

In the future, who will control your home library – access to the abundant storage capacity in your set-top box? In the next, and more powerful, generation of set-top boxes, will the BBC be able, for instance, to help you store and play back all the natural history programmes available from us in a week?

Governments will be cautious of interfering. There are many gatekeepers. The gatekeepers are powerful. They must first make a return on their substantial risk investment, it is suggested. 'Let's not intervene till we can assess the full scope of the problem' governments say.

Let me say with all the force that I can muster that now is the time to act and to apply, with rigour, clear regulatory principles for the digital age. It will be even more difficult later than it is now to dislodge those who will benefit massively from their grip on the gateway.

An approach to regulation

Let me suggest what governments should do:

- let no group in any distribution system both control the gateway and be at the same time a substantial provider of services
- let us have a regulatory regime that champions the consumer and promotes choice. Let us have competing programme guides. Let consumers set up their own personalised programme guides if they want to. Let consumers control the use of the memory in their own TV.

And let us work to this end – starting right now! All of this, I believe, is absolutely in the interests of consumers and all service providers.

Let me unashamedly propose something else. The public pays for the BBC. It is in the public's interest that they should always be able easily to access BBC services – and by whatever means they choose to receive their media. The BBC should remain at the centre and not be relegated to the periphery of the nation's life. There should be a guaranteed and appropriately prominent position for the BBC on every gateway in the UK.

John Birt (1999) 'The Prize and the Price: The Social, Political and Cultural Consequences of the Digital Age', The New Statesman Media Lecture delivered at the Banqueting House, Whitehall, 6 July.

4.18 OFCOM

A New Regulatory Body

The proliferation of regulatory bodies during the 1990s, following the provisions of the Broadcasting Acts 1990 and 1996, prompted contradictory judgements of the same issue among regulators and triggered calls from broadcasters, politicians and media observers for a less complex, unitary system of regulation. *A New Future For Communications* proposed the establishment of OFCOM, a radical and powerful new regulator with a brief to regulate television and radio broadcasting as well as telecommunications. OFCOM incorporates the regulatory responsibilities of the Broadcasting Standards Commission, the Independent Television Commission, Oftel, the Radio Authority and the Radiocommunications agency. OFCOM's major regulatory brief is to protect consumers' interests and sustain programme quality. To that end, OFCOM has regulatory powers based on Competition Act principles and can levy financial penalties. OFCOM also has an interesting 'self-destruct' role. It must constantly review developments in television markets and 'roll back' regulation as market developments render it unnecessary.

8.2.1 The current framework for regulation of communications in the UK is complex. Technology has also moved faster than regulation can keep up. As convergence continues to accelerate, such complexity and potential for confusion will only increase unless regulation is reformed.

8.2.2 We therefore need a simpler and more flexible system . . .

8.5.1 We propose that OFCOM's central regulatory objectives should be:

- protecting the interests of consumers in terms of choice, price, quality of service and value for money, in particular through promoting open and competitive markets;
- maintaining high quality of content, a wide range of programming, and plurality of public expression;
- protecting the interests of citizens by maintaining accepted community standards in content, balancing freedom of speech against the need to protect against potentially offensive or harmful material, and ensuring appropriate protection of fairness and privacy.

8.5.2 In all its activities, the regulator should also give proper weight to:

- the protection of children and vulnerable persons;
- the prevention of crime and public disorder;
- the special needs of people with disabilities and of the elderly, of those on low income and of persons living in rural areas;
- the promotion of efficiency, including efficient use of spectrum and telephone numbers, and the promotion of innovation.

8.6 The internal structure of regulator

8.6.1 We will be discussing the details of how the new regulator should be structured internally with the existing regulators and others. However, we expect that the regulator will be governed by a small body of executive and non-executive members, rather than a single individual. They will be collectively accountable and, between them, should have sufficient knowledge, expertise and authority to pursue the regulator's objectives. They will establish the strategic framework for the regulator's work and resolve any conflicts between the regulator's different objectives in a clear and transparent way. They will operate in accordance with the best principles of corporate governance and better regulation.

- We will enhance the regulatory powers available to OFCOM.

8.9.1 It is important that OFCOM has sufficient powers to carry out its duties. It has to be able to take tough action when necessary and to ensure that regulated companies take the action which is required of them. We therefore intend that OFCOM will have enforcement powers analogous to those of Oftel and the ITC. We will re-base broadcasting regulation upon modern Competition Act principles and give the regulator concurrent powers with the OFT which the ITC currently lacks. In addition, we will give OFCOM Competition Act type powers to levy financial penalties for breaches of the sector-specific regulatory requirements. This will bring the range of enforcement powers into line with the powers of other regulatory bodies, for example the Financial Services Authority . . . We invite views on whether this is an adequate toolkit for regulation in this field, or whether further powers could prove necessary in future.

8.11 Regulation at the minimum necessary level

OFCOM will have a duty to keep markets or sectors under review and roll back regulation promptly where increasing competition renders it unnecessary. It will encourage co-regulation and self-regulation where these will best achieve the regulatory objectives.

DTI and DCMS (2000) *A New Future For Communications* London: HMSO, 12 December, Cm 5010, Sections 8.2.1–8.11.

PART FIVE

Television Broadcasting Policy: Political Communications

THE RELATIONSHIP BETWEEN POLITICIANS and broadcasters has been and remains highly complex. On occasion, politicians seem to exercise ultimate power and control over the media: a dominance that is expressed most starkly in their ability to censor newspapers, radio and television. Britain has not been immune from such censorship. In nineteenth-century England the notorious 'taxes on knowledge' – a series of government imposed fiscal measures designed to restrict the ownership, control and sales of newspapers – inhibited the development of a working-class readership for radical newspapers until the early 1860s. During the twentieth-century, in periods of war, broadcast media have been subject to close control by politicians. More recently, in 1988, a Conservative government issued a notice to all broadcasting organisations outlawing the reporting of the views of certain proscribed paramilitary groups in Northern Ireland (5.1). Such extreme forms of censorship have not always been necessary for politicians to achieve their ambitions to influence news media. Occasionally, government has requested that certain programmes should not be broadcast: this was the case with the television programme about sectarian politics in Northern Ireland entitled *Real Lives*. Government has also attempted (not always successfully) to postpone the broadcasting of particular programmes, as with Thames Television's *Death on the Rock* (5.2). Mechanisms of control, moreover, need not always assume political guises. In 1994, for example, broadcaster Greg Dyke argued that the UK government's growing involvement in the granting of charters and licences to broadcast, as well as with certain aspects of the regulation of broadcasting, had generated a 'culture of dependency' which inhibited the critical autonomy of news media and broadcasters (5.3).

Viewed from an alternative perspective, however, it is broadcasters who seem to be the dominant partner in the relationship with politicians. On this account, the media are judged to be a fourth estate, critical of government and holding politicians to public account. The press is an ever-present watchdog that barks to alert the public to any misdemeanors committed by politicians. Occasionally, the dog will bite! Very occasionally, the wound proves fatal, as the resignation of Neil Hamilton and the imprisonment of Jonathan Aitken illustrated.

Both the above formulations presume that the relationship between politicians and the media is essentially adversarial and conflictual but, on a day-to-day basis, the relationship can also be characterised by cooperation: a cooperation that on occasion can verge on collusion. Both groups remain wary of the harm that the other is able to inflict but, more significantly, both groups have ambitions and interests that can most readily be achieved with the cooperation of the other group. In short, there is a growing mutuality of interests between the groups. Politicians increasingly view media as providing platforms and opportunities to communicate political messages to the public. In an age when politics is increasingly packaged for media presentation and audience consumption, productive and congenial working relationships with news media are central to political success. For their part, broadcasters require the cooperation of politicians as informers about the political scene, as well as performers in political programmes, if the enterprise of political broadcasting is to have any prospect of success. In brief, the relationship between politicians and the media is symbiotic, fulfilling distinctive needs for each partner but uniting them by the overlapping of their fundamental purposes. Consequently, the history of the relationship between politicians and the media is one that oscillates between suspicion and collusion.

In the early days of television broadcasting some politicians were highly suspicious of the new medium, sceptical about its relevance to politics but, paradoxically, fearful of its influence on mass audiences and its ability to promote the arguments of opponents. Winston Churchill, for example, denounced television as nothing less than a 'red conspiracy' and supported the 'fourteen-day rule' – a censorial mechanism which until 1956 prohibited television discussion of any topic likely to occur in Parliament in the subsequent fortnight – on the grounds that 'it would be a shocking thing to have the debates of parliament forestalled by this new robot organisation of television and BBC broadcasting'. The rights of MPs required protection 'against the mass and the machine' (Franklin, 1992: 3). Others saw the potential of television to reach large audiences and were concerned that politicians' access to this influential new medium should be closely regulated. In 1947, the *aide-mémoire* or agreement between the Labour government, Conservative opposition and the BBC, a set of rules which formalised and regulated politicians' access to television and established the formats of ministerial broadcasts and party political broadcasts, was a significant landmark in the history of political broadcasting.

As the new medium came of age it grew in confidence. The emergence of commercial broadcasting during the 1950s, replete with its own independent news organisation (ITN), witnessed broadcasters' retreat from the deference that had characterised their early contact with politicians. Interviewers such as Robin Day pioneered a more robust, challenging and confrontational style of political interviewing which exacerbated politicians' misgivings about television. In 1959 when the House first debated the possibility of televising its proceedings, Members' fears about television 'taking over' the Commons were apparent: such fears were evident in the subsequent twelve debates before the motion was successfully carried. Subsequently broadcasting from the Commons has become routine, but parliamentarians' loudly canvassed concern is that political broadcasters and journalists are ignoring the House and its proceedings.

The extracts below are grouped under four headings in order to capture and illustrate some of the complexity and variation in the relationship between politicians and broadcasters. 'Broadcasters and Politicians: The Relationship Under Pressure', highlights the potential for conflict in the relationship and illustrates how on some occasions the intervention of government in broadcasters' activities can enjoy wide support and hence legitimacy (the ban on broadcasting proscribed organisations in Northern Ireland), while on other occasions a less robust intervention (the postponement of *Death on the Rock*) may none the less be regarded by broadcasters, members of the public and others as undue interference. The extracts concerning impartiality reveal the difficulties that arise for politicians when they legislate to guarantee what they consider to be 'good professional practice' for broadcasters; it also illustrates politicians' suspicions about broadcasters. 'Television and Parliament', explores the politicians on the horns of a dilemma. On the one hand, they are keen to avail themselves of the advantages of televising parliament – advantages which might accrue to them as individuals or to the broad public via the democratising effects of televising proceedings. On the other hand, they are persistently wary of broadcasters and the possible impact of television broadcasting on the proceedings of the House. Finally, 'Party Political Broadcasting' illustrates broadcasters and politicians in more collaborative mood, with each seeing advantage in a formalised system of free access for politicians to broadcasting resources at key stages in the political and electoral cycle.

Reference

Franklin, B. (1992) *Televising Democracies*, London: Routledge.

BROADCASTERS AND POLITICIANS: THE RELATIONSHIP UNDER PRESSURE

5.1 The Broadcasting Ban on Reporting Northern Ireland

Censorship is the most obvious and dramatic form of control which a government can assume over broadcasting authorities: it was last exercised in Britain in 1988. The then Home Secretary Douglas Hurd, using existing powers available to him, issued notices to the BBC and IBA outlawing the broadcasting of statements made by members of certain identified political organisations based in Northern Ireland. The broadcasting ban was open-ended. Roy Hattersley, the opposition spokesperson, denounced the ban as ineffective, imprecise in its terminology and insulting to citizens who should be allowed the right to make their own judgements about these matters. It offered a 'publicity coup', moreover, to the proscribed organisations which would inevitably denounce the government as the 'enemy of free expression'. In an uncharacteristically clumsy defence Hurd announced to the House of Commons that 'this is not a restriction on reporting. It is a restriction on direct appearances by those who use or support violence'.

Douglas Hurd. For sometime broadcast coverage of events in Northern Ireland has included the occasional appearance of representatives of paramilitary organisations and their political wings, who have used these opportunities as an attempt to justify their criminal activities. Such appearances have caused widespread offence to viewers and listeners throughout the United Kingdom particularly just after a terrorist outrage.

The terrorists themselves draw support and sustenance from access to radio and television – from addressing their views more directly to the population at large than is possible through the press. The government have decided that the time has come to deny this easy platform to those who use it to propagate terrorism. Accordingly, I have today issued to the Chairmen of the BBC and the IBA a notice, under the licence and agreement and under the Broadcasting Act 1987 respectively, requiring them to refrain from broadcasting direct statements by representatives of organisations proscribed in Northern Ireland and Great Britain and by representatives of Sinn Fein, Republican Sinn

Fein, and the Ulster Defence Association. The notices will also prohibit the broadcasting of statements by any person which support or invite support for these organisations. The restrictions will not apply to the broadcast of proceedings in parliament, and in order not to impair the obligation on broadcasters to provide impartial coverage of elections, the notices will have a more limited effect during election periods . . . These restrictions follow very closely the lines of similar provisions which have been operating in the Republic of Ireland for some years. . . .

Broadcasters have a dangerous and unenviable task in reporting events in Northern Ireland. This step is no criticism of them. What concerns us is the use made of broadcasting facilities by supporters of terrorism. This is not a restriction on reporting. It is a restriction on direct appearances by those who use or support violence.

I believe this step will be understood and welcomed by most people throughout the United Kingdom . . .

Roy Hattersley. Like the overwhelming majority of citizens in this country the Labour party is dedicated to the defeat of terrorism and we share the natural revulsion at the exhibition on television of support for terrorists and terrorist organisations. But the important task is not so much demonstrating disapproval as defeating the IRA and the UDA and it is against that criterion, together with the consequences for freedom of speech and the practicality of the proposals, that the Home Secretary's statement must be judged.

Will the Home Secretary confirm that nothing that he now proposes reduces the opportunities for the opinions of terrorist organisations to be reported on television or in newspapers? All that he has done today is to prevent personal appearances . . . Has he considered the damaging way in which his proposals will be used at home and abroad, especially in the United States to portray the government as the enemy of free expression? Has he weighted the publicity coup for the IRA against the advantage of keeping its representatives off television? Does he not have enough faith in the British people to accept that such personal appearances only increase the revulsion and contempt felt by most British viewers for terrorists and terrorism?

Can the Home Secretary tell us how the law will define such general concepts as 'representatives of' and 'supporting'? Will he assure us that there will be a more objective test of those terms than simply the government nominating individuals who must not be interviewed on television or radio? That would be an absolutely unacceptable power for any government to possess.

What consequences does the Home Secretary foresee from his necessary exemptions of both the House and the period of parliamentary elections? Is there not something absurd in allowing the hon. member for Belfast West [Mr Adams] were he to attend the House, to voice his views on 'Yesterday in Parliament' while at the same time preventing him being interviewed on that speech as he left the building?. . .

Does not an examination of the detailed results of the proposal demonstrate that it is trivial, worthless and almost certainly counter-productive in the real fight against terrorism? Today's statement is intended to create the illusion, rather than the reality of activity. It will make the government look simultaneously repressive and ridiculous.

Douglas Hurd. The notice that I have given to the two chairmen today is, I believe, clear and precise. It specifies organisations, and I believe that is as clear and precise as such a notice can reasonably be. Of course, it distinguishes between speech in the House and speech outside. If I had not done that, I should have been immersed in considerable argument about privilege, which I wished to avoid as that would have obscured the main issue.

The Broadcasting Act and the Representation of the People Acts lay certain obligations of impartiality on the broadcasting organisations during elections and it was right that that should be respected when we drafted the notice . . .

This step will invoke an immediate flurry of protest from Sinn Fein and the supporters of terrorism, but it will deny them a weapon of which I believe they have made substantial use . . . I believe that the use those people have made of direct access to radio and television has aroused the deepest outrage in Northern Ireland, as I said in my statement. People cannot understand how we are to be taken seriously in fighting terrorism if, after reading a statement by my right hon. friend the Secretary of State for Northern Ireland, for example, the next thing that they see on the news is a supporter of terrorism using direct access to underline or deepen the impression that he wishes to create.

The airwaves are full of points of view with which we all disagree from time to time. In a free society it is our job to argue and, we hope, to out-argue in those discussions. However, we are not talking abut that. We are talking about whether there should be a platform for those whose weapon is not argument but destruction and death . . .

The two notices are from me to the regulatory authorities the BBC and the IBA. It is then for them, as regulatory authorities using their powers of discipline, to ensure that those notices are respected. If they are not respected, that is a matter for my action against the regulatory authorities.

Parliamentary Debates (1988), 'Broadcasting and Terrorism', 19 October, Vol. 138, cols 893–902.

5.2 *The Windlesham/Rampton Report on Death on the Rock*

Governments only occasionally try to resolve conflicts with broadcasters by using the very blunt tool of censorship. More typically, politicians might suggest that a programme should not be broadcast. This happened with *Real Lives*. Such requests, however, are not always conceded by broadcasters. In 1988 Thames Television broadcast the programme *Death on the Rock*, produced by the distinguished team of journalists responsible for the current affairs series *This Week*. The programme examined the shooting of three members of the IRA, allegedly engaged on a bombing campaign in Gibraltar; but after their deaths, the three people were found to be unarmed, and no explosives were ever found. The programme challenged the official version of events and prompted considerable anger among politicians and the press. On 4 May 1988, Sir Geoffrey Howe, then Foreign Secretary, wrote to Lord Thomson of Monifieth, who chaired the IBA, requesting that broadcasting of the programme be postponed on grounds that it would prejudice the inquest in Gibraltar and would constitute 'trial by television'. Thomson rejected the request. The furore in the press was considerable. On 29 April 1988, *The Times* headline denounced 'Trial by TV Row Over IRA Killings Film', while the *Sun* reported the 'Storm at SAS Telly Trial' and the *Daily Mail* reported the 'Fury Over SAS "Trial by TV"'. The protests by politicians and the press became so severe that in October 1988 Thames Television commissioned a special inquiry into the programme which was published as *The Windlesham/Rampton Report on Death on the Rock.* Initially, the commissioning of the report occasioned misgivings among some broadcasters who believed it might be interpreted as an acknowledgement of culpability, but the findings of the report vindicated Thames Television and stated that the programme makers 'did not bribe, bully or misrepresent those who took part . . . and did not offend against the due impartiality requirements of the IBA' (p.142). Windlesham/Rampton also argued that journalists had a right to report matters which 'those in authority' consider 'inappropriate' or 'embarrassing', but reminded broadcasters of the public opprobrium which they might attract when they offend widely held public beliefs. The conciliatory and sensitive report did little to placate politicians' concerns. No. 10 issued a statement saying that the Prime Minister 'utterly rejected' the findings of the report.

169 As the Inquiry progressed, we became increasingly conscious that to subject any programme to such a very detailed scrutiny several months after it had been screened would be likely to inconsistencies or lapses in judgement. Yet of its very nature television journalism, like newspaper reporting, does not depend on absolute accuracy for its validity. Journalists are often writing against the clock, sometimes (as in this case) pursuing inquiries of undoubted public importance, but without the cooperation of some or all of the directly interested parties. They can only work with the sources which are available at the time and cannot be expected to acquiesce in treating certain subjects as being put out of bounds whenever those in authority consider it to be inappropriate or irresponsible for potentially embarrassing or inconvenient questions to be asked. The relatively unrestricted opportunities for investigation which the British print and broadcast media enjoy are only earned, however, if what is known of the other side, be it an official policy or a private interest, is fairly put before the public.

170 How did 'Death on the Rock' measure up to this standard? . . .

171 An analysis of the content of the programme has led us to the conclusion that taken as a whole 'Death on the Rock' did not offend against the due impartiality requirements of the IBA and the Broadcasting Act 1981 . . . We find that the true meaning and effect of the programme was that it pointed towards one possible explanation of the shootings, namely that the deceased might have been unlawfully killed. This conclusion falls well short of the criticism that in effect the programme had posed the single question whether the terrorists had been executed as part of a deliberate plot, and then answered it in the affirmative. But we are aware that to some readers of this report the distinction

may seem a fine one, which is another reason for urging a study of the arguments which we offer to support it.

172 It may be it was the thoroughness with which the programme was produced, and the vividness with which it was presented, that made 'Death on the Rock' a lightning conductor for the intense feelings that the Gibraltar shootings evoked in the minds of the British public. It was evident from Parliament and the press that attitudes were deeply divided. Some people felt that in countering the IRA's brutal campaign of violence . . . the security forces were fully entitled to take such measures as were necessary to protect the people of Gibraltar . . . from planned assassination. Others, while similarly abhorring the IRA's objectives and tactics, were disturbed about the implications of any actions by the security forces, whether in Northern Ireland or elsewhere, which fell outside the specific limitations of the rule of law by which they are bound. The conflict was essentially one of divergent personal attitudes and values rather than of party political divisions. Some reactions were inchoate, instinctive rather than certain; others were forthright and passionate . . .

173 Hazardous though it is to get close to a lightning conductor, even after the storm has passed, we can take heart from the fact that such strongly conflicting views were widely and eloquently voiced on an issue of profound public importance . . . Diverse values freely expressed are unmistakable marks of a free society. It does not always make for a comfortable or popular life for those who have unleashed powerful forces they may not have anticipated but . . . broadcast journalists must not be too sensitive towards criticism of their work or function.

174 We advance the proposition that 'Death on the Rock' reflected the virtues and limitations of television journalism in the late Eighties. The paradox is that while taken overall the programme fulfilled the requirements of a complex regulatory system, its transmission outraged a section of the population at large as well as provoking bitter criticism in Parliament and the press . . . The programme-makers were experienced, painstaking and persistent. They did not bribe, bully or misrepresent those who took part. The programme was trenchant and avoided triviality. Despite the various criticisms which we have noted in our report, we accept that those who made it were acting in good faith and without ulterior motives.

175 Yet we have found that the effect of the programme went beyond its stated intention of laying before the viewers certain evidence giving rise to questions that deserved to be examined by an authoritative tribunal such as a judicial inquiry. The suggestion that the terrorists might have been unlawfully killed was enough to offend those in the viewing public who saw in the programme a subversive and unfair attack on the security forces when they were unable to give their side of the story. The content of the programme was demonstrably unsympathetic towards the IRA in its orientation. Nevertheless some of these viewers found it lacking in identification with the objectives of the security forces. Exactly the same criticism had been made of media coverage at the time of the Falklands War. While the public mood is notoriously difficult to interpret there are sufficient indications that 'Death on the Rock' was out of step with a substantial body of national opinion. Others, of course, took a contrary view and spoke up accordingly.

176 We cannot ignore the realisation that it was the alienated rather than the satisfied voices which brought about the establishment of our Inquiry in October 1988. Whether such a state of affairs is seen as a matter of concern, or simply as the price of independence, is another and larger question. We leave our report with one final reflection. Whatever view is taken of the state of public opinion and the legitimacy of Government intervention, the making and screening of 'Death on the Rock' proved that freedom of expression can prevail in the most extensive, and the most immediate, of all the means of mass communication.

Lord Windlesham and Richard Rampton QC (1989) *The Windlesham/Rampton Report on Death on the Rock*, London: Faber and Faber, 145pp. © 1988 Thames Television Limited, A Pearson Television Company.

5.3 Politicians and the Culture of Dependency

In his 1994 MacTaggart Lecture entitled 'Power, Politics and Broadcasters', Greg Dyke attacked what he described as the 'culture of dependency'. He argued that 'It is not the role of broadcasters to spend their time currying favour with the government'. Dyke claimed it was the relationship between Murdoch and Thatcher which 'really changed the rules of the game'. In his conclusions, Dyke proposes a royal commission on broadcasting, the appointment of more independent broadcasting regulators and argued for a guaranteed income for the BBC for ten years.

So what are the threats to the broadcasters' freedom to challenge, to rock the boat or to expose, which I now believe we have to counter? They are not Norman Tebbitt openly attacking the BBC or Margaret Thatcher ranting and raving about *Death on the Rock*. They are caused by the growth of a dependency culture in which broadcasters are increasingly dependent on the actions of government in some cases for their very existences and, in the commercial sector, for their financial success. This is not healthy for broadcasting.

The old ITV franchise system was once explained to me as a game of pass the parcel: everyone got into trouble with the regulator or even the government at some time during the period of a franchise; the art was not to be in trouble with the regulator at the time of the franchise. Inevitably companies were more cautious in their investigative journalism when a new Broadcasting Act was going through or franchises were up for renewal. But for the rest of the ten-year franchise period the ITV companies were largely strong enough to see off government pressure, usually with the support of the old Independent Broadcasting Authority.

In ITV some of us naïvely believed once the franchises had been awarded in 1991, the old pass-the-parcel rules would disappear and we would be free from the need to lobby and 'stay close' to government for a decent period. Of course, nothing has been further from the truth. For a number of reasons – a combination I suspect of the inadequacies of the Broadcasting Act, the business ambitions of some of the ITV companies, and the changing face of competition – the larger ITV companies now always want something more out of government. This is a potential threat to a politically free broadcasting system and potentially gives enormous power to the government of the day . . .

The problem is that the 1990 Broadcasting Act effectively told ITV companies that being a business was more important than being a broadcaster . . . if you look around the ITV system today, in only four of the fifteen companies is the most powerful executive from a broadcasting or programme background . . . There has been a significant shift in power.

Of course it was the relationship between Rupert Murdoch and the Thatcher government which really changed the nature of the game. The cross-media ownership rules in the 1990 Broadcasting Act were devised to create diversity of ownership – but just happened to exclude News International's majority ownership of *BSkyB*. The result was all other broadcasters and newspaper groups were disadvantaged when compared with News International. It's equally clear that this exclusion was reward for putting the full weight of the Murdoch papers behind the Thatcher government. The lesson: lobbying and currying favour with government was clearly effective . . .

We need to recognise that the ITV companies for their legitimate business interests will continue lobbying government. Last year the powerful ITV companies wanted to change the ownership rules for their own business reasons. Next year . . . the two largest ITV companies, Carlton and Granada who now own 72 per cent of ITN – which the law doesn't allow – will no doubt want . . . to change the ownership rules of ITN. Again they'll be lobbying the government . . . It will take a very brave ITV broadcaster to make or broadcast a controversial programme about government if by doing so it believes it is seriously threatening its chance of persuading the government to change a particular piece of legislation . . .

So what about the BBC? Isn't it now safe for ten years? Can't it occasionally take on the government? Certainly in recent years the BBC does not appear to have been at its bravest. The Charter renewal process has had the same effect on the BBC as the franchise process has had at times on ITV.

Does the government White Paper mean the BBC is now able to be a broadcaster free from the need to keep government on-side? Sadly I don't think it does. First, the government has renewed the charter for ten years not the fifteen it got last time. So by the seventh year at the latest the old game is back in play; everyone has got to keep the government of the day happy . . . But far more important, the government plans to look again at the means of funding the BBC after just five years . . . So the message could well be interpreted as saying step out of line and you could well lose the licence fee . . .

Put yourself in say October 1996. The Blair government has just been elected on a programme of open government. There is a short window of say a couple of years before the Labour government follows the paths of most governments and realises it doesn't want government to be quite as open after all. What in that two years do we want them to do to protect broadcasters from undue government influence and, at the same time, to sort out the legislative mess left by the 1990 Broadcasting Act?

. . . After just a week in government I'd like . . . a government Commission to look at broadcasting . . . We need a Commission made up of interesting and thoughtful people not politicians.

We can assume that the Blair government will go ahead with plans for both a Bill of Rights and a Freedom of Information Act . . . what is important however, is that the Commission ensures that within the Bill of Rights not only is the individual protected against the power of the state . . . but that proper, fair questioning journalism is also protected from the power of the state by statute supported by an independent constitutional court. Secondly, the Commission needs to ensure that the powers given by parliament to the broadcasting regulators should be enacted as part of this Bill of Rights so that the government of the day cannot simply abolish or change their role on a whim. Thirdly, it is important the broadcasting regulators are appointed by and answerable to an authority other than the government of the day. We must never again be in a position where the government of the day can fill the BBC's board of governors with their friends and placemen as the Thatcherites did. Fourthly, the BBC should be given certainty of its income for the whole ten years of its charter . . . Fifthly, the Commission needs to sort out the role and purpose of regulation of commercial television for the next decade . . . regulation needs to be equally applied to all commercial broadcasters which it isn't at present . . . Sixthly, because of what could be the growing tension between some sorts of journalism and the business interests of the commercial broadcasters, the commission should look closely at the viability of a requirement that commercial broadcasting organisations should have two boards – a business board (to protect shareholders' interests) and a broadcasting board (to take account of the public's wider interests).

Finally, we have to be able to offer the ITV companies, Channel 4 and possibly Channel 5, some sorts of certainty in an uncertain commercial world. We have to end the position whereby they believe they can always get a bit more from government. We have to end the unhealthy dependency culture which has grown up in the past five years.

Greg Dyke (1994) 'Power, Politics and Broadcasters', MacTaggart Lecture at the Edinburgh Film Festival, 26 August.

IMPARTIALITY

5.4 The Broadcasting Act 1990 and Impartiality

Throughout the 1980s, the Conservative government seemed to believe that political news on television was biased in favour of its political opponents. This belief led to a series of very public spats between the government and broadcasters, especially those at the BBC. In 1985, for example, the government complained about a *Panorama* programme which portrayed armed members of the IRA 'policing' a roadblock at Carrickmore; later the same year, the then Home Secretary Leon Brittain persuaded the BBC Governors to postpone and re-edit the documentary *Real Lives* which the Prime Minister claimed offered terrorists the 'oxygen of publicity'. A year later Norman Tebbit denounced as 'biased' the BBC's news coverage of the American bombing of Libya, while in 1987 the special branch raided the offices of BBC Scotland and took away journalist Duncan Campbell's notes and research materials concerning a programme, highly critical of government defence policy, entitled *Secret Society*. But the government's concern about bias in television news and current affairs programming was not limited to the public sector of broadcasting. In 1988, the government tried to prevent the showing of Thames Television's programme *Death on the Rock* which contested the government's account of the shooting of three members of the IRA on Gibraltar (see 5.2 above). During the passage of the Broadcasting Bill in 1989, Lords Orr-Ewing and Wyatt decided to address the issue and introduced an amendment which required the ITC to draft a code of conduct for broadcasters concerning impartiality in programming. The amendment constituted a legal and broadcasting precedent; a statutory requirement for impartiality. The amendment, which was eventually successfully incorporated into the Broadcasting Act 1990, generated considerable controversy and a great deal of resentment among broadcasters.

The code was to ensure impartiality in all programming including news and current affairs, but also fictional formats like drama; *Play for Today* as well as *World in Action*. Programme makers argued that the Code was unworkable and suggested that matters such as impartiality were best left to broadcasters' professional judgements rather than involving politicians and bureaucrats in regulatory quangos. The ITC's code reflected some of the complexities involved in defining impartiality (the preferred term was 'due impartiality'), but argued that it did not imply neutrality or balance in any simple 'mathematical sense'. Nor did it invalidate programmes in which individuals might express strong personal opinions, although these perhaps required special safeguards to guarantee impartiality. The code acknowledges that ultimately impartiality requires the broadcasters to exercise 'editorial judgement'. Interestingly, although the impartiality amendment of the 1990 Act and the subsequent ITC code triggered considerable controversy, neither has been evoked to keep broadcasters in line. Following the 1992 general election, when complaints of media partisanship had quite regularly issued from political parties on all sides of the political debate, political broadcaster Glyn Mathias noted the absence of even a single mention of the impartiality clause (Mathias, 1993).

Reference

ITC Code on Impartiality. http://www.itc.org.uk For a discussion of the code see Mathias, G. (1993) 'Competing With Impartiality', *British Journalism Review* 4 (1), pp.16–20.

6. (1) The Commission shall do all that they can to secure that every licenced service complies with the following requirements, namely . . .

(c) that due impartiality is preserved on the part of the person providing the service as respects matters of political or industrial controversy or relating to current public policy.

(2) In applying subsection (1) (c) a series of programmes may be considered as a whole.

(3) The Commission shall –

(a) Draw up and from time to time review, a code giving guidance as to the rules to be observed in connection with the application of subsection (1) (c) in relation to licenced services; and

(b) Do all they can to secure the provisions of the code are observed in the provision of licenced services;

and the Commission may make different provision in the code for different cases or circumstances.

(4) Without prejudice to the generality of subsection (1), the Commission shall do all that they can to secure that there are excluded from the programmes included in a licenced service all expressions of the views and opinions of the person providing the service on matters . . . which are of political or industrial controversy or relate to current public policy.

(5) The rules specified in the code referred to in subsection (3) shall, in particular, take account of the following matters –

(a) That due impartiality should be preserved on the part of the person providing a licensed service as respects major matters falling within subsection (1) (c) as well as matters falling within that provision taken as a whole; and
(b) the need to determine what constitutes a series of programmes for the purposes of subsection (2).

(6) The rules so specified shall, in addition, indicate to such extent as the Commission considers appropriate –

(a) what due impartiality does and does not require, either generally or in relation to particular circumstances;
(b) the ways in which due impartiality may be achieved in connection with programmes of particular descriptions;
(c) the period within which a programme should be included in a licensed service if its inclusion is intended to secure that due impartiality is achieved for the purposes of subsection (1) (c) in connection with that programme and any programme previously included in that service taken together;

and those rules shall in particular indicate that due impartiality does not require absolute neutrality on every issue or detachment from fundamental democratic principles.

(7) The Commission shall publish the code drawn up under subsection (3) and every revision of it, in such manner as they consider appropriate.

The Broadcasting Act 1990, London: HMSO, Part 1, sections 6(1)–(7).

5.5 Impartiality or Censorship?

The week after Lord Wyatt proposed an amendment to Section 6 of the Broadcasting Bill to introduce a code on impartiality, distinguished journalist John Pilger attacked the proposal as 'one of the most blatant, audacious attempts to impose direct state censorship on our most popular medium' (*Guardian*, 8 October 1990: 25). Pilger argued that the requirement for television producers to make additional programmes to 'balance' the sentiments expressed in an initial programme would prove costly and make television companies less likely to commission programmes with any controversial content. Television, Pilger argues, has superseded newspapers as the fourth estate in Britain: this prominence worries those in power. Investigative television

> journalism, moreover, enjoys a considerable reputation worldwide precisely because programmes expose and make public instances of corruption in government and business. Such programmes would subsequently be denounced as 'one-sided'. The true purpose of the amendment was 'control'.

The Arts Minister David Mellor has described a proposed amendment to clause six of the Broadcasting Bill as 'British and sensible'. Mellor is a lawyer; he will understand that the corruption of language is the starting point. Indeed there is something exquisitely specious about the conduct of this affair. Censorship is never mentioned. The code words are 'impartiality' and 'balance'; words sacred in the lexicon of British broadcasting resonant with fair play and moderation: words long abused. Now they are to provide a gloss of respectability to an amended bill that is a political censor's mandate and dream . . .

In July, the Home Office minister Lord Ferrers announced that the government wanted to amend the Broadcasting Bill with in effect a code of 'impartiality' that would legally require the television companies to 'balance' programmes deemed 'one-sided' . . . The point about this amendment is that it has nothing to do with truth and fairness. Charlatans and child abusers, Saddam Hussein and Pol Pot, all will have the legal right to airtime should they be the objects of 'one-sided' journalistic scrutiny. But control is the real aim. The amended Bill will tame and where possible prevent the type of current affairs and documentary programmes that have exposed the secret pressures and corruption of establishment vested interests, the lies and duplicity of government ministers and officials. Thames TV's *Death on the Rock* exemplified such a programme. Unable to lie its way to political safety, the government tried unsuccessfully to smear both the producers of *Death on the Rock* and the former Tory minister whose inquiry vindicated them. The amendment is designed to stop such programmes being made . . .

A skilful political game has been played. Thatcher's stalking horse in the Lords has been Woodrow Wyatt . . . Wyatt's refrain has been that broadcasting in Britain is a quivering red plot: 'left wing bias' he calls it. In the Lords he tabled an amendment to the Bill that would 'define impartiality' . . . Such obsession with political control stems mainly from a significant shift in how the establishment and the public regard the media. In many eyes, television has replaced the press as a 'fourth estate' in Britain. This alarms those who believe television is there to present them, their ideology and their manipulations in the best possible light.

In contrast, much of the public now looks to television current affairs, documentaries and drama documentaries to probe the secrets of an increasingly unaccountable state. Every survey shows public approval of television current affairs and offers not the slightest justification for new restrictions . . . For more than a quarter of a century, Granada's *World in Action* has exposed injustices, great and small and made the sort of enemies of whom serious journalists should be proud . . .

Factual programmes are expensive, especially investigations that require time and patience. Under the new Bill how many companies will now risk controversy if it means having to make two or more 'balancing' programmes? What happened to Ken Loach's *Questions of Leadership* . . . Loach's four films demonstrated how the trade union leadership often collaborated with government against the interests of millions of working people. After months of circuitous delay and decisions taken in secret, the IBA decided that each of the four films would need 'balancing' and that another longer programme would be made to 'balance' that which had already been balanced. Arguing against this absurdity Loach maintained that because his films provided a view of trade unions rarely seen on television, they themselves 'were the balance'. They were never shown.

That Britain already has television censorship ought to be enough to alert us to the extreme nature of the demands of Wyatt and co. Since 1970 more than 50 television programmes on Ireland have been banned, doctored or delayed . . . The effectiveness of the present system often relies on its subtlety. 'Impartiality' serves to buttress what was known in the 1960s as the 'consensus view' which pretends that Britain is one nation with one perspective on events. This is untrue of course, and 'consensus view' is a euphemism for the authorised wisdom of established authority. Thus 'impartiality' is a principle to be suspended whenever the established order is threatened. During the Falklands war the minutes of the BBC's Weekly Review Board noted that reporting of the war was to be shaped to suit 'the emotional sensibilities' of the public, that the weight of BBC coverage would be concerned with government statements of policy and that impartiality was felt to be an 'unnecessary irritation' . . .

Anti-Bill lobbyists have argued that much of British television is among the best in the world. Yes, but this reputation derives in great part from those very 'dissenting' programmes that are the amendment's target and which follow a rich British tradition that has nothing to do with 'balance'. The first documentary makers, among them John Grierson, Denis Mitchell, Norman Swallow and Richard Cawston, presented people and places as they saw them; and their work was moving and often brilliant. For them the issue was not so much 'personal bias' as illuminating those areas of society which had long remained in the shadow. What they revealed was another Britain. John Grierson, for example, was the first to give people the opportunity to tell of what it was like to live with rats, damp and cold. Wyatt and co would have wanted to 'balance' him . . .

The Thatcher government . . . understand the usefulness of media more than any since the war . . . Almost all of its actions since 1979 have been in the name of the doctrine of 'a free market and a strong state', of expanding 'consumer choice' while restricting political choice . . . And of course the 'choice' is as phoney as 'balance' for it excludes the unprofitable and the politically unpalatable.

J. Pilger (1990) 'A Code for Charlatans', *Guardian*, 8 October, pp.25–27.

TELEVISION AND PARLIAMENT

5.6 The Debate about Televising the House of Commons

There were eleven major debates between 1959 and 1985 about televising the proceedings of the House of Commons. The arguments of advocates and opponents of allowing the cameras entry to the chamber were remarkably consistent across these almost thirty years. Many observers had anticipated that the debate introduced by Janet Fookes on 20 November 1985 would be successful (although it was defeated by 275 votes against the motion to 263 in favour) for three reasons. First, there had been an experiment in televising proceedings in the House of Lords between January and July 1985. Second, most European countries televised their parliaments; and third, while previous divisions had been very close, Prime Minister Thatcher was rumoured to be in favour of the cameras and it was expected that Conservative back benches would follow her into the 'Ayes' lobby. In the event she voted against televising, and the House did not support a motion to conduct an experiment in television broadcasting until 8 February 1988 (by a majority of fifty-four votes). A scholar of political communications analysed the arguments which MPs had offered so routinely against televising of the Commons' proceedings and published the findings in the Hansard Society journal *Parliamentary Affairs*. The numbers in brackets indicate the Hansard column number for the 20 November debate.

Advocates of broadcasting foresee substantial consequences flowing from a decision to televise the Commons. Television is considered a vital ingredient in a modern parliamentary democracy, capable of closing the communications gap between parliamentarians and citizens by educating and informing the latter. Television might also serve to halt the twentieth century decline of parliament and save it from political obscurity by publicising its central role as a watchdog of government . . .

The major objections [to televising the Commons] can be grouped under four categories; technical, reputational, party political and procedural, although the categories are not wholly exclusive.

Technical arguments

Members' concerns here centre on the technical difficulties involved in broadcasting. In terms of its lighting and acoustic properties, the House of Commons is far removed from a television studio and, so the argument runs, the equipment necessary to ensure television broadcasts of sufficient technical quality would constitute an unacceptable intrusion.

There are a number of particular grievances under this head which include queries about how many microphones would be necessary, where they would be placed and whether or not they would pick up and transmit the same level of annoying background noise as sound broadcasting (281). It is commonplace to complain that cameras would be bulky and intrusive . . . while cameras sited in the gallery would portray only the top of members' heads . . . It is usual for questions about cost . . . to be raised and . . . one member placed a figure of £2.5 millions on costs suggesting that this would be reflected directly in an increased licence fee.

Reputational arguments

A persistent concern of some members is that the eventual outcome of televising the proceedings of parliament would be a threat to the reputation and stature of the House among voters. This process has already begun with radio broadcasting which 'has done nothing but bring the House into disrepute' (296) and television would simply exacerbate this process.

Members' doubts about television coverage reflect what they consider to be the incompatibility of the two institutions, expressed by the antithetical objectives which they pursue and the values which inspire them. The ultimate telos of television is wrongly judged to be entertainment, which is achieved most readily by alighting upon and stressing the trivial and the sensational; the witty remark is more likely to be televised than the considered judgment . . . These values are not so much alien as irrelevant to the House where to quote Anthony Beaumont-Dark, 'reflection is what this House is meant to be about' (288). Informed and rational debate . . . are the objectives of the House, but these qualities are 'good for debate but not for television' (291).

Party political arguments

A third set of objections to the televising of the Commons articulate the worry of some members that the presence of television cameras would serve the interests of one party to the detriment of others and also serve to misrepresent or distort levels of support for each of the leading political parties within the House. Three specific objections are usually advanced.

First, in the recent debate [20 November 1985] it was suggested that the Conservative and Labour parties were supporting the motion with a cynical eye to the next general election. Both saw political advantage and propaganda possibilities in televising the Chamber (336) . . . A second objection was raised by Alan Beith . . . His concern was that televising the Commons would disadvantage the smaller parties by reinforcing public perceptions of an adversarial two-party system within the House (219–222) . . . This in turn would prompt difficulties of balance and, in one sense of the word, bias . . . This leads directly to a related difficulty. There would be no agreed and uncontentious criterion by which to allocate a 'fair' amount of screen time to the different parties; moreover, the disputes about the legitimacy of different criteria would themselves be inspired by partisan considerations and raise constitutional issues (346–347).

Procedural arguments

Procedural objections range from the relatively minor to the highly signficant; from assertions that specific procedures would change to more worrying and general forecasts that televising the House would change, if not destroy, its essential character.

So far as the former are concerned, there are regular predictions that broadcasting would result in members behaving more theatrically and flamboyantly and that television would promote the 'cult of the personality' (298). In debates members would speak more, interrupt more, put down more questions and speak directly to their constituents rather than the House (353) . . . Ministers would make four statements a day and in debate the 'front bench would monopolise'. The back benches would 'end up something like Cecil B. de Mille's chorus from Samson and Delilah' (307) . . .

These specific procedural changes, if aggregated, could culminate in a serious threat to the essential character of the House. The argument expressed here reveals a deep-rooted conservatism which preaches caution about change and the need to place a high value upon tradition and continuity with the past. It is therefore not surprising to find the case argued most cogently by members such as Enoch Powell and, in 1966, Quintin Hogg (now Lord Hailsham). 'The past generation of members who sit on these green benches' Powell reminded the House 'are the holders of a trust . . . which it is our duty to hand over as little as possible diminished to those who will sit here after us' (309).

Bob Franklin (1986) 'A Leap in the Dark: MP's Objections to Televising Parliament', *Parliamentary Affairs*, Vol. 39, pp.284–296.

5.7 Televising the Commons

The Case in Favour

On 20 November 1985, Janet Fookes (Plymouth, Drake) moved that this House 'approves in principle the holding of an experiment in the public broadcasting of its proceedings by television'. The motion was rejected. During the debate Michael Foot argued in support of the motion drawing heavily on the arguments used by Aneurin Bevan (his predecessor as Member for Ebbw Vale) when the issue was debated in 1959. Foot's remarks neatly illustrate the continuity informing the arguments in favour of televising proceedings in the House.

I hope that we shall have the wisdom to proceed to establish television in the House as soon as possible . . . Many of the arguments against televising our proceedings are the same as those that were used against the original reporting of the House . . . There were many members who said the affairs of the House might be trivialised if they were reported and that great debates might be debased. There was one argument that went beyond that. It was argued that if the proposals were implemented the character of the House would be changed. The character of the 18th Century House of Commons was changed by the reporting of its proceedings, and a very good thing, too . . .

It would be a very retrograde step if we were not to face change here and now. We should have done so long since . . . I shall recall to the House what was said a long time ago by my predecessor, who was then the member for Ebbw Vale . . . I shall quote some of this sentences, which continue to set some of the major arguments. He said:

> 'It was said last week . . . that there was a considerable gulf growing between this House and the nation. I believe that to be absolutely true. There is a lessening interest in our discussions. We are not reaching the country to the extent that we did. It can no longer be argued that the national newspapers are means of communication between the House of Commons and the public. The fact is that parliamentary reporting is becoming a sheer travesty. Apart from a few solid newspapers with small circulations, the debates in this House are hardly reported at all, and such reports as take place are, as hon. members on both sides know, a complete travesty of our proceedings. I am not making an attack upon the newspapers.'

And that probably went for those who were associated with them. I do not think that there are many Members who would consider those words inapposite to the position in which we find ourselves today.

My predecessor then described . . . the method by which television companies select the Members of Parliament who are to be most prominently displayed on the television screen. He used strong language in referring to the method, as he often did in other debates. I am sure that hon. Members will regard the following sentences as apposite. He said:

> 'In fact, there has been nothing more humiliating than to see Members of Parliament in responsible positions selected by unrepresentative persons to have an opportunity of appearing on the radio and television . . . In my opinion there is something essentially squalid . . . in Members of Parliament beginning increasingly to rely upon fees provided by bureaucrats in the BBC and ITV.'

I do not suppose that any of us reject the fees when they are graciously offered. None the less, it is much better that the major debates that are reported are the ones that take place in the House rather than those that take place afterwards between Members on both sides of the House who have been selected by those who run Broadcasting House or the ITV . . .

There will be misrepresentations and misreports and there will be complaints about them, just as there have been complaints about the newspapers' reporting of our affairs. These arguments were brought forward in 1965. For us to suggest in this year that we shall continue to refuse to allow the public to hear what happens in this place by means of television, which is the major form of communication throughout this country, is to deprive the House of its capacities and its rights, and to insult the public.

My predecessor Aneurin Bevan went on to say:

> 'All I am suggesting is that in these days when all the apparatus of mass suggestion are against democratic education we should seriously consider re-establishing intelligent communication between the House of Commons and the electorate as a whole. That surely is a democratic process.'

My predecessor then went on to say that he had not watched television very often, but he believed that some of its reports could bear favourable comparison with reports in the bulk of the newspapers. That was said in 1959. I think it would have been much better if we had decided then to go ahead with television.

I hope that we will proceed speedily with televising the House of Commons though I know there are arguments against it. It has been said that Front Benches and Privy Councillors will have an advantage. This is not necessarily the case with the reporting of proceedings by the press, and I do not see why it should be so with this new form of reporting.

It is also said that televising will infringe the rights of minorities and smaller parties. Sometimes it is said that the Liberal and Social Democratic parties will not have – [interruption]. Perhaps their attendance will improve with the television cameras. It is said – this is part of a larger argument which I must admit I am always rather dumbfounded to hear – that the Liberal and Social Democratic parties have been unfairly treated by the media. The complaint that the two Davids have been unfairly treated by the media strikes me as the basest example of gratitude since King Lear's daughters Goneril and Regan turned upon their father! The House of Commons need not devote too much attention to that aspect. I have not the slightest doubt that minorities and individuals will be able to reshape and guard the process as we proceed.

Parliamentary Debates (1986) 'Televising the House', Vol. 87, 20 November, cols 277–286.

5.8 Televising the Commons

The Case Against

On 19 July 1990 the Commons debated and approved the report of the Select Committee on Televising of the Proceedings of the House and agreed in principle that the televising of the Commons should continue indefinitely; there were some notable dissenters from this view. Roger Gale MP, an ex-television producer, long-standing opponent of television in the Commons and member of the Select Committee, argued against the continuation of broadcasting on technical and editorial grounds. In an essay reviewing the experiment in televising the Commons and making policy recommendations for its future development, Gale argued in favour of a dedicated channel for parliamentary broadcasting to be funded by the public purse.

I was described recently by a journalist as 'an unreconstructed opponent of the televising of the House of Commons'. That, for a journalist, is a tolerably accurate description, although it is also true that my views have modified since the debate that gave the entry visa to the Trojan Horse on 9 February 1988. In winding up that debate for the opponents I offered 'two separate but equally valid grounds – technical and editorial' for the rejection of the motion (HC Debs 1988: col. 277). Let me review the technical arguments first.

Members were offered, in a joint paper of 20 January 1988 prepared by the BBC and ITV, 'remote controlled cameras which could be mounted below the galleries . . . there would probably be seven and they would be slightly smaller than the current generation of news cameras' and 'a modest increase in the existing lighting level in the Chamber . . . particularly below the galleries'. It was immediately apparent that the technology available at that time meant the installation of cameras that would have intruded upon the back benches and a level of lighting that would have been hot and uncomfortable. The first lighting experiment conducted by the BBC engineers produced an almost universally hostile reaction even from those most ardent proponents of the 'experiment'.

'But it works in the House of Lords, doesn't it?' was the question most frequently posed by those eager to get the cameras into the Commons Chamber but blissfully unaware of the nature and requirements of television broadcasting. The House of Lords Chamber is larger and of a very different design from that of the Commons. There are positions available for tripod cameras that simply do not exist in the lower House, where the east and west galleries overhang the back benches, casting deep shadows. 'Why does it work in other legislatures?' was another question that begged all sorts of answers. Most other legislatures that we examined provided either fixed places or a podium for speakers – making the selection of pre-programmed shots a simple matter. Most other legislatures have also abandoned the freewheeling nature of Commons debate in favour of a more formal, more rigid and less immediate structure.

This leads directly to the editorial argument. 'Debate based upon an exchange of views in other legislatures has disappeared,' we said. 'Members go into their chambers and read set speeches to camera; they do not take part in debate.'

The advocates of televising deployed, at every opportunity, the argument that 'the public has a right to see and hear the elected representatives at work' and that somehow the admission of television cameras to the Chamber would enhance democracy. The claim is both naive and ill informed. What we were offered in terms of reporting from the House by the BBC and ITV – who at that time had assumed that it would automatically be they that did the job – was *Match of The Day* and edited highlights used to tart up the *Nine O'Clock News* and *News at Ten* with occasional 'live' coverage of the 'sexy bits' – such as Prime Minister's Question Time and the Budget – and selective forays on to the committee floors. The debate was not about democracy but about journalism and televisual entertainment.

'What is proposed is an experiment, nothing more,' read a letter from the movers of the motion. The House was in fact offered not an experiment but a Trojan Horse. It was abundantly plain that once the cameras were in the press would not allow them to be removed. With the passing of the resolution the name of the game, therefore, became damage control . . .

Funding a dedicated channel

A basic assumption of televising of the House has been that there should be no burden of finance on the public purse. This in itself is a quaint and inconsistent approach. The House has apparently decided, through the voting lobby, that the British public has a right to see the House of Commons at work, but is unwilling to provide adequate resources to achieve this policy objective. Unless we are prepared to accept that editorial control should rest with the BBC and ITV, we are duty bound to make provision for a dedicated channel, as an extension of the decision taken by the House and if necessary – to fund the service that we have already decided the public wants!

The precedents for the public funding of information services are already clear. Through the provision of BBC World Service, the Central Office of Information (COI) Government Information Departments . . . and Hansard, we commit some £450 millions a year to the subsidy of news and information. In this context the funding required to provide dedicated coverage of the Mother of Parliaments is not large. Indeed at some £5 millions a year, a parliamentary television service would be cheaper than the £9.5 million that the government has provided for a service to a maximum potential Gaelic speaking audience of about 80,000 people!

Roger Gale MP (1992) 'A Sceptic's Judgement of Televising the Commons', in B. Franklin (ed.) *Televising Democracies*, London, Routledge, pp.100–116.

5.9 Televising the Commons

The Decline across a Decade

Television broadcasting of the House of Commons began with the State Opening of Parliament on 21 November 1989, following Members' decision of 9 February 1988 to hold an experiment in televising the proceedings of the House. The Select Committee established to oversee the conduct of the experiment, appointed a group of researchers based at the Centre for Television Research at the University of Leeds to examine broadcasters' uses of pictures from the House of Commons in news, current affairs and parliamentary-based programmes across the experimental period. As a result of a unique collaboration between broadcasters and the Commons, the researchers enjoyed access to programmes broadcast not only on the four terrestrial channels (BBC1, BBC2, ITV and Channel 4) but the newly launched SkyNews, and significantly all thirty-one regional outlets of the BBC and ITV networks. The study concluded: 'British television has responded impressively to the challenge presented by its long-awaited entry to the House of Commons.' Across the study period, 'Westminster appeared remarkably frequently and prominently in both national and regional television news services.' The BBC1 *Nine O'Clock News* averaged 3.4 parliamentary stories per programme while the equivalent figure for ITV's *News at Ten* was 2.9 parliamentary stories each news day. In their submission of evidence to the Select Committee, the researchers noted that the experiment represented a 'honeymoon' period between broadcasters and politicians and that subsequent programming (if permission for further broadcasting was approved) might reduce in quantity and character; the past decade has witnessed the fruition of these expectations. Two studies (Franklin, 1996; Straw, 1993) noted a marked and substantial decline in newspaper reporting of Parliament. A study by Stephen Coleman for the Hansard Society in 1999 examined the four nightly news broadcasts by BBC1 and ITN between January and March 1999: 252 programmes across sixty-three days. The study findings suggested 'a major reduction' in parliamentary reporting in news programmes between 1989 and 1999. Equally significantly, the report noted the dominance of the front bench, but especially the Prime Minister, over the back benches in televised parliamentary coverage. The news values and priorities of programme makers in the late 1990s meant that parliamentarians now featured less frequently in news than did celebrities and criminals.

References

Franklin, B. (1996) 'Keeping it "Bright, Light and Trite": Changing Newspaper Reporting of Parliament', *Parliamentary Affairs*, January–February, pp.57–78.

Straw, J. (1993) 'The Decline in Press Reporting of Parliament', unpublished paper, available from the author at the House of Commons.

This study suggests that there has been a major reduction in the coverage of Parliament over the decade since the cameras entered the Commons. Over the whole period, 0.7% items featured Parliament compared with 3.5% featuring non-parliamentary institutions, 7.8% featuring star celebrities and 4.6% featuring criminals, non-parliamentary governmental institutions, 7.8% featuring star celebrities and 4.6% featuring criminals. From 3.4 per day on BBC1 in 1989–90, the figure for stories featuring Parliament has fallen to less than 1% per day in 1999. In 1989–90 the Prime Minister, Margaret Thatcher, featured in 268 actuality excerpts, more than any other MP, but still less frequently than her own Government backbenchers (770 contributions) and less than 20% of the 1,392 occasions in which backbenchers from the two main parties were featured. In 1999 frontbenchers predominated overwhelmingly. Tony Blair featured in 53 stories, more than all backbenchers added together.

The major reduction in the use of parliamentary actuality suggests that Parliament is regarded as being less newsworthy than both broadcasters and MPs predicted ten years ago. The concentration upon leading Government or shadow-government figures suggests that Parliament is frequently used more as a scenic backdrop for the coverage of the executive than as a means of reporting the activities of the legislature.

Two statements can be made about public viewing of Parliament on television: firstly, there is less parliamentary actuality shown on universally available television now than there was ten years ago; secondly, fewer people choose to watch parliamentary programmes now than ten years ago.

ITV broadcasts no regular national coverage of Parliament, although regional channels do run coverage relating to their own areas. ITN produces the *Channel 4 News*, which carries more parliamentary actuality than the main BBC and ITV News broadcasts, as well as *5 News* (which carries very little parliamentary actuality), Channel 4's *Big Breakfast News* (which carries none at all) and Channel 4's political series, *Powerhouse*, broadcasts four weekday mornings each week from the restaurant at 4 Millbank. Whereas in 1992 A *Week In Politics* was attracting audiences of over 600,000 and the *Parliament Programme* was attracting well over 200,000 viewers, in 1999 the *Powerhouse* audience hovers around 100,000. *Sky News*, a satellite channel, provides educational parliamentary coverage, including *Prime Minister's Questions.*

There is more television coverage of Parliament on the BBC today than there was in 1989, though most of this is scheduled outside prime time or on less accessible channels. The BBC . . . with its statutory requirement to provide daily reports of parliamentary proceedings, has been accused of meeting its formal obligation to 'show the green benches' of the House of Commons, rather than seeking to promote such coverage to a mass audience. BBC TV coverage amounts to 255 minutes per week of regular programming on BBC2 . . . and no regular programming on BBC1, although Parliament is occasionally shown on News reports or other current affairs programmes. Regular parliamentary coverage comprises *Despatch Box*, from midnight to 12.30 am on Mondays to Thursdays and *Westminster Live*, from 2.45 to 3.30 pm on Tuesdays, Wednesdays and Thursdays. *Westminster Live* is the most popular slot for coverage including live coverage of PM's Questions each Wednesday; its audience has declined from 815,000 in 1992 to 630,000 in 1999. *Despatch Box* receives an average audience of 270,000 (figures for April 1999) and the average audience for *Scrutiny* is 1.1 million. BBC Parliament shows over 100 hours of live or recorded parliamentary coverage each week and News 24 also shows some, but these channels are only available to cable, satellite or digital subscribers. A good example of the decline in parliamentary coverage since Blumler et al. reported in 1990 is BBC's *Breakfast News:* in 1990 there were 32 Commons events covered during the 15-week period; in 1999, over an 8-week period (April and May) there were only 3 uses of Commons actuality, all concerned with the Welfare Reform Bill over which the Government risked facing a backbench rebellion.

. . . Nicholas Winterton MP claimed that the BBC executives were 'trivialising and making peripheral what goes on in Parliament' (HC Deb c 495) . . . Stephen Pound MP asserted that 'It is a question of democratic accountability. This is about the forum of the nation; the place where decisions are taken that affect the lives of every single man, woman and child in these islands. This is the place where we act and speak on behalf of the people of this nation. We have a duty to be as open and transparent as possible in our activities in this House. The BBC has a concomitant duty to reflect that to the nation.' (HC Deb, c 156)

Not all MPs were unanimous in casting the blame for downgrading Parliament upon the BBC executives. Tam Dalyell MP observed that 'it is all very well for the hon. Member for Macclesfield (Mr Winterton) to say that in the past quarter of a century serious coverage has been reduced, but something else has been reduced: ministerial interest, in both parties, in the proceedings of the House of Commons.' (HC Deb, c 499) Roger Gale MP reflected that 'part of the problem is us: we are boring and announcements are made on the *Today* programme and on *The Word At One*, not in this place.' (HC Deb, c 504)

Stephen Coleman (1999) *Electronic Media, Parliament and the People*, London: Hansard Society.

PARTY POLITICAL BROADCASTING

5.10 The History of Party Political Broadcasting

The first party political broadcast (PPB) was in 1924; the first televised party election broadcast (PEB) was in 1951. In Britain, broadcasters have been acknowledged as playing a significant role in the democratic process by providing parties with opportunities to speak directly about their policies to the electorate both at times of elections (PEBs) and in the 'peacetime' between elections (PPBs). In 1947 a celebrated *aide-mémoire* formalised the previously *ad hoc* arrangements for allocating broadcast time between political parties. In the subsequent half-century, characterised by an expansion in the number of parties and broadcasting outlets, the development of new electoral arrangements and the election of members to newly established political bodies has on occasion generated increasingly acrimonious disputes between political parties and broadcasters and triggered the need for changes to the arrangements for allocating free broadcast time to political parties. The major changes to the system are detailed below.

1924	*First Party Election Broadcasts (PEBs)* – The BBC broadcast unedited party leader speeches during the General Election campaign – MacDonald (13 Oct), Baldwin (16 Oct), Asquith (17 Oct).
May 1926	*First Prime Ministerial broadcast* – Stanley Baldwin broadcast to the nation during the General Strike.
Apr 1928	*Allocation of time between parties for election broadcasts* – Reith tried to persuade the parties to agree among themselves the distribution of broadcasting time for the 1929 General Election. They failed and Reith did the job himself, to 'the equal discontent of all three parties'. This was the first occasion when comprehensive arrangements were made for PEBs. Minor parties were given access dependent on the number of candidates they fielded.
Apr 1928	*First Budget broadcast* – Churchill (Chancellor of the Exchequer) was allowed to make a factual broadcast after his Budget speech. 'He delivered

a good defence of the Budget, supposed to be non-controversial, but it was not' (Reith). The Opposition had no right to reply.

1933 *First Party Political Broadcasts* – Only a few of them, they didn't assume much importance until after WWII.

1934 *First Opposition response to a Budget broadcast* – Chamberlain, Attlee, Herbert Samuel and JH Thomas took part in a political series. This marked the start of regular Budget broadcasts.

After WWII *Committee on Party Political Broadcasting* – Established as an informal body to facilitate discussion between the BBC and political parties.

Feb 1947 *Party Political Broadcasts formalised – Aide-mémoire* drawn up by parties and broadcasters recommended limited number of controversial party political broadcasts be allocated to parties at times other than elections in accordance with their vote at the previous General Election. Also stated that ministerial statements should be allowed for 'purely factual' matters, to explain 'legislation or administrative policies approved by Parliament' or for 'appeals to the nation to co-operate in national policies.' Because statements were to be 'as impartial as possible' there would generally be no reply from the Opposition.

Oct 1951 *First televised Party Election Broadcasts* – Conservatives, Labour and the Liberal parties were each given fifteen minute broadcasts on television in addition to their radio broadcasts.

May 1953 *First televised PPB* – Macmillan (then Secretary of State for Housing) gave a broadcast for the Conservatives.

Sep 1955 *ITV came on air* – Too late for the 1955 General Election.

Apr 1956 *ITV began simultaneous transmission of PPBs* – But did not take all Ministerial broadcasts.

1956 *First reply to a Ministerial statement* – Gaitskell claimed and was allowed a reply to Eden's statement on Suez.

1962 *Allocation rules revised* – Liberals proposed by-election successes be taken into account when determining allocation of broadcasts. Principle accepted by the 'major' parties and put into effect from 1963.

1965 *Nationalists get PPBs* – Committee on Party Political Broadcasting announced five minute allocations to the SNP and Plaid Cymru on TV and radio: the first parties to make PPBs before winning seats in parliament.

1969 *New Aide-mémoire* – Government use of Ministerial statements for controversial matters prompted revision of rules. New *Aide-mémoire* identified two types of statement:

(i) *Explanation of enacted 'legislation or administrative policies' and calls for public co-operation in matters where consensus exists* (to fit within normal programmes and no Opposition replies allowed)

(ii) *Events of 'Prime national or international importance'* (Ministers to be given airtime, with Opposition able to reply, followed by a round-table debate ('stage three') with the two 'major' parties, Liberal Party and representatives of other parties with comparable electoral support).

Jun 1969 *First Ministerial statement under new rules* – Wilson made a broadcast on the

	withdrawal of the Government's trade union legislation. Heath replied and there was a 'stage three' roundtable debate. ITV did not carry the broadcasts.
1974	*Allocation rules revised* – Allocation of broadcasting time for PPBs no longer to be determined by agreement between parties. Rules established – ten minutes for every two million votes at the previous election (with the SNP given ten minutes for every 200,000 votes and Plaid Cymru getting ten minutes for every 100,000).
2 Nov 1982	*Channel 4 began* – And introduced a political comment slot, allocated to the parties on the same ratio as PPBs.
1990	*Broadcasting Act* – Section 36 requires licensees to observe rules determined by the ITC with respect to Party Political and Election Broadcasts. The ITC code states 'Airtime on ITV should be made available each year to the UK parties represented in the House of Commons and to the SNP in Scotland and Plaid Cymru in Wales. The time allocated to each party for Party Political Broadcasts is related to the number of votes cast for them in previous General Elections.' The IBA was no longer to be the broadcaster of the Channel 3 service.
1 Jan 1993	*ITC* – Ceases to be the broadcaster of the Channel 3 and 4 service and becomes the post-hoc regulator.
Jan 1996	*Agreement between Secretary of State for National Heritage and BBC* – No reference is made to PEBs or PPBs. The only relevant requirement on the BBC is to 'treat controversial subjects with due . . . impartiality'.
May 1996	*BBC sought Senior Counsel's advice on PEBs* – Two key points to emerge from the Conference were: (i) Producers' Guidelines state that the BBC submit proposals to the Committee on Party Political Broadcasting. This is a fiction as the business of the Committee is conducted by Murdo Maclean, the Secretary to the Chief Whip. The obligation to be fair and consistent is the BBC's and if challenged in court the BBC must be clear about this. (ii) A decision was taken to drop the concept of 'proven electoral support' for the minor parties and stick to a test of a minimum of 50 candidates.
Sept 1997	*Commercial radio stations* – Virgin Radio, Talk Radio and Classic FM start to take PPBs.
Mar 1997	*Channel 5 came on air* – Required by the ITC to take General Election and European Election PEBs.
Apr 1997	*Referendum Party took the BBC and ITC to Court* – To seek judicial review of their decision to offer the Party only one five minute television and radio PEB. In his judgement, Lord Justice Auld dismissed the party's application saying that the broadcasters had acted in a 'reasonable' manner.
Apr 1997	*Pro-Life Alliance Party took the BBC to Court* – Over the decision (made unanimously by all broadcasters) to remove a 2 minute 13 second sequence from their PEB on the grounds that it would offend against 'good taste or decency' and be 'offensive to public feeling'. Justice Dyson,

	in his judgement, concluded that there was 'no substance in any of the arguments' advanced by the Pro-Life Alliance Party. This judgement was upheld by the Court of Appeal in October.
Apr 1997	*Sinn Fein took the BBC to Court* – Over the decision made to cut two shots from their broadcast in Northern Ireland on the grounds that they were potentially defamatory. The Court upheld the BBC's decision.
Apr 1997	*BNP Election Broadcast* – The broadcasters failed to come to a unanimous view of the BNP broadcast which was eventually transmitted in two versions. The BNP was unable to make all the changes requested by Channel 4 and consequently they did not transmit it at all.
Jun 1997	*BBC and ITV wrote to the Secretary of the Committee on Party Political Broadcasting* – Thanking him for his services over the years and explaining that on legal advice it would be more appropriate for the BBC to receive representations directly from the various political parties rather than through the Committee.
Jun 1997	*Broadcasters formed the Broadcasters' Liaison Group* – To act as a forum in which the broadcasters, the ITC and the Radio Authority can collect information and receive representations from interested parties on the future of PPBs and PEBs.

BBC, ITC, Radio Authority and SC4 (1998) *Consultation Paper on the Reform of Party Political Broadcasting*, London, Appendix 1.

5.11 Reform of the Party Political Broadcast

The Broadcasters' Proposals

Throughout the 1980s and 1990s party political broadcasts proved increasingly unpopular with audiences and broadcasters. Successive research studies revealed their ineffectiveness in reaching audiences; in the 1992 election the Conservatives lost one viewer in five before the PEB started, Labour lost one in ten. Viewers believed the PPBs were too long, a view supported by specialists in political marketing and advertising. For their part, broadcasters believed the broadcasts disrupted the schedules and lost audiences. In an increasingly competitive market for audiences and advertisers, broadcasters were keen to reform this situation. But there were other factors suggesting the need for reform. The televising of Parliament and the expansion of news and current affairs programmes meant that audiences were much better served with political information and commentary than when PPBs were first broadcast. A further key change has been the growing number of elections to new political institutions such as the Scottish Parliament, the Welsh Assembly, the European Parliament as well as the general and local elections. In recommending reform, the broadcasting organisations in their consultation document published in 1998, the option of moving to a system of American-style, paid political advertising was rejected.

Summary of recommendations

Representations are, therefore, invited on proposals to:

- Move the focus of party political broadcasting to election campaigns when parties are directly seeking votes from the electorate.
- Replace the annual series of PPBs with more PEBs to reflect the growth in the number of elected bodies in the UK.
- Retain the system of PEBs for General Elections on the terrestrial TV networks, Radio 2 and Radio 4 with adjustments in Scotland and Wales and the three INR services.
- Introduce PEBs on BBC TV and Radio and UTV [Ulster Television] for the parties standing in Northern Ireland to replace the informal system of 'Campaign Broadcasts'.
- Introduce a higher threshold of one sixth of seats contested, for the minor parties in all elections.
- Establish a system of Election Broadcasts for the Scottish Parliament and Welsh Assembly.
- Increase the number of Local Election Broadcasts for major parties on BBC1 and BBC2 and on ITV from one to two.
- Review the system for European Elections when the current Bill has gone through parliament.
- Cease Budget broadcasts, and concentrate opportunities for Ministerial broadcasts on truly exceptional circumstances.
- Publish new ground rules covering editorial and compliance issues, and technical and delivery specifications.
- Introduce a scheduling requirement by the ITC for broadcasters to place Party Election Broadcasts between 1730 and 2330 and retain a commitment to prime time scheduling on the BBC.

BBC, ITC, Radio Authority and S4C (1998) *Consultation Paper on the Reform of Party Political Broadcasting*, London, p.11

5.12 Party Election Broadcasts

The New Guidelines

Party political broadcasts and party election broadcasts are radically different in form and content from their early predecessors. The black-and-white, head-and-shoulders shots of party spokespersons making statements about policy intentions have been replaced by shorter, tighter edited, highly sophisticated and visually complex film packages, which may incorporate voice-overs, location sequences, background music, appearances by actors rather than politicians and the use of a range of camera shots which closely approximate day-to-day television. The increased use of these complex and changing formats has prompted escalating complaints by politicians about the probity of using certain kinds of materials and filming techniques. But the principles informing party political broadcasting have remained constant despite these changes in formats. The fundamental belief is that parties should enjoy free airtime to appeal directly to voters without any editorial interference from broadcasters. In 1998, however, following the 1997 general election, the political parties asked the major broadcasters to clarify the ground rules or guidelines governing the production of PEBs. The new guidelines are reproduced below.

New Guidelines

Editorial Guidelines are designed to cover compliance issues and the political 'rules' to be observed by all parties. While the parties are responsible for the content of the broadcasts, they are required to observe the following guidelines, which have been agreed between the broadcasters and will be applied equally to all parties:

- All broadcasts must observe the law – for example, on libel, contempt, obscenity, incitement to racial hatred, the Representation of the People Act and all other relevant legislation.
- All broadcasts must comply with the relevant provisions of the BBC Producers' Guidelines, the ITC code on matters of taste and decency and the Radio Authority Codes of Practice (Chapters 5, 6 & 7 of the BBC Producers' Guidelines, Section 1 of the ITC Programme Code and Radio Authority codes of practice and the relevant section of the S4C Compliance Guidelines) and fairness and privacy (Chapters 3, 4 & 9 of the BBC Producers' Guidelines, Section 2 of the ITC Code and Radio Authority codes of practice and the relevant section of the S4C Compliance Guidelines), having regard to the political context of the broadcast.
- Subject to the matters set out above, accuracy is the responsibility of the parties making the broadcasts.
- Impartiality is achieved over the series of PEBs as a whole. There is, of course, no obligation on the parties to achieve impartiality within each broadcast.

- Extracts of recordings of parliamentary proceedings should not normally be used. If something of this nature is required, then it may be used only if it features a speech by a member of the party making the broadcast, and the member's consent has been obtained. The use of general scenes of either chamber or material featuring exchanges between the parties should not be included.
- Extracts from party conference speeches of the party allocated the broadcast may be used.
- Archive or news clips of speeches by members of opposing political parties should not be included. This applies to both visual and audio material alike.
- Broadcasters' own news footage will not be made available for party election broadcasts.
- Candidates taking part in a party election broadcast must not make any references to their own constituencies.
- No individual should be featured or identified in a broadcast in a manner that appears to support a party without that person's consent.
- The use of actors in a broadcast must be made clear to the audience if there is any possibility that the audience could be confused or misled by their appearance.
- No revenue-generating telephone numbers are to be used in a broadcast.

Technical guidelines will also be issued in due course. Tapes for television broadcasts must be received by 1200 on the day of transmission, or the allocation may be lost. This is an ITC Code requirement.

BBC, ITC Radio Authority and S4C (1998) *Consultation Paper on the Reform of Party Political Broadcasting*, London, pp.9–10.

GUIDE TO FURTHER READING

Overviews of television broadcasting and broadcasting policy

Bonner, P. and Aston, L. (1998) *Independent Television in Britain*, Volume V, *ITV and IBA, 1981–92: The Old Relationship Changes*, Basingstoke: Macmillan.

Briggs, A. *The History of Broadcasting in the United Kingdom*, five volumes, Oxford: Oxford University Press. Volume 1, *The Birth of Broadcasting 1896–1927* (1961); Volume II, *The Golden Age of Wireless 1927–1939* (1965); Volume III, *The War of Words 1939–1945* (1970); Volume IV, *Sound and Vision 1945–1955* (1979); Volume V, *Competition 1955–1974* (1995). The 'companion' five-volume history of commercial television, *Independent Television in Britain*, is published by Macmillan with volumes I and II written by Bernard Sendall, volumes III and IV written by Jeremy Potter and the recent volume V written by P. Bonner and L. Aston.

Crisell, A. (1997) *An Introductory History to Broadcasting*, London: Routledge.

Curran, J. and Seaton, J. (1997) *Power Without Responsibility*, 5th edn, London: Routledge.

Franklin, B. (1997) *Newszak and News Media*, London: Arnold.

Goodwin, P. (1998) *Television Under the Tories*, Broadcasting Policy 1979–1997, London: BFI.

Graham, A. and Davies, G. (1997) *Broadcasting, Society and Policy in the Multimedia Age*, Luton: John Libbey Media.

Hood, S. (ed.) (1994) *Behind the Scenes: The Structure of British Television in the Nineties*, London: Lawrence and Wishart.

McQuail, D. and Siume, K. (1998) *Media Policy: Convergence, Concentration and Communication*, London: Sage.

O'Malley, T. (1994) *Closedown? The BBC and Government Broadcasting Policy*, London and Boulder Col.: Pluto Press.

Potter, J. *Independent Television in Britain*, Volume III, *Politics and Expansion 1968–1980* (1989); Volume IV, *Companies and Progress 1968–1980* (1990), London: Macmillan.

Sendall, B. *Independent Television in Britain*, Volume I, *Origin and Foundation 1946–1962* (1983); Volume II, *Expansion and Change 1958–1968* (1983), London: Macmillan.

Seymour-Ure, C. (1991) *The British Press and Broadcasting Since 1945*, Oxford: Basil Blackwell.

Smith, A. (1974) *British Broadcasting*, Newton Abbot: David and Charles.

Television broadcasting policy: public service broadcasting

Atkinson, D. and Raboy, M. (eds) (1997) *Public Service Broadcasting: The Challenges of the Twenty-First Century*, Paris: UNESCO.
Barnett, S. and Curry, A. (1994) *The Battle for the BBC*, London: Aurum Press.
Blumler, J.G. (1993) 'The British Approach to Public Service Broadcasting: From Confidence to Uncertainty', in R.K. Avery (ed.) *Public Service Broadcasting in a Multichannel Environment*, New York and London: Longman.
MacCabe, C. and Stewart, O. (eds) (1986) *The BBC and Public Service Broadcasting*, Manchester: Manchester University Press.
McDonnell, J. (1991) *Public Service Broadcasting: A Reader*, London: Routledge.
Smith, M. (1993) *Public Service Broadcasting*, unpublished MA Thesis, University of Sheffield.
Stevenson, W. (1993) *All Our Futures*, London: BFI BBC Charter Review Series.
Stevenson, W. (2000) 'The BBC In the Future', in *e-britannia*, Luton: University of Luton Press, pp.121–127.
Tracey, M. (1998) *The Decline and Fall of Public Service Broadcasting*, Oxford: Oxford University Press.

Television broadcasting policy: finance

Barnett, S. (ed.) (1993) *Funding the BBC*, London: BFI.
Barnett, S. (2000) 'A Public Service Argument for Broadcasting in the 21st Century', in *e-britannia*, Luton: Luton University Press, pp.153–161.
Blumler, J.G. and Nossiter, T. (1991) *Broadcasting Finance In Transition: A Comparative Handbook*, New York and Oxford: Oxford University Press.
Collins, R., Locksley, G. and Garnham, N. (1988) *The Economics of Television*, London: Sage.
Davidson, A. (1992) *Under the Hammer; The ITV Franchise Battle*, London: Heinemann.
Graham, A. (ed.) (1999) *Public Purposes in Broadcasting, Funding the BBC*, Luton: University of Luton Press.
Wegg-Prosser, V. (1998) *BBC Producer Choice and the Management of Organisational Change*, unpublished Ph.D. thesis, Brunel University.

Television broadcasting policy: programmes

Barnett, S., Seymour, E. and Gabor, I. (2000) *From Callaghan to Kosovo: Changing Trends in British Television News 1975–1999*, London: University of Westminster.
Barnett, S. and Seymour, E. (1999) *A Shrinking Iceberg Slowly Travelling South: Changing Trends in British Television – A Case Study of Drama and Current Affairs*, London: Campaign for Quality Television.
Franklin, B. (1997) *Newszak and News Media* London: Arnold.
Glencross, D. (1994) 'Superhighways and Supermarkets', Speech to the Royal Television Society, 8 March.
Horrie, C. and Nathan, A. (1999) *Live TV: Tellybrats and Topless Darts – The Unusual Story of Tabloid Television*, London: Simon and Schuster.
Isaacs, J. (1989) *Storm Over 4*, London: Weidenfeld & Nicolson.

Street Porter, J. (1995) 'Talent versus Television', Twentieth James MacTaggart Lecture for the Edinburgh Film and Television Festival, reprinted in the *Guardian*, 26 August.

West Yorkshire Media in Politics Group (1986) *Research on the Range and Quality of Broadcasting Services: A Report for the Committee on Financing the BBC*, London: HMSO.

Wilson, R. (1994) *Local Television: Finding A Voice*, Church Stretton, Shropshire: Dragonflair Publishing.

Television broadcasting policy: regulation

Collins, R. and Murroni, C. (1997) *New Media, New Policies: Media and Communication Strategies for the Future*, Cambridge: Polity Press.

Graham, A. (2000) 'Public Policy Issues for UK Broadcasting', in *e-britannia*, Luton: University of Luton Press, pp.93–108.

Hamm, I. and Harmgarth, F. (eds) (1995) *Television Requires Responsibility, Vol. 2, International Studies*, Gutersloh: Bertelsmann Foundation Publishers.

Harvey, S. (2000) 'Broadcasting Policy and Broadcasting Regulation: Who Needs It?', Paper presented to the Manchester broadcasting Symposium, 24–25 March 1999.

Hearst, S. (1992) 'Broadcasting Regulation in Britain', in J.G. Blumler (ed.) *Television and the Public Interest: Vulnerable Values in West European Broadcasting*, London: Sage.

Mitchell, J. and Blumler, J.G. (1994) *Television and the Viewer Interest: Explorations in the Responsiveness of European Broadcasters*, London: John Libbey.

Shaw, C. (ed.) (1993) *Rethinking Governance and Accountability*, London: BFI BBC Charter Review Series, no 5.

Veljanovski, C. (1987) *Commercial Broadcasting in the UK: Over-Regulation and Mis-Regulation*, London: Centre for Economic Policy Research.

Television broadcasting policy: political communications

Blumler, J.G. and Gurevitch, M. (1995) *The Crisis of Public Communication*, London: Routledge.

Blumler, J.G. and Kavanagh, D. (1999) 'The Third Age of Political Communication', *Political Communication* 16(3), pp.209–230.

Blumler, J.G., Franklin, B., Mercer, D. and Tutt, B. (1990) *Monitoring the Public Experiment in Televising the Proceedings of the House of Commons*, published in the First Report of the Select Committee on the Televising Proceedings of the House, Session 1989–1990, Vol. 1, HC 265–1, London: HMSO.

Bolton, R. (1990) *Death on the Rock and Other Stories*, London: W.H. Allen.

Briggs, A. (1979) *Governing the BBC*, London: BBC.

Burns, T. (1977) *The BBC: Public Institution, Private World*, London: Macmillan.

Coleman, S. (1999) *Electronic Media, Parliament and the People*, London: Hansard Society.

Elstein, D. (1999) *The Political Structure of UK Broadcasting, 1949–1999*, unpublished lectures delivered at the University of Oxford by the Visiting Professor in Broadcast Media.

Franklin, B. (1989) 'Televising Legislatures: The British and American Experience', *Parliamentary Affairs*, October, pp.485–503.

Franklin, B. (ed.) (1992) *Televising Democracies*, London: Routledge.

Franklin, B. (1994) *Packaging Politics: Political Communication In Britain's Media Democracy*, London: Arnold.

Franklin, B. (1998) 'Tough on Soundbites, Tough on the Causes of Soundbites', *New Labour and News Management*, London: Catalyst Trust.

Jones, N. (1999) *Sultans of Spin*, London: Gollancz.

McKie, D. (1999) *Media Coverage of Parliament*, London: Hansard Society.

Milne, A. (1988) *DG: Memoirs of A British Broadcaster*, London: Hodder and Stoughton.

Negrine, R. (1996) *The Communication of Politics*, London: Sage.

Negrine, R. (1999) '*Parliaments and the Media: A Changing Relationship?*', *European Journal of Communication*, 14(3) pp.325–353.

Oborne, P. (1999) *Alastair Campbell: New Labour and the Rise of the Media Class*, London: Aurum Books.

APPENDIX A

Parliamentary Debates on Television Policy: A Chronological Listing

1 July 1986	Cmnd 9824	*Report of the Committee on Financing the BBC* Peacock, Prof. Alan (Chair)
3 July 1986	CH	Statement on the Report of the Committee on Financing the BBC 100 c1176–1189; 100 c1180–1193 Hurd, Douglas
10 December 1986	Bill	Free Television Licences for Pensioners Bill Winnick, David
14 January 1987	CH	Statement on Government response to Peacock report on Broadcasting and Television Licence Fees 108 c263–275 Hurd, Douglas
9 April 1987	PGA	The Broadcasting Act 1987
24 November 1987	Bill	Concessionary Television Licences for State Retirement Pensioners Bill Mowlam, Marjorie
16 May 1988	CH	Statement on Broadcasting Standards Council and appointment of Sir William Rees-Mogg as its first Chair 133 c685–695, 133 c6890–698 Hurd, Douglas
19 October 1988	CH	Statement on access to the Broadcast Media by certain paramilitary organisations in Northern Ireland 138 c885–895; 138 c893–903 Hurd, Douglas. Home Office
7 November 1988	Cm 517	*Broadcasting in the '90s: Competition, Choice and Quality* Home Office
13 June 1989	CH	Statement on the Future of Commercial Television and procedures for awarding Licences for Channels 3 and 5 154 c710–724 Hurd, Douglas

7 June 1990	Bill	Pensioners Television Licences Bill Vaz, Keith
1 November 1990	PGA	The Broadcasting Act 1990
13 November 1990	Cm 1303	*Competition and Choice: Telecommunications for the 1990s* Department of Trade and Industry
5 March 1991	Cm 1461	*Competition and Choice: Telecommunications Policy for the 1990s* Department of Trade and Industry
24 November 1992	Cm 2098	*The Future of the BBC* Department of National Heritage Brooke, Peter
24 November 1994	CH	Statement on the future of the BBC including the announcement of the White Paper *The Future of the BBC* Department of National Heritage 214 c741–753 Brooke, Peter
24 May 1994	Bill	Television Licences (Reduction for Poor Reception) Bill Hendry, Charles
6 July 1994	Cm 2621	*The Future of the BBC: Serving the Nation, Competing Worldwide* Department of National Heritage
6 July 1994	CH	Statement on the future of the BBC including the announcement of the publication of the White Paper, Cm 2621 Department of National Heritage 246 c315–330 Brooke, Peter
11 January 1995	Bill	Media (Diversity) Bill Mullin, Chris
21 February 1995	Bill	Television Sport (Public Access) Bill Grocott, Bruce
23 May 1995	Cm 2872	*Media Ownership; the Government's Proposals* Department of National Heritage
23 May 1995	CH	Statement on cross-media ownership including the announcement of the White Paper *Media Ownership* Department of National Heritage Dorrell, Stephen
10 August 1995	Cm 2946	*Digital Terrestrial Broadcasting: the Government's Proposals*
24 July 1996	PGA	Broadcasting Act 1996
15 July 1997	Bill	Television Licence Payments (Age Exemption) Bill Flight, Howard

February 1998	Dept	*Television the Digital Future: A Consultation Paper. Plus A Study to Estimate the Economic Impact of Government Policies Towards Digital Television* Department of Culture, Media and Sport
23 March 1998	Bill	Concessionary Television Licence (Amendment) Bill Swinney, John
21 July 1998	Cm 4022	*Regulating Communications: Approaching Convergence in the Information Age* Department of Trade and Industry/Department for Culture, Media and Sport
21 April 1999	Bill	Digital Television Broadcasting Bill Turner, George
21 February 2000	CH	Statement on the future funding of the BBC Department of Culture, Media and Sport Smith, Chris
12 December 2000	Cm 5010	*A New Future for Communications*

APPENDIX B

Committees of Inquiry into Broadcasting and Television Policy

Further details about each of these Committees of Inquiry are available at www.shef.ac.uk/uni/academic/R–Z/socst/staff/b_frankl.htm#publications

Click on British Television Policy Documents. You will need Adobe Acrobat to download this file.

The Sykes Committee

Title

Broadcasting Committee Report (Chaired by Sir Frederick Sykes) 1923, Cmd 1951, x, 13 Post Office.

Members

Sykes (Chair), Astor, Brown, Bunbury, Burnham, Eccles, Norman, Reith, Robertson, Trevelyan.

Terms of reference

'To consider: (a) Broadcasting in all its aspects. (b) The contracts or licences which have been or may be granted. (c) The action which should be taken upon the determination of the existing licences of the Broadcasting Company. (d) Uses to which broadcasting may be put. (e) The restriction which may need to be placed upon its user or development.'

Context

The establishment of the Sykes Committee was prompted by two factors. First, the British Broadcasting Company was experiencing severe financial difficulties. Founded on 14 November 1922, the BBC was a consortium of leading radio receiver manufacturers which, licensed by the Post Office, had been broadcasting radio programmes to stimulate demand for their radio sets. The newly formed BBC derived its income from royalties on the receivers which its member companies sold and the licence fees paid by listeners but collected by the Post Office. All radios were marked 'BBC' and no receivers of overseas manufacture could be purchased under the company's licensing agreement. The financial crisis for the company arose as a consequence of evasion of licence fee payments by listeners and the use of foreign components to construct 'home-made' receivers on which company royalties were not paid. The new medium of radio was enormously popular from the outset. In 1923, the Post Office issued 80,000 licences and a further million in 1924. But evasion of the licence fee was equally popular; Crisell estimates that between four to five times this number of radio sets were in use (Crisell, 1986: 20). The second factor triggering the Sykes Committee was the allegation, emanating from Beaverbrook newspapers, that the BBC was a monopoly nurturing the ambitions of its six largest members against the interests of smaller manufacturers and the public interest.

Reference

Crisell, A. (1986) *Understanding Radio*, London: Methuen.

The Crawford Committee

Title

Report of the Broadcasting Committee 1925 (Chaired by the Earl of Crawford and Balcarres) 1926, Cmd 2599, viii, 327–349.

Members

Lord Blanesburgh, Fraser MP, Graham MP, Hadow, Kipling, Macpherson, Lord Rayleigh, Royden, Talbot (Dame M.).

Terms of reference

'To advise as to the proper scope of the broadcasting service and as to the management, control and finance thereof after the expiry of the existing licence on 31 December 1926. The Committee will indicate what changes in the law, if any, are desirable in the interests of the broadcasting service.'

Context

The Crawford Committee was to assess the early experience of radio broadcasting and public reaction to the new medium. The Committee's primary concern was with the organisational structures of broadcasting but, amid increasingly articulated concerns that radio might serve as a surrogate for listeners' direct and active participation in cultural events, the Committee considered the content and quality of programmes. The Committee was informed, for example, with a certainty matched only by an equivalent absurdity, 'that the musical programmes offered to listeners are so varied and so easily enjoyed, that the private performer will be discouraged from learning the piano'. Moreover, 'concert-givers will be faced by overwhelming competition that the concert as such will suffer . . . and the standard of performance would consequently fall' (Crawford Committee Report, Cmd 2599, 1926, p.10).

The Selsdon Committee

Title

Report of the Television Committee (Chaired by Lord Selsdon) 1934–1935, Cmd 4793, xi, 921, 27pp.

Members

Lord Selsdon (Chair), Cadman (V. Ch), Angwin, Ashbridge, Brown, Carpendale, Phillips.

Terms of reference

'To consider the development of television and to advise the Postmaster-General on the relative merits of the several systems and on the conditions under which any public service of television should be provided.'

Context

The particular dilemma which the Selsdon Committee was appointed to resolve was to choose between two rival and incompatible systems of television broadcasting technology. John Logie Baird was developing a system in collaboration with the BBC, which used a rather crude mechanical scanner to generate televisual images. The technologically superior competitor system developed by EMI–Marconi used an electronic scanner to generate high-quality pictures using 405 lines with fifty frames a second. Selsdon eventually opted to develop television broadcasting by employing both systems until one proved its undisputed superiority. When the BBC began television broadcasting on 2 November 1936 the Baird and EMI–Marconi systems operated in tandem, which created predictable problems. At a meeting in July 1936 a coin was tossed by Selsdon to decide which company should conduct the opening transmissions: the Baird Television Company proved successful. But by February 1937 the Baird system was dropped because of the evident superiority of the EMI technology. On 1 September 1939, two days before the outbreak of the second world war, the BBC shut down its television service in case the transmitter system offered navigational aid to enemy bombers.

The Ullswater Committee

Title

The Broadcasting Committee Report (Chaired by Lord Ullswater) 1936, Cmd 5091, vii, 617, 77pp.

Members

Lord Ullswater (Chair), Astor, Attlee, Davies, Lord Elton, McLintock, Reading (Lady), Lord Selsdon, White.

Terms of reference

'To consider the constitution, control, and finance of the broadcasting service in this country and advise generally on the conditions under which the service, including broadcasting to the Empire, television broadcasting and the system of wireless exchanges, should be conducted after 31st December 1936.'

Context

The Ullswater Committee was appointed to review the organisation of the new television service and assess its programme content as the first Charter period drew to a close. The Ullswater Committee offered few substantive recommendations for change concerning the organisational structures and finance of the BBC other than the proposals concerning decentralisation of programming to regions, but it did look closely at programme content. As the Committee noted in the introductory preamble to its report:

> We are impressed, as were members of earlier Committees, by the influence of broadcasting upon the mind and spirit of the nation, by the immense issues which are consequently involved, and by the urgent necessity in the national interest that the broadcasting service should at all times be conducted in the best possible manner and to the best advantage of the people.
> (Cmd 5091, para 7)

In the wake of the General Strike, moreover, concerns were expressed about the role of broadcasters in the event of such a 'national emergency'. The question of allocating airtime to highly controversial views and minority views was a significant focus for Committee attention in the context of the rise of Hitler and the intense public debate about rearmament during the early 1930s.

The Hankey Committee

Title

Television Committee Report (Chaired by Lord Hankey) 1945, non-parliamentary, Privy Council Office, 25pp.

Members

Lord Hankey (Chair), Angwin, Appleton, Ashbridge, Birchall, Cockroft, Haley, Harvey.

Terms of reference

'To prepare plans for the reinstatement and development of the television service after the war with special consideration of: (a) the preparation of a plan for the provision of a service to at any rate the larger centres of population within a reasonable period after the war; (b) the provision to be made for research and development; (c) the guidance to be given to manufacturers, with a view especially to the development of the export trade.'

Context

The Selsdon Committee had recommended that the BBC should establish a public television service broadcasting from Alexandra Palace; broadcasting began in 1936. Selsdon anticipated a new industry manufacturing television receivers to develop in tandem with the new industry of television programme making and broadcasting. Both ambitions were thwarted in 1939 when the outbreak of war triggered the closure of the BBC's television operations. Hankey's brief was to make recommendations for rekindling those ambitions.

The Beveridge Committee

Title

The Broadcasting Committee Report (Chaired by Lord Beveridge) 1951, Cmd 8116, Cmd 8117, ix, I, vii, 327pp.

Members

Lord Beveridge (Chair), Binns, Crawford, Lord Elgin, Lloyd George (Lady Megan), Oakeshott, Reeves, Stedford, Stocks (Mrs MD), Taylor, Lloyd.

Terms of reference

'To consider the constitution, control, finance and other general aspects of the sound and television broadcasting services of the United Kingdom (excluding those aspects of the overseas services for which the BBC are not responsible) and to advise on the conditions under which these services and wire broadcasting should be conducted after the 31 December 1951.'

Context

When television services were re-established following the Second World War, there was considerable opposition to the continuing BBC monopoly and growing support for the establishment of a commercial system of broadcasting. The Beveridge Committee, established by the Labour government and charged with making recommendations for the future of broadcasting, became closely focused on these issues. The Committee reported in favour of sustaining the BBC's broadcasting monopoly and also rejected by a majority of seven out of eleven to continue the existing ban on advertising and programme sponsorship on the grounds that they would 'sooner or later endanger the traditions of public service, high standards and impartiality which have been built up in the past 25 years' (para 376). The Committee, however, was genuinely divided, and Selwyn Lloyd produced a minority report proposing the establishment of a British Broadcasting Commission to license up to three commercially funded national broadcasting services. Only months after Beveridge's report was published, the Conservative party won the election and promptly published a White paper consolidating many of Selwyn Lloyd's proposals. It stated,

> The present government have come to the conclusion that in the expanding field of television provision should be made to permit some element of competition when the calls on capital resources at present needed for purposes of greater national importance makes this feasible.
>
> (Memorandum on the Report of the Broadcasting Committee, 1949, Cmd 8550, 1951–1952, xxv, 25, para 7)

The Pilkington Committee

Title

Report of the Broadcasting Committee (Chaired by Lord Pilkington), 1961–1962, Cmnd 1753, ix.

Members

Pilkington, Sir Harry (Chair), Collinson, H., Davies, E., Grenfell, J. (Miss), Hoggart, R., Hudson, E.P., Newark, Prof. F.H., Shields, J.S., Smith-Rose, R.L., Whitley, E. Mrs, Wright, W.A.

Terms of reference

'To consider the future of the broadcasting services in the United Kingdom, the dissemination by wire of broadcasting and other programmes and the possibility of television for public showing; to advise on the services which should in future be provided in the United Kingdom by the BBC and ITA; to recommend whether additional services should be provided by any other organisation; and to propose what financial and other conditions should apply to the conduct of all these services.'

Context

On 30 July 1954, the Television Act established a commercially funded system of television broadcasting in the UK, to be overseen by a new regulatory body the Independent Television Authority (ITA). The BBC's broadcasting monopoly was superseded by what became known as the 'comfortable duopoly'; commercial broadcasting began in September 1955. The fourteen regionally based and privately owned companies incurred heavy financial losses in the early days but, by the late 1950s, profits were so considerable that the House of Commons Public Affairs Committee questioned the ITA about 'excessive profits'. A year earlier Lord Thomson, who chaired the Board of Scottish Television, had famously commented that holding a commercial television franchise was equivalent to 'a licence to print your own money'.

The new commercial broadcasting system quickly became characterised by a distinctive but controversial broadcasting style. News programming became much less formal in presentational style, while drama programmes contained portrayals of violence and more explicit sexual scenes than previously. There were also concerns about the alleged triviality of much of the programming content; the suggestion – made explicitly by Beveridge – was that the newly arrived broadcasting companies were lowering programming standards in order to win audiences and advertisers. These changes in programme style, combined with growing public concerns about levels of company profits, prompted the Conservative government to appoint the Pilkington committee in 1960. Reporting in 1962, the Committee made a number of recommendations (see below). Significant among these was the recommendation that the ITA should schedule programmes for the network and assume responsibility for selling airtime, thereby removing the broadcasting companies from any direct contact with advertisers; this proposal was not adopted. The issue of excessive profits was addressed via the introduction of a 'levy', an additional tax to the standard income tax which companies paid. The first £1.5 million of advertising revenues were exempt but the following £6 million were charged at 25 per cent with any further revenues taxed at 40 per cent.

The Annan Committee

Title

The Future of Broadcasting (Chaired by Lord Annan) 1976–1977, Cmnd 6753, Cmnd 6753 – I, vi.

Members

Annan, Lord (Chair), Goldman, P., Himmelweit, H. (Prof.), Jackson, T., Jay, A., Laski, M. (Miss), Lawrence, H.M. (Mrs) Lewis, D., Mackay, J. (Sir), Morrison, C. (the Hon. Mrs), Nandy, D., Parkes, J.G., Pollock, J.D., Sims, G. (Prof.), Whitehead, P. (MP), Worsley, M. (Sir).

Terms of reference

'To consider the future of our broadcasting services in the UK, including the dissemination by wire of broadcasting and other programmes and of television for public showing; to consider the implications for present or any recommended additional services of new techniques; and to propose what constitutional, organisational and financial arrangements and what conditions should apply to the conduct of all these services.'

Context

The progress of the Annan Committee reflected the political circumstances of the times. The day after the Annan inquiry was announced, Harold Wilson dissolved Parliament, called and lost an election and was replaced as Prime Minister by Edward Heath; within one month, the new Minister Christopher Chataway rescinded Annan's appointment. The Annan Committee was reinstated within weeks of Wilson's Labour government's return to power in 1974. Annan finally reported in 1977 but indecision by the Labour government meant that Annan's recommendation of a fourth terrestrial channel was eventually implemented by Home Secretary William Whitelaw in 1980. The intervening decade had witnessed a major sea change in British political life. The election of the first Thatcher government in 1979 signalled an enthusiasm for markets above public service commitments in deciding the effectiveness of public institutions such as broadcasting, as well as a government reluctance to invest in the public sector.

More specifically, there was a growing disenchantment with broadcasting. Interest groups like the National Viewers and Listeners Association protested against what they believed to be a retreat from traditional standards in programming. A different critique emerged from within broadcasting itself. There was a growing unhappiness with the broadcasting duopoly of BBC and ITV, increasingly seen as a vast and bureaucratic organisation which was conservative with a small 'c', obsessed with the preservation of its own interests, with a stultifying effect on creative and artistic work. Exemplifying this mood, Anthony Smith, an ex-BBC producer, Oxford Research Fellow and later Director of the British Film Institute, proposed a National Television Foundation which would be a 'publishing house of the air', commissioning and broadcasting programmes from independent programme makers, and educational and cultural sources. The NTF would help to release the 'strait-jacket' of the duopoly. The idea was vigorously supported in the Committee by another ex-BBC producer Phillip Whitehead and Professor Hilde Himmelweit. Eventually Annan produced his own version of the NTF which he designated the Open Broadcasting Authority, although he failed to specify an adequate funding mechanism for the new 'Authority'.

The Association of Directors and Producers offered a salvaging proposal; it is tucked away in Chapter 15 (para 7, p.231) of Annan's report. The fourth channel

> should be allocated to the programme makers. The IBA should schedule the channel as a complementary offering to ITV 1. Certainly the ITV companies would contribute but so would independent production companies whose work should be fostered and where necessary financed by the channel. The channel would not need production facilities or studios apart from those necessary for presentation and continuity; all it required was a small staff with a chief executive and executive board and a secretariat under the overall aegis of the IBA. They would purchase and process productions. The IBA would finance the channel by imposing a levy on the ITV companies who would have the exclusive right to sell advertising time on the new channel in their own areas. The channel itself would be a non-profit making organisation.

In truth the proposal was not new, but a reworked version of a 1973 proposal drafted by David Elstein and John Birt – with the support of Jeremy Isaacs – which set as a first priority the need to establish a viable funding mechanism for the new channel while at the same time encouraging pluralism and diversity in broadcasting. Elstein claims that in drafting the proposal he consciously looked back to Pilkington's recommendation 43 which sought to separate the process of commissioning and scheduling programmes from that of selling advertising.

The Hunt Committee

Title

Report of the Inquiry into Cable Expansion and Broadcasting Policy (Chaired by Lord Hunt) 1981–1982, Cmnd 8679.

Members

The Lord Hunt of Tanworth (Chair), Hodgson, M. (Sir), Ring, J. (Prof.).

Terms of reference

'To take as its frame of reference the government's wish to secure the benefits for the United Kingdom which cable technology can offer and its willingness to consider an expansion of cable systems which would permit cable to carry a wider range of entertainment and other services (including when available services of direct broadcasting by satellite), but in a way consistent with the wider public interest, in particular the safeguarding of public service broadcasting; to consider the questions affecting broadcasting policy which would arise from such an expansion, including in particular the supervisory framework; and to make recommendations by 30 September 1982.'

Context

The Conservative Party's success in the 1979 general election produced a government determined to encourage private sector involvement in developing telecommunications, reflecting a broader commitment to privatise public sector industries and to 'open them up' to market forces; the British Telecommunications Act was among the early fruits of such commitments. The Conservative government, like its Labour predecessor, was increasingly interested in the potential of information technology to revitalise other sectors of industry and economy; new technology and private enterprise were to be the twin handmaidens of the new information economy and society.

Early in 1981, Thatcher appointed Ken Baker as Minister of IT and established the Information Technology Advisory Panel (ITAP) composed of leading figures from the IT industries to acknowledge the 'importance of information technology for the future industrial and commercial success of the UK and the central role that the government must play in promoting its development' and to ensure that 'government policies and action are securely based on a close appreciation of market needs and opportunities' (Written Parliamentary answer, 2 July 1981).

ITAP's first report exploring the potential for development of the cable industry argued that high-capacity cable systems could provide expansive services such as television channels but also information and business services both for the home and industry. France, Germany and Japan were conducting trials with cable television systems while America led the world industry with eighteen million subscribers to cable television channels, but the UK cable industry was in decline with five thousand jobs at risk. Consequently, the development of cable would not only halt such decline but also trigger a more general industrial, economic and technological expansion by innovating resources in the field of information technology.

The ITAP report estimated the costs of cabling half of the homes in the UK at £2500 million, but concluded that no public funds would be necessary (private sources would capitalise these developments) and the new television services would be provided without detriment to the range, quality and public service commitments of extant television providers; both conclusions were widely criticised. In its evidence to the Hunt Committee, the Independent Broadcasting Association (IBA) expressed concern abut the uneven playing field on which the extensively regulated terrestrial commercial television services would be obliged to compete for audiences and advertisers alongside the unregulated cable channels. The BBC issued similar warnings about the corrosive effects of cheap, unregulated cable programming on public service broadcasting. The market-driven development of cable services, moreover, would restrict audiences geographically to the densely populated and prosperous areas. However, these concerns seem to have been largely ignored in the final report.

INDEX